Western
PROFILES

TO KNOW   TO UNDERSTAND   TO PARTICIPATE
THE CANADIAN HERITAGE IS YOUR HERITAGE

**ALBERTA HERITAGE
LEARNING RESOURCES
PROJECT**

A Project of Alberta Education
Funded
By
The Alberta Heritage Savings Trust Fund
and
Dedicated to the Students
of Alberta
by the
Government of Alberta
1979

Grateful acknowledgment is extended
to those who assisted in the development
of the Alberta Heritage anthologies

Members of the Selection Committee

Theresa Ford / *Edmonton Catholic School District*
Michael Allen / *Calgary Catholic School District*
Tom Gee / *Alberta Education*
Marg Iveson / *Edmonton Public School District*
Gloria Limin / *Calgary Public School District*
Lorne MacRae / *Calgary Public School District*
Maureen Ross / *Edmonton Catholic School District*

Western Canadian Literature
for Youth

Western
PROFILES

Theresa M. Ford
Managing Editor

Alberta Education
Edmonton

Alberta Education
Devonian Building
11160 Jasper Avenue
Edmonton, Alberta
T5K 0L2

ISBN 0-920794-06-8

Project Director / Dr. Kenneth Nixon
Design / David Shaw & Associates Ltd.
Publishing Consultants / Hurtig Publishers, Edmonton
Illustration / Leoung O'Young
Typesetting / The Albertan, Calgary
Printing / Lawson Graphics Western Ltd., Calgary
Binding / Economy Bookbinding Company Ltd., Calgary

To the Reader

Western Profiles presents a collage of stories and poems about some of the fascinating people who have made their homes in Western Canada. Some of them lived many years ago; others are very much alive today.

Obviously, there are thousands of individuals whose outstanding contributions to the opening of the West and to its present way of life merit recognition in this anthology. It is also obvious that limitations of space prevent in-depth coverage of all these people.

The decision was made, therefore, to include selections about people whom you might *not* read about in other easily available sources. As a result, you will not find explorers, politicians, or missionaries represented here. You will, instead, read about some important native Canadians, sports figures, rodeo riders, and pioneers whose stories will both inspire and entertain you.

Contents

Perspectives

Silhouettes

Personalities

Persuasions & Power

Perspectives

Words to a Grandchild

Chief Dan George

Perhaps there will be a day
you will want to sit by my side
asking for counsel.
I hope I will be there
but you see
I am growing old.
There is no promise
that life will
live up to our hopes
especially to the hopes of the aged.
So I write of what I know
and some day our hearts
will meet in these words,
—if you let it happen.

In the midst of a land
without silence
you have to make a place for yourself.
Those who have worn out
their shoes many times
know where to step.

It is not their shoes
you can wear
only their footsteps
you may follow,
—if you let it happen.

You come from a shy race.
Ours are the silent ways.
We have always done all things
in a gentle manner,
so much as the brook
that avoids the solid rock
in its search for the sea
and meets the deer in passing.
You too must follow the path
of your own race.
It is steady and deep,
reliable and lasting.
It is you,
—if you let it happen.

You are a person of little,
but it is better to have little
of what is good,
than to possess much
of what is not good.
This your heart will know,
—if you let it happen.

Heed the days
when the rain flows freely,
in their greyness
lies the seed of much thought.
The sky hangs low
and paints new colors
on the earth.
After the rain

the grass will shed its moisture,
the fog will lift from the trees,
a new light will brighten the sky
and play in the drops
that hang on all things.
Your heart will beat out
a new gladness,
—if you let it happen.

Each day brings an hour of magic.
Listen to it!
Things will whisper their secrets.
You will know
what fills the herbs with goodness,
makes days change into nights,
turns the stars
and brings the change of seasons.
When you have come to know
some of nature's wise ways
beware of your complacency
for you cannot be wiser than nature.
You can only be as wise
as any man will ever hope to be,
—if you let it happen.

Our ways are good
but only in our world
If you like the flame
on the white man's wick
learn of his ways,
yet when you enter his world,
you will walk like a stranger
so you can bear his company.
For some time
bewilderment will,
like an ugly spirit
torment you.

Then rest on the holy earth
and wait for the good spirit.
He will return with new ways
as his gift to you,
—if you let it happen.

Use the heritage of silence
to observe others.
If greed has replaced the goodness
in a man's eyes
see yourself in him
so you will learn to understand
and preserve yourself.
Do not despise the weak,
it is compassion
that will make you strong.
Does not the rice
drop into your basket
whilst your breath
carries away the chaff?
There is good in everything,
—if you let it happen.

When the storms close in
and the eyes cannot find the horizon
you may lose much.
Stay with your love for life
for it is the very blood
running through your veins.
As you pass through the years
you will find much calmness
in your heart.
It is the gift of age,
and the colors of the fall
will be deep and rich,
—if you let it happen.

The Face of a Thief
Phil Thompson

There was once a wise old Indian man who had heard of some parents who did not bother to send their children to school.

So this wise old man paid a visit to the parents and upon arrival made the statement, "I wanted to see what the face of a thief looked like, and now I see it."

Of course, the parents were set back and the father said, "We are not thieves, we are honest people. If by mistake we have taken something that is not ours, we will gladly return it."

The old man replied, "It is not something you can see, not something you can hear or feel, nevertheless it is something very real. In this day of ours, there are rights and opportunities that belong to us and our children, especially to the children. There are opportunities of going to school. These opportunities belong to the children and they need them. They need them to make their way in life. And any parent who does not ensure that his children get these opportunities is robbing them of their rights. I will say no more."

This wise old man left the same day. However, the next morning all the children of this family were at school.

This is what I mean when I speak of responsibility. For we rob our children when we do not ensure that they get all the opportunities for education.

A War-Chief Dies
Edward A. McCourt

"My heart is on the ground!" Big Bear cried. He spoke in the crowded court-room at Battleford to those who accused him of complicity in the Frog Lake massacre. The tired old chief had surrendered without resistance to the North-West Mounted

Police near Fort Carleton. Now the Law had found him guilty, not of murder, but of treason. The spirit of the chief was broken; he wanted only to die. But first he must say something on behalf of his people, now leaderless and starving. He spoke with impressive dignity. For a little while he was once more a great chief.

"I am dead now to my people," he said. "They are hiding in the woods, paralysed with fear. Cannot this court send them a pardon? My own children, starving and outcast, afraid to appear in the light of day!

"I am old and ugly, but I have tried to do good. Pity the children of my tribe. Pity the old and helpless of my people! I speak with a single tongue (*i.e.*, truthfully); and because I have always been the friend of the white man, send out and pardon them and give them help.

"I have spoken."

Not a man in the court-room listened unmoved to the old chief's plea. But the Law is inexorable.

"Big Bear," the presiding judge said, "you have been found guilty by an impartial jury. You cannot be excused for all the misdoings of your band. The sentence of the court is that you be imprisoned in the penitentiary for three years."

So white man's justice was done, and Big Bear went away behind the grey walls of the penitentiary to eat his heart out mourning the plight of his people. There was never any real evil in Big Bear. According to his lights he had been a good chief. He had nothing to reproach himself with, except that at the end he had lost control of his young men. But even a chief cannot subdue rebellious spirits forever.

Wandering Spirit, like Big Bear, gave himself up to the white men without resistance. A few days after they had released their prisoners, the Woods Crees, starving and miserable, came into Fort Pitt to surrender. With them came Wandering Spirit. The war-chief knew that death inevitably awaited him at the hands of the whites, but he no longer wanted to live. He had led his people to disaster because he had underestimated the power of the Great Queen. The days of old could never be again; and in the new settled life of the West Wandering Spirit wanted no part. Better to die and go to the land of the Great Spirit, where a warrior and hunter could still be free.

The night of their surrender, the Crees pitched their tents at Fort Pitt and ate their evening meal in sullen silence. Wandering Spirit ate nothing at all. Darkness fell. Wandering Spirit came out of his lodge and called in a loud voice to the Indians huddled around their camp-fires:

"All who wish to look on me once more, look now!"

Then he threw himself down on a blanket and stared into the fire. No doubt he reviewed in his mind all he had done, and failed to do, in months past. In all his life Wandering Spirit had never known such a bitter hour. Suddenly he uttered a fierce cry, snatched a sheath-knife from his belt, and thrust it deep into his side.

But for once his aim was bad. The knife missed his heart, and Wandering Spirit lived to stand trial for his part in the Frog Lake massacre. When asked why he had tried to commit suicide, he replied with simple dignity, "I knew there was no hope for me. Perhaps, I thought, if I sacrificed myself, the Government would not be so hard on the rest."

A fierce untamed warrior, Wandering Spirit, capable of cruelty and murder, yet a man who commanded the admiration of all who knew him well. There was a touch of greatness about the tall, sombre Indian, never more apparent than at the last when he tried to atone, through dying, for the sins of all his people.

The night before he died, the war-chief made his last speech, his audience the guards who next morning would lead him to the scaffold.

"I wish to say good-bye to you all," he said. "You have been good to me. What I have done, that was bad. But let me tell you that I never thought to lift my hand against a white man. Years ago, when we lived on the plains and hunted the buffalo, I was a head warrior of the Crees in battle with the Blackfoot. I liked to fight. I took many scalps. But afterwards the red-coats came, and the treaty was made with the white man, and there was no more war. I had never fought a white man. But lately we received bad advice. Of what good is it to speak of that now? I am sorry when it is too late. I only want to thank you for your kindness to me."

And he added, standing very straight and tall, "I am not afraid to die."

To William Cameron he committed a last message. Cameron, who liked and understood Wandering Spirit, had visited the fallen chief several times in his cell in Battleford. The day before his execution, Wandering Spirit spoke quietly and earnestly to the white man.

"Will you say good-bye for me to my family if you see them?" he said. "Tell the Crees from me never to do again as they did this spring — never to do as I did. Tell my daughter that I died in the white man's religion. I want her and her cousins to have that religion too. I am not thinking very much about what is going to happen tomorrow. I am thinking about what the priest has told me."

In Battleford, on a grey November morning several months after the end of the rebellion, six of the Frog Lake murderers marched to the scaffold. Most of the doomed men chanted war-songs, and called on their people to make no peace with the whites. They shouted words of bitter hate and defiance to the end.

But the war-chief, Wandering Spirit, died without a sound.

Bull Head
The Fearsome Sarcee
J. W. Grant MacEwan

Stamikso-Toosan or Bull Head was a big Indian, six feet two inches tall, broad shoulders, strong and ungainly when he walked. His voice was deep like that of a male elk in the rutting season, and when annoyed he could be heard half way across the reserve. By no stretch of imagination was he handsome. His hair was unruly; one eyelid drooped liked a wilted daisy and, when he scowled, his appearance was enough to frighten anybody who did not know him. It was bad enough to contemplate meeting a man of such countenance in daylight; the thought of encountering him in the dark was something upon which nobody in or about Calgary cared to dwell. The worst threat a mother with a naughty child could offer was: "Behave or I'll let Bull Head have you." Mounted Police knew him as a man with an unusual penchant for trouble, "A notorious old rascal," as John Peter Turner, Mounted Police historian, called him. Officers stationed at Fort Calgary wished he would become more amenable or go elsewhere.

But Bull Head was not all bad. Indeed, there was much good about him. If the white man's conduct made him roar with displeasure, the reaction should not have been difficult to understand. He would answer to his convictions rather than to the white man's code of behaviour; and with a feeling of antagonism toward the white oppressors, the Sarcee Chief could think of no valid reason for hiding it. He was not a hypocrite. The result was a period of "cold war" between the Sarcees and their neighbours, with an occasional clash demanding Mounted Police intervention.

In earlier years the pugnacious Bull Head had been a warrior, capable of showing many scars from fighting Crees — and sometimes Blackfoot. His battle record was unsurpassed and the Sarcees — specialists in warfare — were proud of it. There was a tribal tradition. "The Sarcees," said Sir George Simpson, "were regarded in my time as the boldest of all tribes that inhabited the plains."

The Sarcees constituted a branch of a northern tribe which suffered division some 300 years ago. The separation may have been caused by a quarrel about a dog or it may have resulted, as Bull Head believed, from an upheaval over which the Indians had no control. As related by the late David One Spot of the Sarcees, the northern Indians were crossing a big lake when a lake monster with a huge horn in the centre of its head, heaved the ice and sent many of the people to a drowning death. The survivors were divided by the break in the ice. Those on the north side remained in the North while those on the other side wandered southward into buffalo country and became the Sarcees. Members of the new group might have increased to become a tribe of major importance but disease and other tragedies seemed to plague them.

Most disastrous was an epidemic of smallpox in 1870 which left more tribesmen dead than alive. The Sarcees never regained their former numbers. When they assembled at Blackfoot Crossing to negotiate Treaty Number Seven in 1877 their people totalled less than 250. But Bull Head, who had survived smallpox, scarlet fever, famine and the fury of enemies, was there to bargain for his followers. In that company of Indians from five tribes, he was overshadowed in influence by Crowfoot but no Indian figure was more conspicuous than that of the massive Sarcee.

As in the case of Crowfoot, Bull Head acquired his name after the murder of an older brother who carried the name. The first Bull Head was killed in a battle with a Blackfoot, right where the City of Calgary was to be built and then the younger brother took the dead man's name. He was brave and skillful in warfare and became the Sarcee war chief. Then, when the years of intertribal wars ended, Bull Head continued to be the Sarcee leader and spokesman.

Rev. John McDougall met him on the plains in 1872 and tried to disguise his fear of this big Indian at the head of "a crowd of the wildest fellows on the plains". Having no choice, McDougall spent the night in the Sarcee camp and felt "almost surprised that we were alive" next morning. But the missionary soon discovered that the Chief was not as bad as his appearance suggested.

On the Treaty ground in 1877 Bull Head was one of the reluctant signers. He could scarcely bring himself to trust the white man but, in this instance, there seemed to be no practical alternative and on September 22 he and other native leaders submitted by making their "X" marks in lieu of signatures.

Almost at once thoughts turned to the important matter of locating reserves promised in the terms of the Treaty. The Blackfoot allotment was prairie country on the north side of the Bow River, precisely as Crowfoot wanted it. The Bloods were given a big reservation between St. Mary and Belly Rivers and the Piegans were accommodated beside the Oldman River. Bull Head's choice of location would have been westward on the Elbow River but because the Sarcee population was small, Government officials insisted upon placing the tribe on a small piece of land bordering on the Blackfoot Reserve.

Blackfoot and Sarcee tolerated each other and recognized a loose sort of alliance. But there was no feeling of affection and no desire to live as close neighbours. Bull Head protested and Government officials yielded to the extent of making some adjustments in reservation boundaries but without change of location. The Sarcee land would be on the south side of Blackfoot Crossing, regardless of how Bull Head and his people felt about it.

By 1879, buffalo hunting had ended and Indians were hungry. Government rations were totally inadequate and they seemed to be facing starvation. The Sarcees were becoming rebellious and Bull Head was doing nothing to restrain them. Discontent continued to mount until late in 1880 when the

Sarcees were loading tipis, possessions and families on their wagons and driving westward toward Fort Calgary. They vowed they would never return to that prairie reserve.

Days later, just as settlers were noting signs of winter in the November air, the entire Sarcee band arrived to camp on the south side of the Elbow, just a stone's throw from Fort Calgary. There they cast angry glances at the four worried Mounted Police who happened to be the only occupants of the fort at the time. Bull Head called for rations and made it clear that if the police could not furnish them his hungry Indians would feel obliged to take what they needed from the Hudson's Bay Company and I. G. Baker stores nearby. The men in charge of the two stores, G. C. King and Angus Fraser, had every reason to be worried for there was but small hope that a police sergeant, three constables and two storekeepers could control several hundred bellicose natives.

The immediate need was for police reinforcements. The two pioneer farm settlers, Sam Livingstone and John Glenn, agreed and a rider carrying the urgent message was sent at once to Fort Macleod. The response was prompt; Inspector Cecil Denny, Sergeant John Lauder and thirty men, all suitably mounted, rode over the 100-mile trail in two days and found the Indians, as reported, in a mood for war. Bull Head, backed by his armed braves, was asking for more than the police could furnish and the situation remained tense. The Indians wanted a reserve somewhere west of Fort Calgary, as well as guarantee of rations. Indian Agent Norman Macleod, who had come north with the police troop, told the Chief that if the Sarcee wanted assurance of Government rations for the winter they would have to accept temporary camp close to Fort Macleod. But Bull Head did not want to move southward, fearing that if he and his followers spent the winter in the Fort Macleod area they would never be allowed to return to the Elbow River district for which they had a strong preference. The Chief's answer was "No" and it was loud enough to be heard at Fish Creek.

There had to be a showdown. Either the Indians moved to Fort Macleod and submitted to the police plan or the Mounties would have to surrender to the Indian determination to remain close to Fort Calgary. There could be no compromise and the Indians, with much aimless firing of guns, were showing no inclination to yield. The possibility of a night attack upon the fort was not being overlooked and the police were maintaining a constant alert.

If the police plan was to be carried out, Inspector Denny and his men had to act boldly. On the third day after his arrival, Denny assembled his troop for the big test and again notified Bull Head to prepare to move. When the Sarcees failed to respond, the Inspector, with only Sergeant Lauder at his side, strode forward and pulled down the Chief's tipi. To the Indians, it looked like an act of war. Young bucks howled in anger and seemed ready to begin what might have been the "Battle of Calgary". Fortunately, the chief was wise enough to know when to capitulate and instead of instructing his braves to open fire, he signalled to start loading tipis on carts and wagons for the move to Fort Macleod. At sundown on that day the Sarcees were making their night camp at Fish Creek and ten days later they were at Fort Macleod, cold, unhappy but at least assured of enough beef to keep them from starving.

Nor were the Chief's demands for a new reserve forgotten. Government men acquiesced and in the spring of 1881 Bull Head and his Sarcees moved to their new reservation beside the Elbow River, on Calgary's southwest.

Both Mounted Police and white residents in and around Calgary would have been happier if the Sarcees had been located in some more distant part. It might have been better for male and female members of the tribe to be less accessible to town and city streets but there they were, right at Calgary's outskirts where Bull Head, in the years following, succeeded in being alternately a source of consternation and entertainment. Frequently *The Calgary Herald* carried accounts of Sarcee misconduct. Occasionally the Chief was hauled into court for intoxication but because of his great strength, which he did not hesitate to use, an arrest was not something to which the police looked forward with pleasure.

There was the Crow Collar affair of 1883 when the Indian of that name was accused of robbing government supplies at the reserve. The Indian agent laid the complaint and a police sergeant was sent to make the arrest. But Bull Head had intervened and refused to allow the accused to be taken. Next day, Superintendent McIllree, with ten men rode to the reserve and met Bull Head. The officer spoke clearly: he and his men were there to arrest Crow Collar and if there was any interference they would be obliged to arrest the Chief also and take him to the barracks. But Bull Head's attitude was unchanged and the police promptly arrested him. The enraged tribesmen milled about as if they were ready for violence and it was immediately evident that the police were still without the manpower needed to carry out their purpose. To reduce the risk of a clash which could be costly in human lives, the Mounties allowed Bull Head to return to his people while they sent to Fort Calgary for still more men. After another night in which to consider the consequences and the appearance of an imposing troop of armed policemen, the Sarcees gave up the wanted Crow Collar and Bull Head sent word that he would report next day. Finally, Crow Collar and the Chief spent a few days in jail and left after promising better behaviour.

The Sarcee Chief was spending days in jail rather frequently. The charges were never more serious than drunkenness and obstructing but they were numerous enough to make Bull Head feel perfectly at home in the Calgary guardroom. *Calgary Herald* readers expected to see some news about Bull Head now and then. The news as reported on May 28, 1884, was fairly typical:

> Quite a little commotion was caused by the appearance of Bull Head, Chief of the Sarcees, and some of his braves among the crowd at the celebration

Monday afternoon. He was on business and that particular business was to get a horse or its equivalent that he says was taken from his reserve about the 22nd inst. Joe La Rondale sold a roan horse for $45 to a half breed. A few days ago the half breed drove out through the Sarcee Reserve and Bull Head, seeing the horse, said it was his and demanded it. The half breed refused unless he got the money he paid La Rondale for it. Bull Head, with most of his tribe, like loyal subjects, came in to celebrate the birthday of the Great Mother and spying La Rondale on the grounds, with a horse, made his way thitherward and demanded the horse or $45. La Rondale refused either but offered to settle the matter by giving him another horse and $5. Those who saw the horse say it has a sore on both shoulders, is lame and so generally used up as not to be worth $5. Bull Head refused the offer indignantly and, rushing at La Rondale, snatched the reins out of his hand and led off the horse, followed by his warriors who had been silent spectators. La Rondale laid information at police headquarters.

The Chief's name became more and more familiar to citizens who read police news. *The Calgary Herald,* September 7, 1892 told in rather typical terms that "The Mounted Police went out to the Sarcee Reserve and arrested Head Chief, Old Bull Head, and brought him to the barracks on a charge of drunkenness. . . . He was sentenced to two weeks imprisonment and goes about his work with a ball and chain."

But if anybody supposed that jail would reform Bull Head or change him, that person would be sadly mistaken. Indeed, there was reason to believe the Indian with the distinctive personality was actually enjoying his visits to the cells. And local editors entered into the spirit of it all. The *Herald* report on October 23, 1895, told that while the Chief was paying one of his periodic visits to the jail, Mrs. Bull Head was giving an

"At Home and lawn party" on Centre Street, "well attended by representatives of all the first families. Music and a little social hop were the entertainment."

It would have been easy to misjudge the man. This Bull Head who frightened, worried, entertained and shocked the white people around him, was neither wicked nor stupid. He was smarter than most people realized and wise enough to guard his individuality. He may have had a better sense of humour than those who were puzzled by him. Convinced that the Indians had been wronged by a race with essentially selfish motives, he considered it wrong to conform to or adopt their ways. If he, with his own ideas about right and wrong, could confound the greedy and arrogant whites, he was sure he should do it. He could see nothing wrong with stealing horses from people who had more than they could use, or taking food when it was needed, or misleading the Government which had thrust itself uninvited upon him. And he was smart enough to carry out all of these acts. When he had only 250 in his band, he requested Treaty money payments for 400 Sarcees. Challenged about this inaccuracy, he argued that there was enough need and hunger in his tribe to represent a population of more than 400.

When that bid to overcharge the Government failed he and some of his followers resorted to other tricks intended to outwit the white officials. Indian women borrowed babies to qualify for extra payment and some of the braves passed the Lieutenant-Governor's paymaster three or four times, collecting Treaty money each time. It was told that Bull Head, wearing a buffalo skin draped over his shoulders, collected the usual Chief's allowance and then, with nothing except a breechcloth, took a place near the rear of the line and succeeded in passing and collecting as an ordinary brave.

And Bull Head was smart enough to have his own calendar at a time when nobody else had one. It consisted of a bundle containing peeled willow twigs. Beginning at what he believed to be the shortest day of the year, he would remove one twig each day, knowing that when 90 twigs had been removed the winter would be over and the wild ducks returning. When another 90 were removed, the days would be long and hot and after another 90, both Indians and Nature's children, the animals, should be preparing for winter.

The great Bull Head died in 1911, still adhering to his native religion. Pious missionaries had warned him about the impending hell-fire it he did not accept their prejudiced teachings. But his Indian concept of a Great Spirit stood the test of reason fully as well as the conflicting views brought by the white churchmen. He could see no reason for changing.

Of his age at the time of death nobody could be sure. It did not matter; what did matter was his strength of character. Men might call him a savage and a pagan but the fact was that he had strong convictions and was not to be swayed. If, as he believed, the white man's ways were couched in folly, why should he adopt them? The whites were ultimately more numerous and stronger but not necessarily wiser. Chief Bull Head should be remembered as one of the unswerving defenders of Indian rights. Appropriately, a Community Hall on the Sarcee Reservation a few miles out of Calgary was named in his memory, — the memory of a man wiser than most people who saw him realized, wise enough to guard his God-given individuality.

Son of a Great Nation
Carlotta Hacker

In 1835, a five-year-old boy set out alone to find his mother. His name was Astoxkomi (Shot Close), and he belonged to the Blood tribe who lived in the open prairies and woodlands of the region that is now southern Alberta. His father, Istowun-eh'pata, had been killed on a raid a couple of years earlier, and his mother, Axkyahp-say-pi, had recently taken a new husband. She had married a stranger from the Blackfoot tribe.

Astoxkomi had watched as his mother had packed her belongings onto a travois, said farewell to her relatives, and ridden away with the Blackfoot warrior to join his tribe. She had taken Astoxkomi's baby brother with her but had decided that Astoxkomi himself would remain behind to be brought up by his grandfather. Grandson and grandfather were such close friends that she did not like to separate them.

It was true that Astoxkomi adored his grandfather, but Axkyahp-say-pi had not reckoned with the boy's love for her. Slipping quietly out of camp, he picked up his mother's trail and set off after her. He was on foot, while she was on horseback, but she was travelling slowly because of the travois. If he ran fast enough, there was a chance he would catch up.

The child may or may not have been aware of the dangers he faced in setting out alone and unprotected. He could have been attacked by one of the many grizzly bears which roamed the countryside in those days. He could have stumbled onto an enemy patrol. He could have lost his way. But he never in his life lacked either determination or bravery. On he ran, following the trail that had been left by the marks of the travois. Hours later, way out on the open prairie, his mother saw the small figure running towards her. She had no choice but to turn back. The boy would have been missed and his relatives would be searching anxiously for him. So back they all went. Sometime later, when the newlyweds once again set out from the Blood camp, Astoxkomi and his grandfather were travelling with them.

This is one of many famous stories about the boy who was first called Astoxkomi, then took the Blackfoot name of Kyiah-sta-ah (Bear Ghost), and later took his dead father's name of Istowun-eh'pata (Packs a Knife). A male Indian sometimes had as many as eight or nine different names during his life.

Each name replaced the previous one as he grew to manhood or performed a special act of bravery. Astoxkomi was a teenager when he earned the name that he was to make famous throughout Canada and the world: Isapo-muxika (Crow Indian's Big Foot). He kept this name for the rest of his life, it was shortened to Crowfoot by interpreters.

Because of his determination at the age of five, Crowfoot was brought up among the Blackfoot instead of among the Blood tribe. This was not quite like changing his nationality. The Blood, Blackfoot, and Piegan Indians all spoke the same Algonkian language and were all part of one nation, which was called the Nitsitapi (Real People) and was known to outsiders as the Blackfoot Confederacy. The Sarcee and Gros Ventre tribes were allies in the confederacy although they did not speak Algonkian. The Crow, Cree, Stoney and all other neighbouring tribes were the enemies.

The Indians of the Blackfoot Confederacy were in a very strong position at this time. Their hunting grounds stretched southwards into the United States and northwards as far as the North Saskatchewan River. The Rockies were the boundary of their territory to the west, and they spread eastward far into present-day Saskatchewan. Although they did not believe that they actually owned this land, they refused to allow other tribes on it. It was their hunting preserve. Neighbouring tribes were attacked if they trespassed on Blackfoot territory, just as the Blackfoot were attacked if they strayed beyond the limits of the confederacy's hunting grounds. However, this did not prevent frequent raids into enemy territory for hunting and plunder — and especially for glory.

In these raids, the Blackfoot had a great advantage over their enemies: they were better supplied with guns and horses. Because of their geographical position, they could get horses from the American Fur Company posts on the Missouri, and guns from the Hudson's Bay Company on the North Saskatchewan River. Most tribes did not have this choice of trading companies and trade goods. The Blackfoot had another great advantage over their neighbours. Because of their reputation for fierceness, very few traders or missionaries had ever entered their territory. So their civilization remained intact.

They had, of course, made a few changes in their way of life since their first contact with Europeans. They no longer grew tobacco, for it was easier to get it through trade. They used European goods, such as iron kettles, axes, blankets, and guns. But they continued to use spears and bows and arrows when hunting buffalo. A musket took too long to reload when a rider was galloping alongside the herds.

Horses had brought the greatest change to Blackfoot life. Besides providing speed and agility in hunting and warfare, they were important as beasts of burden. With horses — instead of dogs — to pull the travoises, the Blackfoot could take large quantities of goods from camp to camp. And they no longer had to leave much of the buffalo meat at the scene of a hunt.

By the time Crowfoot was born, the Blackfoot had owned horses for a hundred years. The animals had become part of their lifestyle. They were used like money to buy things, and a man's wealth was reckoned by the size of his herds. The aim of forays was often to capture enemy horses.

Since the animals played such a important role, Blackfoot children were placed on horseback almost as soon as they could walk. Crowfoot would have been a competent rider by the time he was five. By the age of ten, he would have been looking after his stepfather's horse herd, getting up before dawn each day to take the animals to water. As a ten-year-old, he would also have started to ride out on buffalo hunts, learning the techniques from his elders.

The life of the Blackfoot revolved around the buffalo, and they used every part of these shaggy beasts for some purpose. The hairy hides served as bedding or were made into winter clothing. The dressed, hairless skins were made into lighter clothing or used to make tipi covers or ceremonial headdresses. The hair was fashioned into ropes, bridles, and ornaments. The rawhide served many purposes and was one of the materials used for waterproof containers. The bones were made into tools; the horns into cups and spoons. And the meat provided the staple food. Berries and roots supplemented the Blackfoot diet, but buffalo meat was the real food. During a hunt, choice portions were eaten raw, but generally the meat was boiled or roasted. If it was to be preserved, it was dried in the sun and either boiled and made into pemmican or simply stored as dried meat.

The women and girls performed most of these household tasks. A young boy like Crowfoot did not have to learn how to tan buffalo hides or preserve food. But, like Blackfoot girls, he was taught to respect his elders and to observe the taboos connected with the sacred medicine bundles. Much of his education was aimed at physical fitness. He played body-building games with other boys of his age, for he was expected to become a strong fighter. His stepfather and the other men of the band carefully trained him toward this goal from early childhood.

Crowfoot's stepfather was called Akay-nehka-simi (Many Names), and he belonged to the Biters band of Blackfoot. So it was among this band that Crowfoot grew up. Each of the tribes of the confederacy was divided into a number of bands, which lived separately from each other for most of the year, following the buffalo across the plains during the summer months, and camping in sheltered wooded areas during the winter.

The members of a band were generally related, and the chief acted as a father, seeing that all under his care were protected and well fed. The chief had no official power except his influence — though this could be considerable. If his followers disliked his leadership, they could join another band or form a new one. Blackfoot society was very democratic.

It was a well-ordered society, based on a firm religious

faith, a strong moral code, and a real concern for the good of the community. Crowfoot was brought up to practise generosity. The Blackfoot believed that the rich should give to the poor, and that the strong should help the weak. Orphans were fed and clothed. People who were too old or ill to hunt were provided for by healthy young men. Crowfoot was also taught to be a sociable band member, to perform his duties without grumbling, to accept teasing without causing strife, and to be faithful to his people. And a desire for bravery — the greatest manly virtue — was instilled in him from a very early age. Cowardice was despised and ridiculed. So were anti-social vices like lying, cheating, and stealing.

Anyone who did not conform to these high standards was either shamed into better behaviour by ridicule or punished by one of the men's societies. There were several men's societies in the confederacy, each consisting of people of much the same age. Later, when Crowfoot was a young man, he joined an age-grade society called the All Brave Dogs. Like most other men's societies, the All Brave Dogs were part policemen and part soldiers. They protected the band when it was on the move and took turns at guard duty, acting as sentries to keep watch for enemies. Often they settled minor disputes between fellow Blackfoot. They were most active at the time of the Sun Dance when it was their duty to keep order in camp and to see that each man did his share of hunting, and provided meat for the feasts and buffalo tongues for the ceremonies.

Tribal virtues were emphasized during this festival. Boys like Crowfoot received their greatest inspiration as they sat at the edge of the Sun Dance circle and listened to the most daring men recounting their exploits. Glorious battles would be relived to draw the admiration of the audience.

Such long and involved festivals had not been possible before the era of the horse. But, with horses, the Blackfoot found they had leisure. They had time to develop their culture and hold lengthy religious and social functions. They had time for art and craftsmanship, time for games and sports. And they had time to raid their enemies to gain glory — and a fresh supply of horses.

They were at the height of their civilization when Crowfoot was a small child. Prosperous and powerful, they were lords of the plains, unthreatened by the hunger that had haunted their ancestors, and unthreatened as yet by the handful of Europeans who lived on their borders. The buffalo were plentiful, and as long as summer followed summer, there seemed no reason that their civilization should not grow from strength to strength.

But the confederacy experienced the first of many disasters shortly after Crowfoot's mother remarried. First there was an outbreak of diphtheria and then, in 1837, a smallpox epidemic. An Indian had caught the disease from a passenger on an American Fur Company steamer on the Missouri, and before long it was sweeping the plains, spreading from tribe to tribe. The Blackfoot had no immunity against smallpox, and whole bands died of the disease. Some young men committed suicide when they caught it, rather than suffer the terrible disfigurement it caused. About 6,000 people — two-thirds of the entire Blackfoot nation — died during this epidemic.

Crowfoot was only seven years old at the time, and fortunately he and his family were among the survivors. But it was a sign of what was in store, and the first of many tribulations he would have to face. For he was to live through the years of great change, when the buffalo vanished from the prairies and European settlers moved in and the railway spread its line of steel across to the Pacific.

The harm done to the Blackfoot during these years was seldom intentional, no more intentional than the smallpox epidemic. Often it was caused simply by thoughtlessness. Sometimes it was the result of government policy — to do what was best for the European population of Canada. But the result was always the same: to reduce the strength of the Indian people.

Young Crowfoot naturally had no idea of the hard times

ahead as he admired his elders at the Sun Dance or wrestled playfully with his friends. He was training to be a soldier. But, even as a youth, he began to exhibit the wisdom and strength of character that enabled him to lead his people — as successfully as was possible — through their most difficult years of social change.

Dan George
A Noble Man
Terry Angus & Shirley White

It is Academy Awards Night, 1971. Crowds of people are clamouring to see their favourite stars as they arrive and file into the Los Angeles Music Center. Flash bulbs pop and spotlights play over the throngs picking out famous faces and award nominees. The tension builds as limousine after limousine glides up to the Music Center and lets out its own famous passengers. As each door is opened by a chauffeur, the crowd of onlookers presses even closer to catch a glimpse of people they see normally only on the screen.

When the door of one particular limousine swings open, a small bronze-skinned, craggy-faced man with shoulder length silver hair steps spryly out to the sound of mild applause. The man squints in the glare of television lights and looks slightly uncomfortable. The Hollywood glamour and glitter is a long way from the world of Burrard Inlet, British Columbia, where Chief Dan George has lived all his life. After nodding slightly to acknowledge the crowd, the 71-year-old Co-Salish Indian moves in to take his seat at Hollywood's annual awards night.

As Dan George sits among the famous celebrities, the television cameras often zero in on his handsome, almost regal, face. Finally the moment comes. An actor on stage reads the list of nominees for Best Supporting Actor in 1970. Dan

George's role as Ol' Lodgeskins in the film *Little Big Man* is described. Dan draws a breath of anticipation as the envelope is opened. The actor on stage utters the now famous words "And the winner is . . ." There is a pause. Then the name follows. John Mills is named for his role in *Ryan's Daughter*. Dan George sits back in his seat almost relieved. At least the whole thing is over and he can return to the environment where he is most comfortable.

Dan lives in a small white cottage which overlooks the water on Burrard Reserve No. 3. He was born on the reserve in 1899 and has been there all his life. As a child, he lived as his people had always lived, helping his parents collect seafood and berries, preserving the food, and storing it away for winter use. He learned crafts and the traditional ways of the Co-Salish tribe. Until he was 16, he attended St. Paul's Boarding School in North Vancouver.

At 19, Dan George married Amy Jack, a beautiful girl from a neighbouring reserve and settled down to work. In 1920 he went to work on the British Columbia docks for 40 cents an hour. The work was hard and the days long. Toiling in groups of four, the men on the docks would pack 12 m lengths of timber and hoist them into the huge ships that came into port from all over the world. One day swinging timber suddenly broke loose from a bundle, crashed into Dan, and tossed him. It smashed all the muscles in his hip and left one leg shorter than the other. After 27 years, Dan George's working days on the docks had abruptly ended.

But Dan's career was not yet over. A few years after his accident he was elected chief of his tribe and, for the next 12 years, he dedicated much of his time to the work of leading his people. He was voted out of office in 1963. Since then he has been named Honorary Chief of both the Shuswap and Squamish tribes.

The other career that began when Dan lost his job on the docks was as an entertainer. Soon he was known locally in

Burrard Inlet. His real break came in 1960, when he was approached to fill the role of Antoine on the CBC television series "Cariboo Country". Over the next five years, he became deeply involved with television and professional theatre work. He also performed on radio and gained a reputation as a public speaker.

With his appearance in Walt Disney's film *How to Break a Quarter Horse* he made his entrance into motion pictures in the United States. Since then he has worked on American television and stage. His experience with *Little Big Man* and the Academy Awards left him bruised, however. The $16,000 that he received for the movie part turned out to be a fraction of the figure that had been offered other actors for the same role. And when he didn't win an Oscar he realized how fickle the world of Hollywood could be. "I'm glad in a way that he didn't get it," remembers his friend, broadcaster Hilda Mortimer. She was one of the people who accompanied Dan to the Awards ceremony and saw how he was treated. "We sat in a room together the next day and waited for all those promised people who never came. The magazines. The agents. The studio people."

Perhaps, though, it is another aspect of his career that has become most significant. He is well known as a spokesman for the Indian people. His wise countenance and unique husky whisper combine to command almost immediate attention and respect. His habit of punctuating his soft-spoken words with pauses of silence has a spellbinding effect. "Years ago, I dedicated myself to try to do something that would give a name to the Indian people," Dan has said. It may be that his public speaking is doing as much for this goal as his acting career.

A particularly fine example of Dan George's effectiveness as a speaker was illustrated on July 1, 1967, when he spoke in Vancouver's Empire Stadium to a crowd of 32,000 people. The occasion, of course, was Canada's centennial celebration and the milling throng that had gathered was in a buoyant holiday mood. It took the Chief only minutes to achieve complete silence and seriousness among the celebrating Canadians as he delivered an eloquent but bitter "Lament for Confederation" in which he poignantly stated that Canada's first 100 years had not been good to the Indian people.

And so it is not surprising that Dan George still lives on the reserve at Burrard Inlet in his little white cottage far from the fast-moving world of Hollywood. Leaving the reserve, he feels, is for another generation. For him it is home and he is happy to be with his people.

Alex Janvier
Inge Vermeulen

What is the difference between the successful career of a white man and that of an Indian?

"It's a lot harder to come by," says treaty Indian Alex Janvier — and he should know. It took at least 20 years of struggling against prejudice and indifference until he was accepted as an artist, first on the local, and finally on the national art scene. Today, at the age of 42, Janvier has "arrived". His works show up in important collections, he is in demand for exhibitions, and the critics hail him as one of the most prolific Indian painters of the west.

Alex doesn't pay too much attention to this sudden public recognition. In his own stubborn way he has known all along that he was a good painter. The present artistic and commercial success only proves that he was right.

As he slouches comfortably in a big chair that fits his stocky build, dressed in a casual shirt with rolled-up sleeves, he doesn't look at all like a famous man. He looks like an ordinary nice guy — an Indian, son of a chief, but not in any way resembling the Hollywood Indian image. The straight black hair of his race covers his round head like the cap worn under a helmet during the Middle Ages. Compared to the jovial fullness of chin and cheek, his dark eyes seem small, their expression guarded when he listens. But as soon as he begins to talk, they register his emotions so vividly that his statements become totally believable.

The other outstanding physical feature about this soft-spoken man is his hands. Cradled around his tea mug, they are so perfectly shaped that they look strangely elegant. It is easy to imagine the fingers serving as delicate tools to a painter who works with meticulous care and attention to fine lines in drawings and boldly colored "hard edge" acrylics.

The Janvier paintings lining the walls of the living room are unique. This artist doesn't bother to paint pretty trees, romantic barns, or Indian scenes on the reserve. . . . His Indian heritage, and the talent for expressing symbolism that comes so naturally with his people's traditions, are expressed in the clean lines of paintings and gouaches that are carefully planned compositions in color. His subject matter is closely related to his concerns.

"This is my way of commenting on pollution," he explains, pointing out a large white painting with the image of a red and black eagle hovering over "the soul of an insect". Two fat black dots symbolize death for both; a green dot, seemingly wandering off the picture to the right, mourns the demise of other living creatures already exterminated by the effects of pollution.

Not all of his paintings proclaim the message in such unmistakable terms. A viewer, unaware of Janvier's title at the back of the canvas, might easily be deceived by the brightly colored lines and shapes, wandering over the surface through intricate paths, meeting in harmony, or ending abruptly. But once acquainted with the title, some people are shocked by the sting of *Mass Hate, No One Cares, Nothing in the Budget,* or *Insoluble Answer.*

Ignoring the Treaty is a title with special meaning for Alex, his non-Indian wife Jacqueline, and their three young children. Alex's treaty number, 287, assigned to him on his birth at the Cold Lake reserve, appears on every one of his paintings next to his signature.

"It's a reminder that I'm a diplomatic slave to the Indian Department."

What other "advantages" are associated with being a treaty Indian?

Jacqueline laughed. "We get $5.00 a head annually, free education and free health care."

Alex's eyes flash with anger when he talks about meddlers who tried to interfere with his goals at a most crucial time during his art training. After his second year at the Alberta College of Art in Calgary, he received word from Ottawa that it had been decided to shift his training to commercial art.

"I was furious. The last thing I wanted was designing packages or painting signs. My mind was set on getting a degree in fine arts."

Thanks to the efforts on his behalf by two of his famous art teachers, Marion Nicoll and Illingworth Kerr, Ottawa reversed the decision and he graduated with top marks in fine arts.

"I was lucky to have these people stand up for me and encourage me, because I sure didn't get much encouragement from anybody else. My fellow students were so prejudiced that I began to become prejudiced myself."

As Alex learned after graduation when he applied for jobs, his Indian background was not the only strike against him. "I was stuck with a loaded situation: I had a French name, I was a Catholic, an Indian, and to top it all, I was an artist!"

After weeks of battling the "Don't call us — we'll call you" syndrome, he finally landed a job as an instructor at the University of Alberta Extension Department. But he was really more interested in painting than in teaching others, and after two years he returned to the reserve to paint and help his brother raise cattle.

Much to the surprise of his family who didn't think very highly of painting as a career, Alex was approached by an Edmonton commercial art gallery who offered him a one-man show.

Public reaction was mixed: puzzlement, delight, and acceptance — at least to a degree. One of the show's paintings was presented to Prime Minister L. B. Pearson whose wife wrote to say how proud they were to own such an outstanding work of art by a Canadian Indian.

That was in 1964, a time when, Alex Janvier says, Canadian Indians didn't count much around Edmonton. A time when it was legitimate for an Edmonton hotel to inform the gallery director that he couldn't have lunch there with Alex Janvier.

"We don't serve Indians," he was told.

Alex Janvier came to expect prejudice, and he got his full share. He was refused lodgings in hotels, he says, robbed of his money, cheated by white businessmen, and ignored by government agencies.

"I'll never forget what happened when I asked for a Canada Council grant. They sent me a form and asked me for proof of my background. Was I a landed immigrant, or did I have the status of a Canadian citizen?"

By the time he'd filled out the form, explaining that he had been delivered by an Indian midwife in a loghouse on the reserve, and that baptismal records were the only proof of his birth, he received the Canada Council's regrets. He had missed their deadline.

"As I said in one of my titles: *Let Red Tape Do It.*"

Disillusioned again, but too proud to ask for money from other sources, he struggled through his lean years without government assistance, working for a pay cheque here and there, farming on the reserve, and painting as much as possible.

The Canadian event of Expo brought a long, overdue change, illustrated sarcastically with a Janvier title: *The Unpredictable East*. These three words sum up Alex's reaction when the federal government commissioned him to paint a nine-foot circular mural for the Expo's Indian Pavilion.

"You should've seen my father's face when he saw the cheque for the mural. He'd never dreamt anybody would be foolish enough to *pay* me for painting. That cheque made all the difference in his attitude towards my work."

Alex's own attitude towards his work continued to be strained by the financial difficulties resulting from the slow public acceptance of his style.

"To remain honest — and true to myself — I couldn't bend my style and churn out commercial paintings. I just had to wait it out until the public became brave enough to live with my paintings."

It took courage indeed to buy a Janvier canvas. His paintings — and the underlying ethnic messages — were strong enough to completely overshadow the pleasant landscapes on most people's walls. But gradually public taste conformed to Janvier's unconformity. As more and more paintings sold, he became known and accepted not *despite* but *because* of his style. His Indian heritage had changed from a liability to an asset.

But it took Jacqueline's insistence to convince him of this. "I was too scared to jump into freelancing," he said. And then he pointed to his pretty blonde wife. "If it hadn't been for her stubborn pushing, I might still be working in 9 to 5 jobs to make ends meet."

Jacqueline, a former school teacher he met on the reserve, expressed the confidence typical of a white person: "I told him we'd be all right, and I'm proud that we dared to become independent. It's about time white people learned that treaty Indians can be successful too."

She is tired of being classified as a member of a dependent

minority group, and her eyes flash as she recalls the druggist who asked her for her welfare numbers.

"As if Indians were automatically welfare cases."

The Janvier family's income from Alex's work far exceeds that of welfare payments. His paintings sell in commercial galleries all across Canada, and private and public commissions keep him working steadily. In fact, Janvier paintings are reaching the status of investment art, and it looks as if Alex is in danger of becoming a member of the artistic "establishment".

So why does he still add his treaty number to his signature?

He no longer needs to prove his point. Has he become a rebel without a cause?

He is thoughtful for a moment. And then he admits that he is emotionally attached to 287. It stands for his own and other Indians' protests against a group that regards people as mere numbers.

"Maybe the day will come when governments change their functions. When I can see really significant action in Ottawa, then I might quit 287. But I suspect it'll be a long time yet before I become an Indian without his number."

Payepot
The Sioux-Cree Chief
Abel Watetch

'Way back in 1816 a party of Plains Crees were encamped near what is now the border between Canada and the United States. One very sultry day, when storm clouds had gathered low overhead, rumbling with the breath of the Thunder Bird, a son was born to a young Cree couple.

It was the custom of the Crees to name a child for whatever object or incident was first observed when the wail indicated a new life had begun. As this little Cree's cry began there was a great flash of lightning leaping across the blue sky. So the newcomer was named Kisikawawasan Awasis, or Flash-in-The-Sky-Boy.

He had a grandmother in the camp and this wise old woman felt that the child would some day be a great leader of the Crees, a medicine man, perhaps a chief. So she took over the care of the infant while the young parents resumed killing and preparing food for the band.

Not long after his birth, some of the hunters, far out on the prairie, came upon a lonely white man, who had been left behind by a party of explorers because he was ill. The hunters took the man back to camp and gave him shelter and food and tried to nurse him back to health. They did not know that the man had smallpox.

Smallpox was the terror of all Indians, since the first terrible epidemic had spread like fire among them a generation before this time, killing thousands of their kith and kin. The one instinct of the Indians was flight. So when they realized what had happened, they rode off in all directions, abandoning all those who were unable to follow them. Survival of the few depended on their ruthlessness, for there was nothing they could do to combat the horrible disease.

Presently there was no one left in the camp but the grandmother and her helpless charge. Neither of them was infected with smallpox, but the outlook was grim for there was no one to hunt for them and no other food within the reach of the old woman.

With the stoicism of the Indian she began setting up a shelter for herself and the child from the bits and pieces the others had left behind them and contrived a little tepee from oddments of buffalo hides.

She kept the child alive by going about gathering old buffalo bones and boiling them in a kind of bag made of buffalo hide hung on stakes, dropping hot stones into the water, to make soup.

Autumn was approaching and the old grandmother had no

means of coping with winter weather that was not far off. But she went bravely on, buoyed up by her secret belief that this was a child destined for greatness.

Some dogs had also been abandoned and one day as she was sitting with the child on her knees, she noticed that the dogs were uneasy and restless and sometimes howled. She pricked up her ears, because it seemed to portend that something was not far off.

It was some time before a party of Sioux (also a hunting party) came from the south, right to the campsite. She was terrified of the traditional enemy of her people and had hidden in her shelter. The Sioux, when they saw human bodies lying about, turned to ride away. But one of them saw a movement under the shelter and so they rode over to the pile of skins.

When they found the old lady with a fine boy in her arms, they took them both prisoners and rode off with them towards Dakota.

In the Sioux country the woman and the child were well cared for. The boy grew up speaking Sioux and was taught all the skills of a Sioux hunter and warrior.

When he was about fourteen years of age, a Cree war party surprised this band of Sioux and since war was a game and a skill, just as was buffalo hunting, they attacked the Sioux camp and put them to rout. Then the grandmother, seeing the attackers and hearing their familiar voices cried out that she was a Cree and pointed out Kisikawawasan Awasis, telling them who he was. She convinced them, and the victorious Crees rode away to the north carrying the boy and his grandmother with them, back to their favourite country, the headwaters of the Qu'Appelle River. This was about 1830.

In the camp of his own people, Flash-in-The-Sky-Boy had to learn to use his own language and to pick up the habits and customs of the band. Naturally he was an object of great interest, for he could now tell them a great deal about the Sioux they had not known before. The Crees laughingly called him "the Sioux Cree" or Nehiyawapot. This came to be accepted as the name of the band for now they had the skills of the two cultures, their own and the Sioux, at their command. To this day the Cree name for Payepot's band is Nehiyawapot. A brother of Flash-in-The-Sky-Boy gave him a nickname, Payepot, which is "a hole in the Sioux" meaning probably that he had made a breach in the secret life of their enemies, the Sioux, and had brought them intimate knowledge of the Sioux way of life. The nickname stuck to the boy and he became known to history as Payepot.

As he grew to manhood he proved to be remarkable in many ways. He was a famous warrior, a revered Medicine Man, a great horse thief, bringing in many fine horses for the use of the band. And he was also a man of vision and wisdom and was called to sit in the council of the Rattler's tepee, the council of the bravest. In the rain dance he acquired a reputation for magic in rain making.

No one knows when Payepot became a chief but doubtless it was when he was a mature man, at the height of his skill as a hunter and warrior which may have been in the 1840s. If so, he was a chief for more than sixty years.

Canada's "Indian" Senator
Jacques Hamilton

James Gladstone, in a way, is the personification of all the history of Alberta.

His memories go back to a childhood when he lived in a tee-pee on the open prairie, when transportation was a horse and a travois, and when the buffalo still ran free.

Now in his eighties, he talks with easy familiarity of men we associate with the very beginnings of our heritage — Col. Macleod, Jerry Potts, the famous Indian chiefs, a grandfather who built Fort Whoop-Up.

"All this was open country then," he muses in his home in Cardston. "Wherever we went we camped, and there was nothing to disturb us and no one to chase us away. All this land was ours. It belonged to us."

By "us", of course, James Gladstone means Alberta's Indian people. And that "us" is, at the same time, his favorite private joke and the greatest honor of his life.

"What Indian is in me," he explains with a twinkle of his blue eyes, "is from Winnipeg. That's where my grandfather married this girl — French half-breed as far as I can learn, according to the name of her and all. Best I can do is about an eighth Indian — by blood."

But "blood" isn't what counts with Jim Gladstone. By choice — and by appointment — he is an Indian, and the greatest statesman his people have.

Raised as an Indian boy, he spoke Cree before he spoke English, and was fluent in Blackfoot by the time he was 12.

From childhood on, he made it his destiny to fight for the rights of his people; a fight he still continues, and which paid off in the unique honor at age 33 of being legally adopted as a full treaty Indian by the Blackfoot.

He remembers that day as the greatest of his life. Greater even, perhaps, than the day in the 1950s when he heard that John Diefenbaker had appointed him a member of the Canadian Senate — the only "Indian" ever to be elevated to such high status in the Dominion.

And if anyone ever wants to question just how Indian Jim Gladstone really is, all they have to do is look back to the day he made his maiden speech in Canada's upper house — in Blackfoot.

"You think Indians got a good deal in this country?" he demands abruptly. "Well they haven't. And I'm not going to stop fighting till they do."

Jim Gladstone makes that a determined promise.

But, then, Jim Gladstone has all Alberta history within his life-span.

And, in the end, that kind of determination and promise may very well be what our Alberta heritage is all about. . . .

Jerry Potts
Andrew Suknaski

1

jerry potts
crow black eyes
and moustache a raven feather
wrapped around the upper lip —
in the famous photograph
he stands
as though the west wind
is curving around his shoulders
as though the wind
has suddenly shifted
and a northeast wind
twists
his hips and spine

jerry potts
better known as *kehyokosi*
in his time
among the plains indians
where his legend began —
kehyokosi
beloved bear child
born somewhere
before 1840 to *namopisi*
crooked back
of the bloods
and andrew potts from scotland
bear child
who later rises to fame
and is
an honoured warrior
among the blackfoot

his father
working for the american
fur trading company
is a factor
at fort benton the day
a young clerk
haggles with a blackfoot
who finally bears a grudge
out into a willow grove
hides
and waits patiently for sundown
and revenge —
the clerk leaves work early
and old andrew potts is left
with the daily chore
closing shutters
the blackfoot finally sees
an arm reaching into evening twilight
and empties a buffalo gun
into the old man's chest

bear child's story
becomes vague at this point
some claim
he is then adopted by alexander harvey
a wild
and lusty trader
on the upper missouri
a man
who abandons the boy
five years later
the boy
then adopted once again
by andrew dawson
a gentle scot

others tend to believe
the more colourful story:
bear child a young boy
skilful with a rifle
and how the evening his father dies
he follows
the murderer's trail day and night
back to camp
where the blackfoot
arrives whooping and boasting
about his act —
how the boy shoots him dead
with a single shot
in front of the man's own tepee
how the boy is honoured by the old men
for his bravery
and is taken in and taught
the blackfoot way of life
how to hunt
and track —
how he is later respected
and further honoured
in inner councils

once he is chosen
above all other chiefs
to lead the forces
of the blackfoot confederacy
against piapot and 700 assiniboine
and cree —
300 to 500 of the enemy die
and bear child
leaves the battlefield
with 19 scalps
dangling from his belt —

this
the last battle among indians
of the northwest
and the end of bear child's
indian life

2

our guides
except for louis leveille
had all been hopeless —
a few of us rode
down to fort benton in 1874
we had heard of potts
that he was the finest guide
one could hope for
he joined us
the first day we arrived

the day we rode home
he rode far ahead of colonel french
and the rest of us —
when we caught up to him
in the evening
he'd already finished skinning
a young buffalo
there was a crystal spring nearby
and he'd already
started a campfire

there was something uncanny
about the way
he led us unfailingly
to different waterholes fed by springs —
one evening
by the fireplace at fort walsh
while we smoked and drank

colonel steele commented:
— *potts has a kind of sixth sense*
always knows where he is
in a blizzard or even
complete darkness

the winter of 1875
potts led four of us
from fort brisbois to helena montana
200 miles away —
we were picking up money ottawa had sent
for the force
on our first day
we arrived in fort macleod
and the wind was from the northeast —
it was a cold
and truly miserable day
and it continued to drift
out on the open prairie
all of the next day
on the third day the drifting
turning into a wailing storm
but potts wouldn't stop
finally
he led us down a bank of the milk river
it was evening
and the storm had worsened
and we couldn't see a thing
so we set up camp —

a small buffalo herd pressed in upon us
to seek shelter
by the river bank
we spent two days and nights
at that place
and it grew colder and colder

till some of the men began to panic
and were certain
we would freeze to death —
then potts decided
he would guide us to a shack
at rocky springs 30 miles away
while we rode south the storm
died down
but by the late afternoon the wind
rose again
and our tired horses stumbled along
our progress seeming
something mechanical
we followed potts
with our blind confidence
till it was twilight —
potts seemed a ghost from a dream
as he rode
in the storm ahead of us — suddenly
he reined his horse
to a halt
and slowly dismounted
riding up
we suddenly found ourselves
beside the shack
we had reached rocky springs
as potts groped for the doorhandle
we suddenly realized
he was nearly
completely snowblind

3

then there was the day
grayburn took his turn on herd duty

watching over our horses
three miles from fort walsh —
upon returning home late
in the afternoon
he realized he'd left
a lariat and axe behind
and returned
to retrieve the articles

that evening
when the young policeman didn't return
we sent out a search party —
when it grew too dark
the men finally returned
having found nothing

the following morning
i joined another search party
led by potts
a light snow had fallen
during the night
and tracks had disappeared —
we circled the area
where we thought our horses
had been grazing
and coming to our tracks again
potts noticed
a bright patch of blood
within a hoof print —
he then rode south towards a tree
when we got there
we found a hat
hanging on a branch

beyond the tree
and down in the coulee
we found grayburn's body

then one of the men found the horse
tied to a branch
of a chokecherry tree
the horse had been shot
through the head —
potts silently circled the coulee
for a while
as we all waited
he then returned
having reconstructed all
that had happened —
he quietly mumbled:
they two injun
ride while with grayburn
slow down
when he ahead
shoot him in back
i questioned him:
how do you know this potts?
he replied:
three trail
two bare hoof mark
injun pony
grayburn trail deeper
his horse
have horse shoe

star child the murderer
was arrested
some time later —
a jury consisting of ranchers
found him *not guilty*
however
a few years later he received
five years
for horse stealing

4

me teach schofield be guide
teach him injun way

tole him:
wear buckskin
feel better
after day in saddle

teach him kindle campfire
injun way
use two three
small twig
put plenty buffalo chip round —
he laugh at me
first time i do this
i tole him:
damnfool whiteman
build big fire
stand long way off —
injun build small fire
squat down close

one evening we ride
jack rabbit jump up
over hill —
i take gun one hand
shoot him dead
one shot
funny schofield surprised — say:
jerry
where you learn to shoot that way?
i tole him:
you hungry
you shoot good

that night campfire burn low
we talk

drink bottle whiskey —
i put small piece buffalo fat
in coals
injun style
small fire wake up
i tole schofield
when fire die down:
this country
get too damn soft
for me

Death of a Son
Hugh Dempsey

By June 1885 the rebels were beaten, the dreams of native
self-government were shattered, and the white man had become unchallenged master of the Canadian West. Poundmaker was in jail, refugees were fleeing into Montana, and
everywhere was the chaotic aftermath of a brief but bitter
war.

When Crowfoot learned that his adopted son would face
trial in Regina, he sent an anxious letter to Governor Dewdney
asking for mercy.

> I, Crowfoot, having lately heard that Poundmaker
> has been arrested and taken to Regina for having been
> connected with the rebellion, I wish to say that I sent
> word to him to remain loyal, but my words did not
> reach him until he had been persuaded into joining the
> half-breeds. He being my adopted son and we having
> been together a great deal in past years, I have great
> affection for him and would request the Great Mother,
> through her Chiefs in Regina, as a personal favor to me,
> to grant him pardon, with the understanding that he

remains loyal in future and I promise to use my influence to the same end.

Now that the rebellion was over, Canadians were screaming for the blood of those who had led the fight, so Crowfoot's request was turned down. The Cree chief stood trial, even though evidence indicated that he had done his best to avoid conflict and to save the lives of any whites who became prisoners of the insurgents. He had taken his followers to Battleford when they were hungry. And tried to get their regular rations, but the Indian agent had fled, and the chief was powerless to stop the pillaging which followed. Later, in Colonel Otter's unprovoked attack at Cutknife Hill, only through Poundmaker's actions did the white force avoid annihilation. He had been loyal to his people but, unlike Crowfoot, he had wanted to protect the whites even during the height of the rebellion. He told the court:

> I am not guilty. A lot has been said against me that is untrue. I am glad of what I have done in the Queen's country. What I did was for the Great Mother. When my people and the whites met in battle, I saved the Queen's men. I took the firearms from my following and gave them up at Battleford. Everything I could do was to prevent bloodshed. Had I wanted war, I would not be here but on the prairie. You did not catch me. I gave myself up. You have me because I wanted peace. I cannot help myself, but I am still a man. You may do as you like with me.

Poundmaker, the adopted son of Crowfoot, was found guilty and sentenced to three years in Stony Mountain Penitentiary.

When the Blackfoot chief received the news, he was too sick to be angry. He had been bedridden for several days and was feeling the effects of the old musket ball his body still carried as a souvenir of his warring past. His condition was so grave that the Indian agent feared for his life and said that "if he died, it would be hard to replace him."

During the rest of the summer, Crowfoot carried out some of his duties, but his illness, the imprisonment of Poundmaker, and further sickness in his family made him surly and short-tempered. He helped the Mounted Police obtain the surrender of some horse thieves, one of whom was his son-in-law, but his health was too poor for any active participation in daily life. In October, when the treaty payments were made, Crowfoot was presented with one hundred dollars from a thankful government "for keeping loyal".

Early in December another of Crowfoot's children died of tuberculosis, leaving him with only three children in his own lodge. This was pathetically different from the twelve children who were crowded into his tipi at the signing of Treaty Seven. Some had since grown up and left him, but on Christmas Day, when he learned that another of his children was ill, he went to the Indian agent to be assured that Poundmaker was still alive and well. The agent took down a message from the sick chief and forwarded it to the penitentiary.

> Dear Poundmaker, I send you word that the Agent and other white men say you are well used, and I should like you to send word if it really is true. . . . I have such a feeling of lonesomeness of seeing my children dying every year and if I hear that you are dead, I will have no more use for life. I shake hands with the Agent and Mr. Dewdney, and I know they will do what they can for you. I would like to hear from you direct, how you are treated. Your father, Crowfoot.

The reply, which was received early in January, did much to hearten the ailing chief. Poundmaker assured his father that he was being well treated and had no complaints. With it was a message from Governor Dewdney, giving his sympathy to Crowfoot for the tragedies in his family and promising to visit Poundmaker to see that he was well.

The winter of 1885-86 was a mild one on the Blackfoot Reserve, but it also was a hard one. The Canadian Pacific trains, belching sparks as they thundered past, set one prairie fire after another until the whole area was a blackened ruin. Crowfoot tried to get compensation for the tribe, but the Montreal company took no action. The impatience of the chief started more rumors of war. These were pounced upon not only by sensational newspapers but also by those who were eager to heap further discredit upon the prime minister's Conservative regime. Politically, the western rebellion had been a severe blow to his party, and the execution of Riel as a traitor had opened a wide rift between English and French Canada.

Rumors were spread that the Bloods were joining with American tribes to make common war on the whites. An alliance between the Kutenais, Stonies, and Blackfeet was proclaimed. As the stories spread, they became wilder and more fanciful and all predicted a rebellion in the spring of 1886. The *Toronto Mail* sent its top reporter, George H. Ham, to Blackfoot Crossing to check the facts. He arrived about a week after Crowfoot had received Poundmaker's letter, so the chief was in good spirits. The reporter quoted him as saying:

> Why should the Blackfeet create trouble? Are they not quiet and peaceable and industrious? The Government is doing well for them and treating them kindly, and they are doing well. Why should you kill us, or we kill you? Let our white friends have compassion. I have two hearts — one is like stone, and one is tender. Suppose the soldiers come and, without provocation, try to kill us. I am not a child — I know we shall get redress from the law. If they did kill us, my tender heart would feel for my people.

Death of a Son 59

The rebellion and the tragedy in his family had wrought many changes in the great chief. He was fully resigned now to the domination of the white man, but at the same time he knew that some were really sincere about trying to help his people. He was willing to work with these officials to aid his tribe in accepting the life which had been thrust upon them. He still balked at some of their proposals but no longer had the heart nor desire to fight. Some of the spark went out of the chief during the rebellion year, and from that time on he withdrew more and more into his personal life. Only on special occasions would he rise above his sickness, sadness, and sense of defeat to give dynamic leadership to his tribe. He had led the Blackfeet through the plains, into a treaty, and onto a reserve. Now he found that the controls were in the hands of those who issued rations and gave out treaty money. Like every other chief in the country, he could choose between being a leader without power and a chief who would break loose from his chains and in the process destroy his people. His choice, governed largely by his illness, was to give the Blackfeet all the diplomatic leadership he could provide. But, realistically, he no longer tried to run the reserve. This was being done by Indian Agent Magnus Begg, whom Crowfoot found to be an honest and dedicated man.

In February, Governor Dewdney took the first step to gain Poundmaker's release from prison. He dispatched a telegram to Begg, asking him to get a letter from Crowfoot. On the strength of this plea, Poundmaker was set free on March 4, after serving only about six months of the three-year sentence. He no longer was a handsome and dignified leader but a man whose health had broken down completely in those few months. One of the reasons for the quick release was the fear that he might die in jail. When he went back to his own reserve, Poundmaker was met with hatred by the surrounding white population. For five weeks he rested, then set out for Blackfoot Crossing to see his beloved father. There were three in the party — Poundmaker, his wife, and a young nephew. It took them nine days to cross the open prairies to the Blackfoot Reserve, as they had only one horse among them; the others had been seized after the rebellion. On May 21, the man who had been convicted of making war against the queen stopped wearily in front of Crowfoot's lodge.

The chief was happy to see Poundmaker, for less than a month earlier the son who had been sick since Christmas had died of tuberculosis, while another was confined to bed and was not expected to live. Saddened by these further tragedies in his family, Crowfoot welcomed the son whom he had never expected to see again.

Early in May, the other sick child passed away, leaving only one baby daughter at home, two daughters who were married, a grown son who was going blind . . . and Poundmaker. The Cree chief was the only son who had reached manhood without being disabled or deformed, so it was upon him that Crowfoot bestowed all his fatherly love and affection. For the first time in weeks the chief was happy and alert. He recovered from the illnesses which had plagued him since the rebellion and was pleased when the time came for the Sun Dance. When a messenger came from the Gros Ventres in Montana asking if he would join them in a fight against the American soldiers, he laughed it off. He sent the young warrior back with advice that the Gros Ventres should forget about fighting and settle down to their new life.

Poundmaker's health also improved during the weeks in Crowfoot's lodge, so it was with sadness that the Cree chief finally announced that he must return to his own reserve to build a new life for his followers. He would stay only until the Sun Dance was under way.

Situated on the flats near the Bow River, the great Sun Dance camp was an impressive sight. Hundreds of lodges were pitched in a great circle, with the brush-covered holy lodge in the center. Crowfoot, as always, was camped with the

Moccasin band and, although he did not join in the sacred rites, he favored this type of religion over anything the white man had to offer.

On July 4, Crowfoot and Poundmaker were guests at one of the ceremonies where holy food of thick saskatoon berry soup and bannock was passed to each man. As Poundmaker sipped a spoonful of soup, something became lodged in his throat and he started to cough violently. Suddenly the blood gushed from his mouth and in a few moments he was dead.

The doctor's diagnosis was that a burst blood vessel had caused the death. The Blackfeet, however, had their own theories, based upon their religious beliefs. According to one tale, when Poundmaker was released from prison some of his people said he should have been hanged. Worried about their threats, he went to a shaman, who said he would have a good life as long as he did not eat any saskatoon berries. When he was handed the bowl at the Sun Dance, he said, "I think I'll take a chance," but when he took one swallow he died.

Crowfoot was grief-stricken by the loss. His only healthy son was taken from him during a year when all his children were dying. In a few months his lodge had become an empty shell where there was only sadness and mourning. His favorite son, his most beloved son, was dead.

Red Crow
Mekaisto of the Bloods
J. W. Grant MacEwan

Blood Indians in what became Southern Alberta remembered Chief Red Crow or Mekaisto, the way the Blackfoot remembered Crowfoot and citizens of the United States remembered Abraham Lincoln. He possessed everything an Indian admired. Although much of his seventy years was spent in fighting Cree, Crow and Snake Indian neighbours, Red Crow emerged as a man of good sense, exhorting his people to live in peace. On July 15, 1944, a cairn was dedicated to the honour of this man who was among the signers of Treaty Number Seven, this man who was regarded as a prophet and spoke for many years on behalf of his tribesmen.

Born about 1830, his birth place was believed to be a short distance south of where the City of Lethbridge now stands. His father was Black Bear and for some years the young fellow was known as Sitting White Buffalo. . . . While still a mere boy he and another youngster of his age and disposition stole away with a party of Blood warriors going for Crow Indian horses. After arriving in Crow country the Blood Chief announced that the task of stealing the desired horses would be difficult and dangerous; nobody except mature and experienced braves were to go. The two boys were being instructed to return to the Blood camp.

But the boys refused to go back. They were eager for adventure and when the adult Bloods rode away without them, the two boys went by themselves, creeping into the Crow encampment by night, taking two horses found tied beside the lodges and some trophies which had been hanging outside what they supposed was the Chief's tipi. As it turned out, the two boys returned home with the best horses and the most valuable trophies taken in the course of the entire expedition. The old warriors were embarrassed.

In due course Sitting White Buffalo became a Blood brave. The qualifying ceremony was part of a Sun Dance and this young man was one who inserted thongs under the skin of his breast and then swung and tugged against the leather ropes which tied him to the central pole of the Sun Dance lodge until skin and inflamed and painful flesh broke to release him. Having demonstrated such capacity for the endurance of suffering the young man was admitted to the noble fraternity of braves or warriors.

On his first legitimate warpath he failed to win the glory every young Blood sought; it was against the Crees and he returned without scalps and without stolen horses. But thereafter his record was one to fill every young male with envy and every young female with admiration. Most of his many forays against enemy tribes were directed at the hated Crow and Snake Indians of southern districts.

On one of his earliest entries into Snake country he captured a horse which was still wild and unbroken and allowed the animal to drag him almost into the enemy camp where, still undetected, he was able to cut out forty of the Snake horses and head them north toward home territory. For a young man working alone it was a great feat and it allowed him to make gifts in the form of horses to all his friends.

Stealing horses from the Snake Indians became something of a specialty with Red Crow. No sooner would he deliver a band of stolen stock than he would be away for another and Snakes and Crows were particularly anxious to catch him and get his scalp. The technique, generally, was to sneak into the area of an enemy camp under cover of night, catch a good horse, mount it and drive the rest of the horses away leaving the enemy horseless and helpless. It was the glorious pastime of horse stealing and there was nothing to equal it.

And what Indians were more proficient in horse stealing than Red Crow's Bloods? The editor of the *Macleod Gazette*, in October 1885 estimated 300 stolen horses on the Blood Reservation alone with the number increasing steadily. Most of these were from Indian camps in Montana. The Bloods loved the game and were reluctant to give it up. One of those who learned the art of horse stealing from Red Crow was Bernard Tall Man who died at the age of eighty-seven in 1961. He was pertinacious more than lucky. On one horse stealing expedition to Montana he was arrested by a United States marshal and sentenced to two years in penitentiary. After serving sentence he returned to the Crow camp to try again to get the horses. Again he was captured by United States officers and again sentenced to two years in penitentiary. After the second release from jail he settled down to farm on the Blood Reserve, near Cardston, but he did not forget the Crow horses and on the third try was successful.

Of course, not all the horses in that time of widespread stealing were moving in the same direction. The *Calgary Tribune* of May 23, 1888, told of 31 horses being taken from the Blood Indians on a recent day, these having been spirited away by Gros Ventre Indians from south of the border. The editor added: "A party from the Blood Reserve has gone in pursuit and there will be gore if the marauding party is overtaken." On one expedition Red Crow succeeded in getting a band of horses from the Crows only to find that here were the same horses which his Bloods had lost just a few days before.

For all prairie Indians, war and horse stealing went together and, ignoring the dangers, they saw such activities as intertribal games; the enemy was for killing and enemy horses were for stealing. But as a game, this one had no rules to impede an ambitious man's progress.

Red Crow could recall being with a party of Bloods going south to Crow country and passing a big band of Crow warriors obviously on the way north to attack the Bloods. As it was, the two parties passed a few miles apart and the Bloods saw the Crows while the Crows were unaware of the Bloods. At once, Red Crow's warriors recognized an opportunity to gain an advantage over the enemy and quickly divided their warrior force, sending half the fighting men back north to a position where they could effectively ambush the invading Crows; and at the same time sending the other half south to attack the defenceless Crow camp before the Crow invaders could return. The result was double victory for Red Crow and his Bloods.

Such was Red Crow's life for more than forty years yet, strangely enough, he came to old age without wounds or scars from arrows, bullets or axes.

Blood conduct had been more or less like that for

generations — raiding, warring, hunting — but by 1870 the winds of change were blowing briskly. Chief Black Bear died that year and was succeeded by his son, Red Crow. The rise of a great leader should be seen as a matter of importance at any time but more subtle were changes involving whiskey traders, decline of buffalo and the coming of the white man with written laws and strict ideas about enforcing those laws.

Traders from Montana built Fort Hamilton, a few miles south of where the City of Lethbridge arose, and Blood Indians, ready to exchange buffalo robes for poor and diluted whiskey, became the best customers. In the course of a drunken celebration they set the fort afire and watched it burn to the ground. The Fort Benton men lost no time in rebuilding. The second and bigger trading post became known as Fort Whoop-Up.

Having no understanding of the dangers in the white man's nefarious brew the Indians became willing victims and soon suffered demoralization. Traders without conscience took buffalo skins from the Indians, passed the trade whiskey through a hole in the stockade, made sure the gates were closed and bolted, and laughed as the inebriated natives took to pommelling and massacring each other. Seventy Indians were said to have been murdered outside the walls of one trading post in a single year.

Red Crow was among those who patronized the whiskey traders when they first came to the Alberta country but afterwards was opposed to the use of whiskey by Indians. Donald Graham who was hunting on the plains in 1872 and '73 and whose narration, as edited by Hugh Dempsey, was published in the *Alberta Historical Review*, Winter 1956, told of an episode near the Elbow River post operated by Fred Kanouse. "A Blood chief named Maycasto (Red Crow) had brought a considerable quantity of liquor back to his camp with him and of course they celebrated when they got there. After the festivities had got pretty well along, a few of the young fellows thought they would have a bit of fun at the old chief's expense. So one said: 'Old Maycasto is too drunk now to help himself and he has been pretty mean to us sometimes. We will tie him up and get even with him.' They made a laughing move toward him but the chief drew his revolver and in less time than it takes to tell, there were two dead Indians and several more wounded."

Red Crow had a violent temper. There was no doubt about that. He also had the sense to see the whiskey trade as an evil and then he cooperated with the police to stamp it out.

Communication was primitive and most crimes arising from drinking bouts outside the whiskey traders' posts went unnoticed for a time, but by 1873 the Government of Canada was ready to provide law enforcement for the area. The North-West Mounted Police came into existence and late in the next year the main body of the new force halted at a point on the Oldman River after a long and trying march across the plains and built Fort Macleod.

Not waiting for the Police to come to him, Red Crow visited Assistant Commissioner Macleod at the new fort. He wanted to know how the Police proposed to operate. The officer explained the principle on which his men would administer justice for all people, Indians and whites alike. The Chief welcomed an end to the whiskey trade and pledged his cooperation. Indeed, he gave it even to the point of travelling all the way from his camp to Fort Macleod, carrying a mouthful of whiskey which had been given to him by a trader. This the Chief deposited in a police cup as evidence.

Later, the Chief said: "Three years ago when the Mounted Police came to my country, I met and shook hands with Stamix Otokan (Col. Macleod) at the Belly River. Since then he has made me many promises and kept them all — not one of them has been broken. Everything that the Mounted Police have done has been for our good. I trust Stamix Otokan and will leave everything to him."

When the Chief was not entirely convinced that police action was right he could be obstinate. There was the day when police officers set out to arrest two Bloods on charges of cattle stealing but the action resulted in an uproar in the camp and the two men were forcibly taken from the police. A bigger and stronger detachment of law officers was sent at once to the reserve with a message for Red Crow: "The wanted men must be surrendered immediately." The Chief was well aware of the temper of his people and hesitated. He said he would consider the request. But that did not satisfy the police and they presented him with another message, to the effect that he had to personally turn the wanted men over or the police would at the end of an hour take them by force. Red Crow knew the police meant exactly what they said and just as the hour was about to elapse he appeared with the wanted men.

But on another occasion, when the police were looking for horses stolen from Gros Ventre Indians in Montana, the trail led to the Blood Reserve. After finding the horses there the police arrested four suspects and took them to Fort Macleod for trial. Before the hearing started Chief Red Crow came forward to turn over to the police his own son, reporting that he, too, had been on the particular horse stealing expedition to the Montana reserves.

Red Crow appeared to be overshadowed by his contemporary, Chief Crowfoot of the Blackfoot. But Crowfoot respected Red Crow's judgment and wanted it when decisions affecting all Indians had to be made. Both Chiefs were signers of Treaty Number Seven and although Crowfoot was recognized as the "Chief of Chiefs", negotiations were delayed for three days in order to have Red Crow present. The Blood Chief and his people were hunting and with typical Indian disregard for time he failed to appear on the day set for discussions — or the next day. Most writers tell that the delay was requested by representatives of the Government of Canada but there is strong evidence that it was Crowfoot who wanted to have his wise friend present when the important decision had to be made. Finally Red Crow arrived and the negotiations were carried through without further delay.

By the terms of the Treaty a large reservation area in what became Central Alberta was to serve Bloods, Sarcees and Blackfoot. But the plan was poorly conceived and when the Bloods travelled into Montana in 1879, looking for buffalo herds, they returned only as far as Fort Macleod, refusing to go to the north side of the Bow River. The buffalo and other game upon which the Indians had depended were gone and the tribesmen were hungry and depressed. They camped along the Oldman River and managed to convince the government representatives that they should remain in that area. A year or two later a new reservation comprising 540 square miles was established between the Bloods' temporary campground and the St. Mary River. There they settled, built log homes and cultivated to grow grains, potatoes and turnips. There the old Chief Red Crow, accepting the new order as inevitable, settled down to become a good example to the rest of his tribe. This man who could boast a long list of successes as a killer, this man who was a proven expert in stealing horses, settled down to become a man of peace and a law-biding citizen.

"We have had enough war. I think we can live without it," he said. "If civilization can tame the buffalo so that they are like cattle, the lesson is one that I should not forget."

He was the first of the Bloods to build a log house, the first to grow grain and the first to keep cattle.

When trouble erupted at Duck Lake on the South Saskatchewan River in 1885 and every Indian felt the lust to join in rebellion, Red Crow considered carefully and then acted firmly. He refused to allow the couriers carrying inflammatory messages from Louis Riel's men to come on the Blood Reserve.

Red Crow continued as Chief until the time of his death, August 28, 1900, to be followed in the high office by his adopted son, Crop Eared Wolf. By that time the elder was past

80 years of age. Most people would say a man of such age is too old for leadership, but the Bloods saw him as a man of superior judgement, still the man they wanted as their Head Chief. And not even at his passing did the Bloods forget the tall, lean figure and face that was good looking but not handsome. Perhaps they continued to remember the violent temper he displayed when a young man, so violent that he killed a brother who made some insulting remark about his appearance. They would remember him as a man who gave the missionaries every opportunity to work on the reserve but rejected the white man's religion for himself, saying: "the faith of my fathers is my choice." They might remember him as a man with a twinkle in his black eyes and a good sense of humour. Certainly they would remember him as the quiet forceful personality, the unchallenged spokesman and leader of his people for three decades.

Tom Three Persons
Cowboy Champion of 1912
J. W. Grant MacEwan

Tom Three Persons was the Blood Indian whose bronco riding championship in 1912 brought about as much public surprise as Seager Wheeler's world championship for wheat, won only a few months earlier. Nobody expected a Saskatchewan homesteader to win the highest international honours for wheat in 1911 and nobody expected an Indian from the Blood Reserve to stagger into town and outride and outpoint the continent's best rodeo cowboys assembled for Calgary's first Stampede.

Tom Three Persons, as he appeared at that pioneer Stampede, was tall, powerful and handsome and looked like a movie hero. Indeed, Hollywood would have welcomed such an Indian personality at any time. But it was the rodeo triumph more than the personality that brought cheers from Indians and whites alike. "The Champion is a Canadian," people were saying with astonishment and glee. "And an Indian at that! How do you account for it?"

But there was nothing so strange about the event; Tom Three Persons had the muscle and determination to succeed in just about anything he attempted. He had been an outstanding athlete, and in later years he demonstrated clearly that an Indian living on a reserve could be a good business man and a successful farmer and rancher. Just prior to his death in 1949 he had about 500 high-grade Hereford cattle and almost 400 horses on his ranch land between Cardston and Standoff. Tom liked fast horses and some of those in his band were thoroughbreds and candidates for race tracks. Indeed, this Indian's comfortable home just east of the big St. Mary River irrigation dam, his bank account and his herds would have been enough to bring satisfaction to most neighbours living outside the reserve.

Tom was born right there on the Blood Reserve — the biggest Indian Reserve in Canada — and even as a boy his fearlessness and dexterity in handling horses won local attention. When old enough to be employed, he worked for neighbouring ranchers and became an expert roper as well as horseman. He gained his first rodeo experience while employed with the Quarter Circle Two Bar Ranch. Entering competition for the first time, at Lethbridge in 1908, he won in riding and then went on to compete at Havre, Montana.

The story goes that the Mounted Police at Fort Macleod recognized Tom Three Persons's skill in breaking horses long before 1912 and made it a point to have him in custody whenever they had fresh bronco stock requiring the attention of a fearless trainer. It would seem that Tom cooperated by consuming enough liquor to warrant arrest at any time the police needed him and he was serving time at Fort Macleod when the rodeo performers were converging upon Calgary in

1912. It was a most inopportune time for a young cowboy to be in jail but he had a few friends working for him and through the good offices of Glen Campbell, Indian Commissioner for Canada and also a great rider, he was able to gain release in time to enter the Calgary contests.

The police officers were sorry to see their favourite Indian "customer" leaving ahead of schedule but they wished him well as he took leave to travel northward. He had no worries about a hotel reservation because many of his Blood friends were already on the Stampede grounds, having brought their tipi homes with them. Arriving in the big city of 50,000 people, Tom simply moved in with his Indian friends.

There was no doubt about the high calibre of the Stampede, as Manager Guy Weadick had planned and organized it. The best rodeo performers from as far south as Texas had answered Weadick's call: "The big prize money is here; come and get it." And to put the best cowboys to proper tests, Weadick secured the wildest cattle and the most unruly bucking horses available in both United States and Canada. The most famous of the equine outlaws secured for the contests was the black gelding, Cyclone, an explosive bucker which had taken the conceit out of hundreds of rodeo performers by plunging them to the ground. The only comfort in drawing an animal reputed to be the continent's most wicked bucker was in the knowledge that nobody was expected to stay with him and the humiliation of a fall was minimum.

The powerful black horse had his own peculiar way of rearing on his hind legs, almost to the point of toppling over backward, then bringing his front end down heavily with muzzle almost touching the ground. If a rider did not fall off over the cantle of his saddle he could easily go off in front. And if these simple expedients failed to unseat the cowboy contestant Cyclone had a huge store of violent tricks of other kinds, always more than enough to accomplish his purpose.

This was the horse Tom Three Persons drew for his final

ride. Up to that point in the week his score was good, but Cyclone had been the means of downfall for every other cowboy who tried to ride him at Calgary. The outlaw had treated them all alike; good riders such as Clem Gardner had been dumped and with no more ceremony than riders of lesser stature. Most people were saying: "This will be the end of the Stampede for poor Tom. He'll just last for three or four jumps on Cyclone."

The young Indian may have been worried but he did not admit it. He studied the big black brute, considered the horse's peculiar style and manner, then buckled on his goatskin chaparejos. With no change of expression, he declared himself ready for the dangerous test. Snubbed and saddled, Cyclone was unruly as always, impatient in his eagerness to get along with the routine of dumping another rider. Tom checked the cinch to make sure it was tight, pulled down his high-crowned cowboy hat to ensure its security on his head and mounted.

"Let him go," he called. At once Cyclone was in motion, straining every muscle and groaning in anger. He had been through this hundreds of times and must have known it would not take long.

Guy Weadick, writing in *The Canadian Cattlemen*, September 1945, described the performance:

> When the horse was first turned loose the Indian hit him in both shoulders with his spurs — and hard. This was something the old pony was not used to and it surprised him. He went into his usual high rear and when he came down there was no tight, restraining rein holding his head and the Indian hit him again with his spurs in both shoulders. Then Cyclone got mad and really started in to buck and did everything in the list to try and unseat the rider who kept hitting him with his spurs at every jump. The horse finally quit bucking and stood still. The judges ordered the pickup men to get the horse. The ride was over.

Spectators could hardly believe it. An Alberta cowboy — "an Indian, of all people" — had mastered the invincible Cyclone. The cheering became boisterous. Indians normally undemonstrative, shouted their delight. The excited onlookers were not waiting for the judges to announce their decision; they knew very well that Tom Three Persons was the new World Champion in the Bucking Horse section and winner of a beautiful handmade saddle, a belt with gold buckle and one thousand dollars in cash.

Apart from the Victory Stampede produced in 1919 by Guy Weadick, the event did not take place again until 1923, when the Calgary Exhibition adopted the stampede as an annual feature. Tom Three Persons returned regularly to compete but did not repeat his riding success of 11 years before. His achievements after that memorable day were in other fields of endeavour. . . . There was nothing dull about Tom Three Persons.

Even in marital matters his experience was varied and, to outsiders, somewhat confusing. George Gooderham, whose long service with the Department of Indian Affairs qualified him to judge, pronounced Tom Three Persons as "the most colourful and best known Blood Indian of his time".

As Tom grew older — Mr. Gooderham wrote — he travelled faster, the saddle horse being replaced by the motor car. He found, however, that his favourite "spirits" did not blend so well with the car as they had done with the trusted saddle horse. One day he was forced to buy two Fords to get home. The first was smashed up when it veered and hit a bridge girder. Fortunately, it was not too late in the day to buy another. His life was filled with romance as well as action and trouble.

Not many Indians or whites at that time had the financial resources to allow the purchase of a second car about the way a man might be expected to buy a replacement for a worn tire. But in spite of a pronounced cowboy recklessness the Tom Three Persons operations were highly profitable, with most revenue being from cattle and grain. Exercising the imagination of a seasoned business man, this Indian decided during the '30s when prices were sadly depressed that it would be a good time to start building a herd of cattle. There was lots of grass and water on the Reserve and most of it was not being used. With money saved from wages he bought cattle and placed his brand on them. He traded horses to get more cattle and by the time prices had recovered after the War his herd had grown to a substantial size and his income for 1948 was said to have reached $50,000.

Although a modest fellow, he was proud of his home and ranch near Spring Coulee. He had every reason to be proud. Frequently he was mentioned as the biggest operator and most successful Indian rancher in Canada.

"Now and then he'd come in for repairs," said Dr. J. K. Mulloy, who was the official medical officer at the Reserve. "He'd break an arm or some ribs and when his own brand of 'medicine' failed to kill the pain, he'd come looking for help." On one of his visits to the hospital, an X-ray showed Tom to be carrying a hypodermic needle deep in his body. If it had bothered him he did not complain, but in searching for an explanation somebody recalled Tom coming to the hospital at Cardston years before, seeking attention for a broken arm. The medical man in charge found it necessary to administer an anaesthetic but the patient's heart, battered by many a gale, gave signs of stopping right there. The attending doctor called for adrenalin and quickly plunged the hypodermic needle into what looked like a dying man. But the muscular reaction was violent and the needle, deeply imbedded, broke off. It was not the proper moment to start probing for a needle, and when the search was undertaken the thing could not be found. Tom carried it for the rest of his days.

Tom's most serious accident occurred when herding horses in 1946. It resulted in a fractured pelvis and the great cowboy did not fully recover. Remaining lame, he generally carried a piece of poplar to serve as a cane when walking. His only complaint was that injury was keeping him out of the saddle. But in the summer of 1949 he was taken ill at his home and Ralph D. Ragan, Indian Agent at the Blood Reserve, brought him to a Calgary hospital. There, after a month or so, he died at age 63. Funeral services were held at St. Mary's Catholic Church, Cardston, and hundreds of people, palefaces and Indians, gathered to pay tribute to a popular and successful Indian and a fascinating personality: devil-may-care cowboy, great rider and successful rancher leaving a valuable estate.

Walking Buffalo
A Man for Our Time
Johanna Wenzel

Walking Buffalo didn't sail the seven seas, he didn't scale the Himalayas, nor did he write a bestseller. But he is well remembered in Canada and other parts of the world as a man with a special message. Long before he reached his nineties this Indian, from the Stoney tribe in Southern Alberta, had built a bridge between two civilizations. It wasn't a private property bridge — better yet, it could be used by anyone in either direction. Unlike the Bow River crossing near his old log house, his bridge of dialogue was never washed out.

With his death in December 1967 Walking Buffalo concluded over half a century as the most popular, the most photographed Indian of the West. Part of his appeal was the elaborate feathered dress and the buffalo horns he wore in parades at the Calgary Stampede, and at Banff Indian Days.

He was a chief, a man of stature; he understood people and he understood himself.

Walking Buffalo had managed to find a compromise between his old beloved world and the strange new Canada taking shape. With good reason could he have wished the white race back over the Atlantic, or right into it, then returned to his broken people and help restore their freedom and dignity. But it never came to that. The white man stayed and multiplied and took over the country. That is history. Walking Buffalo was level-headed. He accepted facts. In his opinion negotiation was the only way to deal with the newcomers. He gave up the freedom to roam and hunt, to settle wherever he pleased, as his father and grandfather had done before him. The bond with nature, however, and his need to live in the wide open country, he never compromised. This is where he found order, logic, example and strength.

Walking Buffalo was born in the Morley area, forty miles west of Calgary, in the 1870s. The exact year is difficult to establish, because records vary. But he thought it was March 20, 1871. His mother, Emma Kaquitts, died when he was still small. When Thomas, his father, asked the two grandmothers to raise the child they were glad to oblige. Walking Buffalo remembered these two women with affection. From them he learned the history of the tribe. At school age he entered the McDougall mission in Morley. The Rev. John McLean gave him the name George McLean, but for the rest of his life he was equally well known as Walking Buffalo (a name inherited from his grandfather), and Tatanga Mani.

In his teens Walking Buffalo attended the industrial school at Red Deer, where for a year and a half he learned carpentry. Subsequently he became an RCMP scout and found out how the law was enforced. Meanwhile the missionaries at Morley had made plans for his future. They thought he should study medicine in Winnipeg. But his father and uncle wanted him to return to help with farming at the reserve. Being fluent in

Assiniboine (the Stoney language) and English, he was in constant demand to translate between the tribe, the traders and government officials.

After teaching for a while at the Morley School, George McLean turned his interest to tribal politics, and soon became band counselor, then chief.

In 1896, Flora Crawler, daughter of Chief Hector Crawler, became his wife. Hector was a respected medicine man and healer, and George learned many of his medical and mystical secrets.

On a large clearing near the Bow River, surrounded by pine, poplars, willows and spruce, and some distance from the other reserve houses, George built his own fine log house. He had a vegetable garden, and raised poultry, cattle, sheep and hogs. Naturally there were horses. Walking Buffalo owned some beautiful ones, and he was a good rider.

His main contact with the outside world came through attending the Banff Indian Days, where he rode in the parade for 77 summers and talked to thousands of strangers. His popularity was equally evident at the Calgary Stampede. There he pitched his tent in the exhibition grounds alongside Natives from other tribes for the annual festivities. Local visitors and international tourists alike were always on the lookout, not only for a glimpse into the Indians' colorful past, but especially for a man who had found his place in the present world as well. Walking Buffalo was their man. He was real and articulate. Over the years he had evolved his own philosophy, made up of Indian beliefs, Christian thinking and his own brand of common sense. It served him well. Thus when the "white savages" (a term he used with glee, but without malice) came to him for his secret of peace of mind, he simply pointed to "nature's university", where he got his continuing education.

In the years after World War II he joined Moral Rearmament, a group promoting international peace and understanding. That association took him and a few Native friends on several trips to Asia, Africa and Europe, where he spoke as a goodwill ambassador. One of his fellow travellers was Dave Crowchild, a chief of the Sarcees. On these trips Walking Buffalo gave his message from his heart. He talked of how much better life becomes with more kindness and how rich the world already is because of its diversity. He asked for cooperation among all people, but never suggested that to do that the races should mix. "Trees don't mix," he said, "a birch is always a birch, and a pine will always be a pine. I would like to see the Indians remain what they are." He addressed the *Bundestag* in Bonn, and had talks with government leaders in New Zealand and South Africa.

At home he was a fun-loving, lively person, but he was concerned for his own people at the same time. The large consumption of alcohol worried him. He saw what it was doing to white people, and that the break-up of Indian homes and families could be traced to the same cause. He had touched alcohol once, and then decided that life was too valuable for another round.

Walking Buffalo was of barely medium height, but his eyes radiated such strength, integrity and compassion that he was someone to look up to.

He and Flora had three daughters and one son. On his wife's death in 1949 George mourned, "Without a wife the home and the man fall apart." Later he married Maggy Hunter, widow of Chief Enos Hunter. In his final years however, when Maggy too had died, his daughter Mary Kootenay cared for him. He had meanwhile moved to a new house, a little bungalow, which had been built close to his old log house, offering a few more comforts. He even had a television, but was not impressed with the world as seen through video. "It's much better to go out into the world yourself, than to see it in your living-room," he said. "It's not real."

Dr. J. W. Grant MacEwan, Alberta's former lieutenant-governor, was a good friend of George McLean. He was so impressed with the old Indian that he wrote one book, and a chapter in another, on the man. To illustrate George's sense of humor Dr. MacEwan writes about some Scottish tourists who stopped off at Morley for pictures of the Indians. One of the Scots played the bagpipe. "I am Scottish too," replied Walking Buffalo, "my name is McLean. Just listen to our music." The Indians sang, with loud and piercing voices. "Coyote music, just like yours!" George explained with his broadest grin.

In the 10 years since his death more Indian leaders have emerged. They have articulated well the need for recognition of old claims and new rights for all natives. Nothing would have pleased him more than to see the substantial input of his people into the Berger Inquiry, which concluded in 1977.

Walking Buffalo moved from the travois into the space age, from the peace and tranquility of the foothills to the roar and thunder of the industrialized world. Despite all that he found a place for himself. He did not need a department of environment to tell him that "progress" has polluted water and air, that it has damaged wildlife and land, and that the balance between man and his world is in trouble. He lived his life in low gear, letting nature be his yardstick, his instrument panel, his television screen and his church.

He was a man for our time, a man for all times.

Volunteer
Debby Caplan

It's 3:30
and you leave the freshly-painted school
and you get on the bus
and you transfer from the comfortable to the uncomfortable,

And you get off the bus
and you sign your name in the book

and you put on the brightly-coloured smock with the tear in the
    front
and you rise in the elevator,

And you go through the wired door
and there's an indian kid crying by her bed
and the kid speaks cree
and you can't speak cree,

And you talk through a smile
and a hug
and a crayon and a doll and some paper
and the kid smiles,

And you hold her hand
and you give her a tour of the goldfish bowl
and the hanging easter bunnies
and the kid laughs,

It's 6:00
and you try to explain through a wave and a shrug
that you wish you could stay
and you care but you can't,

And you take off your smock with the tear in the front
and you put on your coat
and you pass by her room
and an indian kid is crying near her bed,

And you go through the door
and you go down in the elevator
and you get on the bus
and you transfer from the uncomfortable to the comfortable,

With an indian kid crying in your head.

Silhouettes

Grandfather

George Bowering

Grandfather
            Jabez Harry Bowering
strode across the Canadian prairie
hacking down trees
                        and building churches
delivering personal baptist sermons in them
leading Holy holy holy lord god almighty songs in them
red haired man squared off in the pulpit
reading Saul on the road to Damascus at them

Left home
            Big walled Bristol town
at age eight
            to make a living
buried his stubby fingers in root snarled earth
for a suit of clothes and seven hundred gruelly meals a year
taking an anabaptist cane across the back every day
for four years till he was whipped out of England

Twelve years old
                        and across the ocean alone
To apocalyptic Canada
                        Ontario of bone bending child labor

six years on the road to Damascus till his eyes were blinded
with the blast of Christ and he wandered west
to Brandon among wheat kings and heathen Saturday nights
young red haired Bristol boy shoveling coal
in the basement of Brandon college five in the morning

Then built his first wooden church and married
a sick girl who bore two live children and died
leaving several pitiful letters and the Manitoba night

He moved west with another wife and built children and
    churches
Saskatchewan Alberta British Columbia Holy holy holy
lord god almighty
                struck his labored bones with pain
and left him a postmaster prodding grandchildren with
    crutches
another dead wife and a glass bowl of photographs
and holy books unopened save the bible by the bed

Till he died the day before his eighty fifth birthday
in a Catholic hospital of sheets white as his hair

Grant McConachie
Jacques Hamilton

It was October 1932 and two brothers, who patrolled line 150
miles north of Edmonton for the army signal corps, returned
to their cabin after a day of work.

The Sen brothers, after a day in the cold air, decided to
light their stove which they had rigged so that it was fed by line
from a nearby pocket of natural gas.

The stove, unknown to them, had sprung a leak and, when
they went to light it, it exploded in their faces.

Both were blinded and burned badly about the face, chest,
arms and hands. They were critically injured and knew it.

Fighting against the pain, one of the brothers used his elbow to tap out a message on the telegraph key, telling headquarters in Edmonton of their situation.

A trapper, who lived nearby and who had rushed over when he heard the explosion, arrived and, following the directions of the brothers, rigged a telephone onto the line so that he could talk to Edmonton.

The man on the other end of the line was Major James Burwash, commanding officer of the corps in Edmonton, and he didn't need much of a description to realize how seriously hurt the brothers were.

But what he also realized, that they didn't yet, was that there was no way to save them.

By 1932 the airplane was already firmly entrenched as the ambulance of the north. Its speed in getting medical help to the injured and in getting the injured out to hospital, had already been demonstrated many times.

But there are two times in the year when the bush plane can't fly. In the bush, the plane has to rely on skis to land on ice or on floats to land on water. During spring break-up and the fall freeze, when rivers and lakes were neither open water nor firm ice, the bush plane was grounded.

And it was fall freeze-up now. Any pilot who tried to land to help the Sens would crack up his airplane and stand a good chance of losing his own life.

Still, Major Burwash couldn't just stand by and listen while the two men died. He put out a call for a bush pilot, any bush pilot.

"At least we can talk about it," he decided.

The man who answered his summons wasn't just any bush pilot, he was the youngest and wildest of them all, a man named Grant McConachie.

No account of northern aviation, or of Canadian aviation for that matter, could leave out Grant McConachie. He started out as one of the most reckless of the barn-stormers and ended up as president of CP Air, pioneering that company's service to Australia and the Orient.

He was a visionary, one of the first to see the possibilities of commercial air service in the north and one of the first to pursue it.

There wasn't enough ice to land on any of the rivers or lakes near the Sen cabin; the trapper confirmed that.

"Then what about beach space?" McConachie asked. "No," the trapper replied, "bush right to the edge of the water."

McConachie was dogged. Wasn't there, anywhere nearby, a lake with some kind of beach space?

It seemed there was, 10 miles from the cabin. It wasn't much of a beach but water was low at this time of year and there might be enough level area to get a plane down.

McConachie outlined his scheme to the major. He had a plane, a Fokker he used on the barn-storming circuit, sitting in a hangar nearby. It was still on wheels.

Get him a doctor and medical supplies, get the trapper to move the Sens to the lake and light a smoky fire to define wind direction, and he and his mechanic would go in.

If they banged up the plane on landing, well, the doctor was there for the Sens and the whole party could just sit it out until enough ice formed to send in a ski-equipped plane for them.

Burwash considered. There was no way he was going to risk a doctor on a hair-brained borderline expedition like this. But he would get a doctor to instruct McConachie on what to do and provide him with the needed medical supplies.

If McConachie and his mechanic wanted to risk it on that basis, fine and thank you — even if it does sound insane.

McConachie got on the improvised telephone and gave the trapper instructions. Get them over there at daybreak, he said, and make sure that fire gives enough smoke.

The trapper promised to follow instructions.

At dawn the next day, McConachie's mechanic, Chris

"Limey" Green, climbed into the enclosed "cabin" inside the fuselage of the Fokker and listened as McConachie, in the open cockpit ahead of him, ran up the engine and taxied out for take-off. Inside the cabin, already lashed firmly to the floor, was a box of medical supplies. Not that the Sens were likely to get the benefit of them, as Limey gloomily saw it.

As the plane gained speed and lifted into the air, he considered the major drawback to McConachie's scheme, a drawback the 23-year-old pilot hadn't mentioned to Burwash the night before, but that he had been considering ever since.

The wood-and-canvas Fokker was a beautifully responsive flying machine. It moved along with the greatest of ease. Stopping, however, was another matter.

It had no wheel brakes. Instead, it had a tail hook that was supposed to catch in the ground on landing and drag the plane to a halt. On frozen beach and shore ice, the hook would simply skid along the surface.

The lack of wheel brakes also posed a problem in steering. In the air and during the early stages of a landing, a plane is moving quickly enough to be guided around by its rudder. But as speed drops, the rudder becomes ineffective and the pilot steers by touching one or the other or both of the wheel brakes.

If and when the Fokker slowed below the point of rudder response, it was going to go where it wanted, which might possibly not be where McConachie or Green wanted.

These problems, McConachie decided, would solve themselves. He was a superb pilot and he knew it. He was also a superbly confident man. Even if they piled up he was sure he and Limey and that precious box of medicine would get through unharmed.

Limey may or may not have shared these optimistic visions, but at least he was along and that was what counted.

McConachie spotted the lake and glided down towards it.

"It was a big lake covered with thin ice," he recalled later. "I could see the trapper's cabin and the three men on the shore.

"The shore line, which appeared to be clear of obstructions, was frozen marsh overgrown with bullrushes, and there was a narrow margin of sand, just enough for one wheel, between the overgrowth and the lake ice. I figured if I could set one wheel down along that sand margin, the other on the flat shore ice, there was just enough room for the wing tip to clear the trees. Nothing to spare, though.

"The trapper had followed my instructions and had a fire going so the smoke would give me the wind direction, but he got a little over enthusiastic and there was so much smoke that it blinded me completely as I flew in low over the beach on the landing approach.

"After two attempts I had to give up that idea and decided that, instead of landing into the wind, which is normal so the head-wind will give you the slowest possible ground speed, I would have to try a landing down-wind. This, of course, stacked the odds higher against me because the wind would be pushing me along faster instead of acting as an air brake.

"However, there was no choice, so I had to rely on my experience with this particular aircraft to bring it in at the lowest possible airspeed. It was like treading an invisible tightrope. Just a shade slower and I knew the plane would stall and drop from the sky out of control. I kept the nose high, with a lot of power on, so we were actually wallowing down through the air in a power stall, practically hanging on the propeller.

"Then, just as the wheels were rattling over the first of the bullrushes on the shore, I chopped back the throttle completely. I cut the ignition switches to minimize the danger of fire if we cracked up, and pulled the control column full back to complete the stall and uttered a small prayer.

"It was pretty rough as we plopped down into those bullrushes. I thought the first impact would drive the undercart right up through the floor. Then we bounced and jolted along the beach. There was a frightful moment when I thought we would keep going right through the trapper's cabin. Without brakes, and with the tail-skid hook dragging uselessly on the rock-hard surface, there was nothing I could do to slow the landing run. Luckily, we rolled right up to the door of the cabin and came to a stop almost beside the bug-eyed trapper and his two patients."

McConachie saw immediately that the Sen brothers were in very bad shape. As Limey began inspecting the plane for damage, McConachie pulled out the box of lotions and ointments and bandages and began giving the injured men first-aid.

But he could see from their condition that, if he waited for the lake to freeze before he took off again, they would both die.

He asked Limey for the results of the inspection. Visibly, Limey told him, the only damage was that the fabric underbelly of the plane was split from end to end, apparently from passing over the stake of an otter trap on the beach.

Limey began sewing and McConachie turned his mind to the problem of taking off along the beach.

Again the lack of wheel brakes faced him. Without them, there was no way to hold the plane back and push up to full throttle and make a short take-off. The Fokker was built to run along, gaining speed, until it was going fast enough to become airborne. There wasn't room enough for that on this beach.

Finally he found the solution:

> We hauled the aircraft back as far as we could up a slight slope and tied the tail to a tree, running the rope over a stump we could use as a chopping block. I told the trapper to stand by with his axe while I ran up the engine to full power, then to chop the rope when I waved my hand.
>
> Meanwhile Chris had loaded the heavily bandaged patients into the cabin and made them as secure and as comfortable as he could.
>
> We were taking off into the wind, and I figured that with the down-slope and starting with full power we had a good chance of making it. I pushed the throttle wide open, waited for the engine to pick up full revs, then

gave the signal. The trapper swung his axe, the rope parted and away we went rumbling through the bull-rushes.

With full power from the start, the blast of the slip-stream over the rudder gave me full control, so it was not too difficult to thread the needle of the narrow beach between the trees and the lake. We didn't seem to hit any obstructions, but suddenly, just before the wheels left the ground, there was the most terrible vibration. I thought it would shake the plane to pieces.

I throttled back as much as I dared but by this time there was no other choice. We had to either take off or crash, so I manoeuvred the Fokker out over the lake, just skimming over the tree tops, figuring it was better to crash through the ice than into the trees if we had to go in.

The shuddering continued. It increased when I put on more power, diminishing as I pulled the throttle back, but I couldn't figure out what it was. The engine seemed to be working all right. Chris couldn't find any damage to the fuselage. However, we were able to gain some altitude and continue the flight.

To the worried McConachie and to his agonized patients, the trip back to Edmonton seemed endless. But finally they landed and the Sen brothers were whisked away in waiting ambulances.

Reporters and photographers who had got wind of the flight were also waiting. Under normal circumstances, McConachie was a man who didn't mind a little publicity, but on this occasion he forgot all about the newsmen as soon as a pale Chris Green called him around to the front of the aircraft and pointed at the propeller.

It was split in two, end to end. All that was holding it together, and all that had kept it from flying off the shaft during the flight, was a thin metal strip. Possibly aided by the kind of luck that rewards those who perform the impossible.

Punch Dickins

Jacques Hamilton

Grant McConachie, for all he represented the epitome of the skill and daring and "What the hell, let's give it a try" breed of bush flier, was much more important in the end as a visionary.

His conviction that the airplane had an important, commercial role to play in the north led to the developement of an industry and played a large part in making it possible for people to live normal lives in a country where they would otherwise perish.

Clennell H. "Punch" Dickins was another kind of visionary and, though his approach to flying was the opposite of McConachie's, he, too, pursued a vision into aviation history.

And, as McConachie himself would gladly yield in later years, Punch Dickins was "the" pioneer flier of the north.

Columnist Jim Coleman once wrote of Dickins that he was "as modest and unassuming a gent as ever pulled on leather helmet and goggles".

That holds true even today. Whether sitting over coffee in his Victoria apartment or standing at the podium making one of his few public speeches, Dickins is a hard man to get to talk about himself.

He has, for example, never told the story of how he won the Distinguished Flying Cross during the First World War.

"The war is over," he says and quickly changes the subject.

But a quick glance through the headlines of the past half-century gives some idea of his place in aviation history:

DICKINS TOOK LIFE IN HANDS FLYING TO WATERWAYS AFTER HIS PLANE HAD BEEN DAMAGED . . . DICKINS FLIES 74,630 MILES IN SINGLE YEAR'S PIONEERING OVER BLEAK NORTHERN TRAILS . . . FLIES INJURED MAN HERE: HAZARDOUS MERCY FLIGHT . . . PUNCH DICKINS BRINGS BACK GREAT DAYS OF BUSH FLYING . . . DICKINS AWARDED O.B.E. . . .

And what the headlines don't add is the part he played in development of great bush planes like the Beaver and Otter. Or the many flight-safety practices that he created.

It was Dickins who pioneered the northern pilot's rule that you always carry enough emergency equipment and food to feed and shelter those on board in the event of a forced landing.

The first emergency radio to go into the air in the north went in Dickins's plane.

And for all the risks he took on his many flights he had only one minor crash in his whole career.

Dickins has earned many names for himself during his flying career, "Snow Eagle", "White Eagle", "Flying Knight of the Northland" and (in Greece) *"Ponts Ntikins"*.

The "Punch" he earned as a child when an aunt described him as a "fat little punch".

Like virtually all the early bush pilots, Dickins learned to fly during the First World War.

He was 17, with one year of university behind him, when he left Edmonton to fight in France. There, in combat, he listed seven kills and won his unexplained DFC.

In the years that followed, his aerial survey flights filled in the map of the north. He set off on search flights that routinely carried him to the North Pole and back.

He was the pilot for the expedition that discovered the huge uranium deposits on Great Bear Lake.

It was during this period that Punch Dickins had his vision and decided to pursue it.

His vision was a simple one by today's standards: air mail for the north.

At the time his idea was generally considered extravagant and impractical.

Dickins felt otherwise. He had already pioneered air mail flights across the prairies and he knew, from personal experience, what was involved in extending it to the north.

He also knew better than most what the mail means to

those in the north. When you live a thousand miles back in the bush, with no normal contact with the outside world, mail becomes as precious as gold. To get it only once or twice a year is simply not enough and Dickins saw that.

In 1924 he prepared a report on the feasibility of the idea, but the postal department was unmoved. He refused to give up the idea and used every opportunity to badger the post office to try it.

Finally, in 1929 the post office relented and a test-flight was authorized.

Dickins set off on the flight in January 1929. On board his Fokker with him were his engineer, Lew Parmenter, postal inspector T. J. Reilly and Fred Lundy of Western Canada Airways.

They were in the air only 20 minutes when ice particles in the carburetor caused engine trouble and they had to turn back.

It took two days in Edmonton to remedy the fault, then they set off again. They were forced by a blizzard to land at Lac La Biche, only half-way to the first day's goal of Fort McMurray. The next day they took off again and made it to McMurray.

Lundy left the party and remained at McMurray to set up a company base.

Dickins prepared to set out again. The journey from this point on, he knew, would be the real test of the experiment and he laid his plans carefully.

From post to tiny post they flew, leaving precious mail for the residents and picking up the letters they had written.

Word of the flight had been radioed ahead and, in every settlement, there was an enthusiastic crowd waiting.

Fort Chipewyan was the first, then on to Fort Smith. Fort Fitzgerald, only 16 miles from Smith, was to be saved for the trip back as they were to pick up a heavy cargo of furs there before again touching down at Smith.

But at Fort Smith, Dickins's characteristic caution changed the plan.

The river level had dropped early in the freeze and the surface of the ice was dangerously rough.

After bumping in for a landing, Dickins turned to Parmenter: "I think this calls for a change of plans," he commented. "We're to bring back a heavy cargo of furs and I wouldn't want to land on this with a loaded plane. Better go to Fitzgerald now and miss them both on the way back."

The decision made, they took to the air for Fort Fitzgerald. But the ice there looked even worse.

"I'm not going to take the chance," Dickins decided. "It will put airmail back 10 years if we crash."

So they flew on to Fort Resolution on Great Slave Lake. There, Reilly stayed to handle some post office business.

Dickins and Parmenter pushed on, fighting through snow and fog to Hay River, Fort Providence and, finally, Fort Simpson.

It was time for the return journey and they took to the air again with a heavy cargo of fur and mail. Their first stop on the way back would be Fort Resolution.

The wind was blowing snow across the ice there and, unseen by Dickins, piling it into hummocks.

Landing, the Fokker struck one of these and the undercarriage buckled. As the plane pitched forward the propeller struck the ice and twisted and bent.

There on the ice Dickins and Parmenter stood and gloomily surveyed their propeller.

They had no spare parts and no radio communications at Resolution. An Indian set out by dogsled for Fort Smith, where there was a radio, with an appeal for a flight with the needed parts.

Dickins watched the Indian leave and knew it would be a long time before any spare parts could arrive. He was driven by a sense of urgency; this was what he meant by the comment that a crash could set northern airmail service back a decade.

Dickins and Parmenter scoured the post in the hope of finding some way to get the plane flying again.

At the Roman Catholic mission, they found a piece of waterpipe that, on inspection, proved good enough to make the needed repairs to the undercarriage.

But what about the propeller?

They stood, at 40 below zero, and examined it. One tip was bent. Carefully they bent it back, hopefully to its original configuration.

The other blade was a serious problem. It was curled around and they lacked the proper tools to straighten it.

"Well, we have nothing to lose, so let's give it a try," Parmenter said. Dickins nodded and they slowly started to pull the blade around.

The metal was strained and brittle with cold and, though they pulled gently, it snapped under their gloves, leaving the blade nine inches shorter than the other.

When their initial dismay passed, Dickins asked: "Do you think the old bus would fly if we cut off the other end to match the broken one?"

Parmenter lifted his shoulders. "Again we have nothing to lose," he answered.

So they started to saw. It took five days of work in the bitter cold before the two ends matched.

The other repairs finished, Dickins taxied the plane out for a test. He built speed, everything seemed okay, so he added speed and the plane lifted easily into the air.

The plane flew, but Dickins and Parmenter didn't want to risk an attempt to fly out fully loaded and lacking those nine inches on either end of the propeller.

They took off empty and headed to Smith, arriving only a day later than the Indian they had sent out with the message. From Smith they flew to McMurray where a new plane was waiting for them.

With it they returned to Resolution and picked up the cargo of mail and furs, then completed the historic experiment.

Confronted by Dickins and by his shrinking propeller, the post office had to admit that, with these kind of men and machines around, airmail might just work in the north after all.

Regular service started with the Christmas flight of 1929.

Dickins returned to his "ordinary" work. Like making the "ordinary" first flight down the length of the Mackenzie to the Arctic Ocean. Or the "ordinary" year when he piled up that record 74,630 miles of travelling.

Bishop Bompas
Ed Tait

When Christmas dinner was over, the factor turned jokingly to William Bompas. "Young man, if you weren't a clergyman, I wouldn't believe your story. It's fantastic — you say you left England the last of June, and here you are on the Mackenzie River, Christmas Day. Through the north country in the dead of winter! It's an unheard of thing!"

Bompas smiled. "It was a rough trip," he admitted, "but here I am, and very pleased to be at Fort Simpson, I can tell you."

"And we're glad to have you, Mr. Bompas. Any man who can reach Fort Simpson in winter is a guest of honour. I'm interested in your trip. Suppose you tell us the whole story."

"Very well, sir," agreed William Bompas. "The story begins last spring when Bishop Anderson of Rupert's Land preached a particular sermon in London. I was in the audience and enjoyed every word he said. The Bishop is a fine man and an excellent speaker. He described the prairies, the forests, the lakes, rivers, half-breeds, Indians, trappers and traders in such an interesting manner I was fascinated by his tales. Then he spoke of the need for a young man to take the place of a sick missionary on the Mackenzie River. The appeal of the Bishop was so strong I volunteered at once and was accepted by the Missionary Society of the Anglican Church.

"Frankly, I was advised not to travel in northern Canada during the winter months, but I was so anxious to reach my field I decided to risk the journey, hoping to reach Fort Simpson by Christmas."

The factor laughed. "And you made it right on the dot."

"Yes," continued Bompas, "but there were times when I thought I would never live to see the Mackenzie River. After crossing the Atlantic, I landed in New York, and then continued my journey by railroad to St. Cloud. From the end of the railway, I made my way northward in a wagon to the Red River. Friends advised me to carry a Union Jack as protection against the Indians. I took this advice seriously and tried to buy a flag, but was unable to do so. Finally I made a crude one by sewing bits of red, white and blue cotton together. This I placed in a prominent position on my wagon and hoped that it would be respected by the Indians."

The factor raised his eyebrows. "Did you have any Indian trouble?"

"Just once. A band of Sioux warriors in war paint halted me at one point. They looked at the flag, inspected the wagon and then went off without bothering me. They appear to be on friendlier terms with the British than with the Americans."

"You were lucky," exclaimed the trader. "They might have shot you and taken your scalp."

"After arriving at the Red River, I was fortunate enough to get a place in a brigade of Hudson's Bay Company boats and travelled in two months' time to Portage La Loche. By this time there were unmistakable signs of approaching winter, so I hired two Metis and a canoe. We went down the Athabaska to Fort Chipewyan, encountering some bad storms and floating ice on the way. I was tempted to stay at the fort, but after some hesitation employed another canoe and three men. We pushed northward again, moving down the Slave River until it was completely frozen over. Leaving the canoe we marched through the woods until we reached Fort Resolution on the shores of Great Slave Lake. There I was most fortunate in meeting the mail carriers who offered to guide me the rest of the way, and as you know I arrived here at Fort Simpson today."

"I congratulate you, Bompas. I am sure you have been very modest regarding your troubles and hardships. It was a remarkable journey and one which will become famous in the north country, I warrant."

William Bompas enjoyed the hospitality of Fort Simpson until Easter time when he went to Fort Norman to take up the work for which he had come. He was a good student by nature, with a remarkable ability in languages. In a short time he had learned enough of the Indian tongue to teach and preach to the local natives. Not content merely to speak the language, he began the difficult work of translating portions of the Bible, hymns and psalms. This proved to be a monumental task complicated by the fact that there were several dialects used by the Indians. The translations were later printed in England and copies were returned to the missionary for distribution.

Later it was decided that William Bompas should extend his work to a wider field. He was given a "roving commission" which permitted him to travel and work wherever he felt the need was greatest. This pleased him very much and proved to be a very excellent arrangement. The country which was his mission is about one million square miles in extent, including the Mackenzie River, the Yukon, the Peace and the Athabaska. Scattered throughout this broad region were tiny settlements, trading-posts and Indian camps.

Travelling by canoe, on foot, or by dog sled in winter, he hurried from place to place, baptizing babies, burying the dead, marrying young people, preaching sermons and distributing his books. It was a hard life, often cold, wet, exhausting. He was tortured by mosquitoes and struck by snow-blindness, but he never spared himself so long as he reached the settlements he wished to visit.

After eight years of this rigorous life, he returned to

England and while there was consecrated as Bishop of Athabaska. His leave in the Mother Country proved to be an important one in another way, for he returned to the northwest with a wife. Mrs. Bompas was eagerly welcomed at Fort Simpson. She was a warm-hearted woman who later took into her home a little Indian girl, Owindia, whose mother had been murdered.

For twenty years Bishop Bompas worked unceasingly in the north: he saw his area staffed by eleven missionaries and served by ten mission stations and six churches. His early dreams had been realized. By 1892, he and Mrs. Bompas were living in the Yukon and some years later they witnessed the great gold rush that drew miners from many countries. Rough though the miners may have been, they respected the aging Bishop, and on one occasion presented Mrs. Bompas with a fine gold nugget as a Christmas present.

The Bishop's life of long service came to an end suddenly in 1906 at Caribou Crossing. In the words of Tennyson, "God's finger touched him and he slept."

Bill Peyto Alone*
Gordon Burles

It's time to go; I've had enough!
Damn this town, all those
pettifogging shopkeepers and
piddling government men — especially
that interfering muddler, Jennings.
There are too many of them, and
you never know what they're up to.
I fought in their war — I guess

*Bill Peyto was a packer, trapper, prospector, guide and park warden around Banff from 1887 to his death in 1943.

I had to do that; but they're not
going to make a hero of me for it.
It was tough enough; but, by God,
we're men, aren't we?
But I don't care. As long as
they do as they're told
when they're out here around
Healy Creek. They're such greenhorns!
Someone's got to help them,
doesn't he? And those damned police!
They'd better leave my guns to me.
A man needs his gun: there are dangers
you can't always predict, you know.
No bear's going to take me before
my time, either: when he comes
stealing my grub, he'll learn
about it from this gun barrel.
Anyhow, I've been around and had fun:
I'm let alone when I want it.
Soon I'll be back up in the larches.
There's snow on the ground now
and I'll see who's been bothering
my cabin. It's mighty pretty there
when no one's around: we'd better
like it while we can, because
we're not going to be around long!
Damnation, I s'pose that wife's
going to cry. By God, that's God's
affair, or somebody's, I don't know.
Whoever made the mountains made me
and I'm not waiting: I'm going.

Jimmy Simpson of Num-Ti-Jah
Ruth Gorman

Some five years ago *Holiday* magazine sent a photographer across Canada to capture, in the camera's quick eye, a study of their vast neighbour to the north. The only person they photographed in Alberta was Jimmy Simpson, and probably rightly so because in Jimmy you can find the history of the West.

He was almost, but not quite, a remittance man. He almost became a sailor on the clipper ships that sailed with the Victoria fleet, he was a friend of the West's greatest artist, Charlie Russell, and he worked on the CPR when it was making that spectacular classic engineering feat that electrified the world — the building of a railway across the high Rockies. After that he was a trapper who grew to know and like the Indian and speak his language. He was one of the first big game guides in the Rockies and had been an intimate friend of thc forgotten greats of yesteryear as well as movie stars, writers and artists of today. He was a patron of the arts, and is himself an artist who paints and sells as many as thirty fine watercolour canvases a year. He designed and built a unique inn, all of logs, in the heart of the wilderness and to top it all he is still fit and hearty at ninety-five.

But the best thing of all about Jimmy is Jimmy the person. Each morning and each night of a summer, this spry, alert man stands erectly, face-on into the brisk wind that blows off the icy Bow Glacier just across the beautiful, constantly changing colours of Bow Lake. No matter how cool that wind is he never wears a coat — just a neat wool shirt and always a stiff-brimmed mountie's hat flipped neatly to the back of his head. Without glasses, his sharp blue eyes take in all the beauty of the glacier — his eyes instantly catch a jumping fish or a bird moving in the fir trees and finally, in the morning, satisfied with all that beauty, he goes into the great log hotel he built. The chef has seen him coming and has ready the same breakfast of bacon and eggs that Jimmy has had for fifteen years. After enjoying his breakfast he walks out into the tall pines behind the Inn. Suddenly as though from nowhere, appear dozens of birds. They circle him on the ground, perch on his hat and eat from his hand the remnants of his breakfast that he always shares with them. After that Jimmy is now ready for a full day's work. It could be painting another picture or it could be a long walk to check up on where the pack horses are.

When I was there he had decided to fix the pot-holes that the terrible cloudburst the week before had washed out in the gravel road leading from the Banff-Jasper highway to the hotel. He doesn't have to do this but chooses to do it because he enjoys being active. He had worked out a system for his road mending. Methodically he wheeled an iron wheelbarrow to a special spot on the lake's edge where the gravel has been washed to a fine consistency. He shovelled the gravel into the barrow, trundled it back down across the lakeshore, up a hill and then neatly shovelled the gravel into each pot-hole. While I watched him he made eight trips! A very fat lady tourist stopped, stepped from her car, took his picture and wagged her fat, nail-polished finger at him, coyly simpering, "Hard work never killed anyone." I waited for an explosion but none came. Instead with a concealed twinkle in his eye, Jimmy gravely replied to her, "No Ma'am, but a lot of people died young trying to avoid it." That must be the secret of Jimmy's full enjoyment of life. He is always enjoying a little joke and usually it is about himself.

In fact it was his too-quick ability to see a joke that landed him in Canada when he was seventeen. He says he was shipped out of England because he was the black sheep of the family. He was raised by a very dour uncle who entertained high hopes that his nephew would follow in his forefathers' footsteps and eventually at least become the mayor of their small village, but

Jimmy was a constant disappointment to his uncle. His final wicked act consisted of laughing right out loud in church at a most inappropriate time. The young minister of the village had been caught kissing the pretty organist. The villagers, led by uncle, expelled the poor man from the church. The broken, but defiant young parson preached a fine farewell sermon which he closed by saying he wanted no further spoken condemnation or condolences from anyone — he would simply leave their village forever, and by that act express his acceptance of their judgment. But Jimmy noticed that as the minister marched out of the church, he had, pinned under his coattails, a branch of the traditional kissing mistletoe and young Jimmy unfortunately let out a loud whoop of laughter. That did it! Before he could further disgrace the family, uncle sternly shipped him to Canada with enough money to get to Winnipeg to buy a farm.

A good look at the sod farmhouse and its grim surroundings was enough for Jimmy. Two days later he was back in Winnipeg, ensconced in a boarding house on Arthur Street where, as he says, he "cheered Winnipeg up with some good fresh English money". The money also cheered up all the other boarders and everyone had a high-ho time until Jimmy's money ran out. When he took stock there was just enough money left to get him to Calgary, so off he went looking for greener fields.

When he arrived in Calgary in 1886, he right away bumped into friends from Winnipeg who told him they were just on their way to a wash-out at Golden where the CPR were hiring men. Jimmy didn't have the price of the fare but they said, "never mind", and pulling down an upper bunk, they pushed Jimmy in and closed it. However, the conductor was wise in the ways of the West. He pulled down the bunk and kicked poor Jimmy off the train near Castlegar. So Jimmy didn't just go to the mountains like Mohammed — before he could even see them, he was literally flung into their midst. As the young man walked along the tracks, through the wilderness, he found their strange beauty.

For a while he was a pick-and-shovel man for the CPR. Then the youngster sailed on a clipper ship from Victoria to the wild Gold Coast city of San Francisco but somehow the mountains called him back. And it was fortunate that they did, because on the next trip the clipper made, Captain Anderson and his crew ran guns in to the Alaskan sealers. The sealers were only allowed spears in those days and rumour had it the Russians caught Captain Anderson with the guns. Anyway, the ship and the crew were never seen again.

Near where his hotel is now, Jimmy set up trap lines and hunted. The Stoney Indians became his friends and he learned their language and their skill in the woods. At ninety-five he still loves the outdoors. In winter, he says, he often longs to go out alone in the mountains and pull down the great snow-covered fir boughs for his bed and light a great fire and watch the Whiskey Jack perched overhead. He chuckles when he tells you about one winter he spent alone with his traps. He decided he should snowshoe seventy-five miles over to Tom Willson's horse ranch at Kootenay. It was a terrible trip. He carried no blankets and could only make about fifteen miles a day. Tom, who was spending the winter alone too, was delighted to have someone for Christmas dinner. They got out a bottle Tom had been saving and had a gay old evening. The morning after, Tom had a hangover and was pretty crochety. As he was lighting up the stove he turned to Jimmy and said, "When did you say you were going back?" So Jimmy went — right then! Back seventy-five miles. They both had all winter to think over what they had meant to say!

Jimmy became very proficient as a guide. In those days the wealthy of New York and Europe made a point of going on big game hunts in the Canadian Rockies — as did leading scientists and famous writers. Jimmy enjoyed his trips with these men and, with his own upbringing and keen interest in books and art, they too enjoyed his company. Once he got caught by the park warden poaching within the Park limits. His good friend, lawyer Paddy Nolan, tried to get him off but he was fined $126.00 and his license was lifted. Typically, Jimmy Simpson even enjoyed the punishment. He signed on as a cook to hunting parties and as soon as they got deep into the wilderness, as the cook, he would guide the party out to get the food for dinner. He kept at this until the government was begging him to buy a license. However, despite this episode the government usually chose him to guide their important scientific expeditions.

For over sixty years he was a big game hunter and guide and he never had a failure.

Most of the men Jimmy hunted with were great men, like Otto Kahn, chairman of the Metropolitan Opera House. Knowing that Jimmy was an opera buff as well as an artist, Otto Kahn would take Jimmy to his opera box, when Jimmy was in New York, and introduce him to artists like Caruso and Geraldine Ferrar.

Fortunately the girl Jimmy married was a Scotch girl with a background similar to Jimmy's. She too came from a home where they enjoyed music and collected good books.

It was in the Simpson home that the first play in Banff was put on by the Banff Drama Club. It was "The Land of Heart's Desire". Mrs. Simpson along with Mrs. Henry Greenham who ran a private school called the Mountain School, Mrs. Kennedy, the wife of Banff's dentist, and Mrs. Robinson, the wife of Banff's doctor, got together and formed a drama club. The ladies of the drama club wrote to the Department of Extension for help and the department sent Mr. Corbett to help them set up a summer drama school. During the first summer they all taught in it and from that small core eventually emerged today's magnificent Banff School of Fine Arts. However, Mrs. Simpson says Banff would never have had the world famous school if it hadn't been for Dr. Cameron. They all dreamt dreams but it was his labour and dedication that alone made the dream the magnificent reality it is today.

Mrs. Simpson is still very active and still very pretty. She is careful not to tell her age but says it is over sixty years since she first came to this country as a young girl and met Jimmy. Both still slight and still handsome, they make a delightful couple. He always refers to her with a twinkle as "The Madam", saying she won't let him do anything and she says, "Oh Jimmy — he doesn't do anything anyone else's way — just his own way," but she says it with quiet pride.

They went to New York on their honeymoon. It was there, at the studio of his friend, Ed Bordein, that Jimmy met Will Rogers, who was then playing in the Follies, and artist Charlie Russell. All these men had much in common. All were men who had left good families to live a carefree life in the West. These congenial Westerners, stuck in a great city when they really only loved the outdoors, indulged in the escapism of constantly telling yarns from morning to night.

Charlie told him about the time his friends decided he should begin to take some art lessons. A wealthy and famous New York instructor was picked out but when the untidy Russell called on him he didn't even ask to see Russell's work. Instead the instructor said "My good man, do you know how to draw a straight line?" Charlie just walked over to the window and said, "You see the saloon on the corner over there? Well a straight line is the shortest distance between two points and that's what I'm taking," and walked out.

Jimmy was fascinated with Russell and his immense speed with paint brush or clay. He tells a story of one afternoon when they were all sitting around a wooden table in a well-known New York saloon. Russell put both arms under the table and brought out a perfect buffalo he had made of plasticine which he then stuck on top of an empty bottle. A few seconds later he grabbed it off the bottle and in a few minutes produced, again without looking down, a fine mountain goat head. When they all had a good laugh he rolled the plasticine in a ball and threw it down on the sawdust floor that was covered with bottle caps and cigar butts.

Charlie Russell painted two pictures for Jimmy — a sketch of a bronc about to fall on his rider, called "Man Killer", and one of a western hunter, riding a roan and carrying his gun down on the left side of his saddle like Jimmy always carried his. Mr. Simpson has given these originals into the safekeeping of the Glenbow Foundation. He feels they should belong to the public but he has filled the walls of the great lounge of Num-Ti-Jah and its lovely dining room and game room with Russell prints.

Jimmy's love of art and artists has been a lifelong affair. He was instrumental in getting the great Carl Rungius to come to the Canadian West where Rungius would paint his way to world fame and fortune. Jimmy had seen an animal drawing by this German artist in a magazine so he just sat down and wrote him. According to Carl's wife, Rungius threw away the letter and it was she who recovered it from the wastebasket and persuaded him to reread it. Jimmy had written telling him about the magnificent wildlife in the Canadian Rockies waiting to be painted. Through a friend, a CPR pass was arranged and the European artist came West.

Jimmy tells how, in those first few weeks, he led Carl over a mountain draw and how suddenly they came across a bear digging frantically for a gopher. Another terrified gopher was standing straight up behind the bear, watching the kill with fascination, unaware that stealing up behind him was a fox. Seeing at one glance this whole panorama of nature's fierce struggle for survival, Carl broke into excited German and it was five whole minutes before he could get back into English. But Carl painted that scene and stayed on the rest of his life in the Rockies. Jimmy had thirty canvases of Rungius's but like his Russell originals they are now in the Glenbow, preserved for posterity.

Of his own painting he says that he "just caught it like a five-year-old catches measles". His wife says his mountain goats are his best. About five years ago he threw away all his oil paints and brushes because it was "too easy". Now he paints in the more difficult medium of water colour. Unlike other water colours, with their calm, washed look, his are vivid with wild colour. He says he paints "winter in summer and summer in winter" and in his mind's eye he sees and paints, on one canvas, all the vivid colour and beauty he has seen in over seventy years in his beloved mountains.

Jimmy built the great log inn Num-Ti-Jah as just one part of his life. Long before the park limits were extended he used to trap the marten ("Num-Ti-Jah" is the Stoney Indian word for marten) around Bow Lake. With the consent of the park officials he built a log cabin so his hunting parties could change and clean up before going on to civilization at the Chateau Lake Louise, twenty miles west. With the advent of the car he realized the great pack trips and hunting parties would disappear so he designed a new cabin. When guests gaze with awe at the two great two-storey octagonal buildings, constructed entirely of giant logs on a natural stone foundation, and the two massive stone fireplaces, they always ask Jimmy if he actually built them himself. He says, very seriously, "Yes, but I had one wonderful helper — John P. Seagram." Actually Jimmy drinks very little but he did get the lumber cut in the forest near by and he cut the logs himself with the help of nine Swedish workers who, every ten days, took a few days for a blow-off in Field. In one winter they put up the first eight-sided building. The second one was added in 1935. It too is eight-sided, so from every one of the inn's guest room windows there is a magnificent view of lake, mountains or the Bow Glacier. With the change in our climate, that glacier has retreated almost half way up the mountain but it is still a glorious, unforgettable sight.

How does a man who has led such an adventurous life feel

about getting old? Jimmy misses his many lifelong friends who are now gone. At the funeral of an old poker friend, he just slipped a pack of cards into the coffin and said "Play solitaire until we get there Friend." But Jimmy loves people with all their idiosyncrasies and he loves exchanging yarns — and what yarns he has to tell! Half the time, with a twinkle in his bright eyes, he is pulling your leg but after a while you don't care — you just hope he will keep on telling his yarns forever.

He has a strong inner faith in life. He says he's only been in a church three times in this country — once to fix a pew, once to go to a wedding and once to win a dollar bet from his old friend, Norman Luxton. Norman bet him a dollar he wouldn't go to church ever. He had lost so many bets to Norman he decided he would win this easy one, but with a chuckle he confesses, "And when they passed the collection plate, guess what? I found I only had a $2.00 bill in my pocket so I guess I lost that bet too!"

He says the mountains have a profound effect on a man. He once had a tough guide who had done nearly everything bad there was to do in life but one day as they came over a mountain and gazed down at a beautiful valley in which soft white clouds were floating, he heard the guide mutter, "And they say there is no God."

He feels he has been exceptionally lucky in his family. His pretty wife is still with him. His two daughters, Kathryn Mary and Mary Louise, became top professional skaters. They astounded New York critics with fifty-four continuous fantastic displays of fancy skating. The "Simpson Sisters" skated on tiny squares of ice "the size of postage stamps" — like their father they were always original, an accomplishment in a rather stereotyped art, and varied their performances each night. Unfortunately Kathryn, who had married Paul Brown of the Boston Gardens, died suddenly while still a young woman. This is the great sadness of their lives. Their only son, Jimmy Junior, on his return from the last great war, fortunately decided to take over where his father left off. He and his beautiful Alberta-born wife run Num-Ti-Jah and Jimmy Junior is, according to his father, a better hunter and guide than he was, which means "never a failure".

Jimmy has enjoyed both good health and the strange strength he has in his slight frame all his life. In all his adventurous life he's only had one serious casualty — he damaged his left eye on a glacier trip and now it sometimes gets snow-blinded. Once a charging moose broke his arm but as Jimmy says, "That moose should have gone to Ontario. He stuck his nose around the end of the lake there and I shot him with my other arm!"

He says if he were told it was his last day, and at ninety-five he knows that can't be too far away, he would laugh right up to the last minute and then say, "God save my soul". And this grand old man probably will be laughing the rest of his life and yarning or maybe painting a bit or pushing a heavy wheelbarrow up a hill on that last day.

His favourite yarn is one told by his old friend, a man he admired — Bob Edwards, famous editor of the Calgary *Eye Opener*. Maybe there's a clue in his choice. It's about procrastination although this grand old man has never put off either a job or a joy for a moment in his long life. Edwards's yarn was about a bee in a meadow who, while sitting on a pretty flower, was swallowed up by a great bull. The bee was furious at this turn of events and decided to sting the bull in the throat, but then decided to wait as it would be more effective if he stung him in the stomach. However when he got down there it was so nice and warm that he decided he should wait and enjoy a little sleep — when he woke up the bull was gone!

A wonderful old man is Jimmy Simpson who has added so much to the Alberta scene!

Personalities

The Men That Don't Fit In

Robert W. Service

There's a race of men that don't fit in,
    A race that can't stay still;
So they break the hearts of kith and kin,
    And they roam the world at will.
They range the field and they rove the flood,
    And they climb the mountain's crest;
Theirs is the curse of the gypsy blood,
    And they don't know how to rest.

If they just went straight they might go far;
    They are strong and brave and true;
But they're always tired of the things that are,
    And they want the strange and new.
They say: "Could I find my proper groove,
    What a deep mark I would make!"
So they chop and change, and each fresh move
    Is only a fresh mistake.

And each forgets, as he strips and runs
    With a brilliant, fitful pace,
It's the steady, quiet, plodding ones
    Who win in the lifelong race.

And each forgets that his youth has fled,
  Forgets that his prime is past,
Till he stands one day, with a hope that's dead,
  In the glare of the truth at last.

He has failed, he has failed; he has missed his chance;
  He has just done things by half.
Life's been a jolly good joke on him,
  And now is the time to laugh.
Ha, ha! He is one of the Legion Lost;
  He was never meant to win;
He's a rolling stone, and it's bred in the bone;
  He's a man who won't fit in.

The Cactus Bloom
Ellen Neal

The difficulties encountered
While settling the west,
Can be likened to the cactus
Struggling to bloom.

Those who make it
Become a bit prickly.

George "Kootenai" Brown
Jacques Hamilton

George Brown was a man who couldn't have existed outside the era of the opening of the Canadian west. And possibly that era couldn't have existed without George Brown.

He started out as a quick-triggered soldier of fortune and ended his days as an irritable old civil servant arguing with Ottawa about lost fire pails.

He was a law unto himself, and even that law was made

only to be broken. Tall, powerful and fast, he went through life afflicted with the kind of temper that draws guns and sometimes pulls triggers.

His genteel British accent never managed to hide a tongue so rough that those who knew him said he invented a new curse every time he opened his mouth.

In later years, he wore his pale blond hair hanging to his shoulders; some say in imitation of his friend Buffalo Bill, but perhaps it was only a wistful effort to cling to a fading era.

Poisoner of wolves, slaughterer of buffalo, gambler, Indian fighter, whisky trader — George "Kootenai" Brown was all these things.

But he was also a man with a vision, a vision that led his life out in a long, looping circle from the Rockies and, in the end, brought him back to the Rockies again.

It was his determined following of that vision that redeemed him and that lets us remember him as one of our great mountain pioneers.

It was 1865 when George Brown first set foot in what is now Alberta. His education was behind him — Eton and Oxford — and so was the finishing school of a soldier's life in Panama and the life of a drifter in the western United States.

Behind him, too, was the darkest incident of his life. In Montana a fight had flared across a poker table and he had killed a man. No one, today, knows just what happened.

Brown himself kept the incident a secret and, although there is some evidence he was arrested for the shooting, there is no evidence he was ever brought to trial.

Probably the closest Brown ever came to talking about the incident was once, in his old age, when he told a friend that the sweetest words in the English language are "Not Guilty".

Whatever happened, he had headed north after the incident, lost himself in the gold fields of the Cariboo.

Now, two years later, he and four companions were riding down the east slope of the South Kootenai Pass and out onto the open prairie. They were bound for Edmonton where they had heard there was gold to be found.

As Brown recalled later, "We had no very clear knowledge of where Edmonton was, and there was no one to tell us."

Brown was convinced that the party should stick close to the mountains and head north, but his companions didn't agree. Reluctantly he followed their directions, and he almost didn't live to regret it.

Unknowingly, the party's looping route carried them into the heart of Blackfoot country.

At that time, the Blackfoot nation was at the peak of its power. Still uncrippled by white man's diseases, white man's whiskey and white man's bullets, the Blackfoot in 1865 were one of the fiercest and most efficient fighting forces in history.

Apart from Brown's party, there probably weren't more than a few white men in all Alberta at the time. And, learning from the experiences of tribes to the south, the Blackfoot were anxious to see even these few white invaders driven out of their lands.

Years later, Brown remembered that trouble wasn't long in coming:

> One day, at a clump of cottonwood trees, we stopped to eat. Well, as we were eating we were suddenly surprised by a flight of arrows from the direction of the cottonwood trees and we knew that our first war party had begun.
>
> We all thought our time had come. The Indians had no firearms, but they were all young bucks, 32 of them, no old men or war women. All young warriors. A war party out for anything they could get. They had lots of arrows and they let them fly.
>
> We got up and started shooting at anything we could see. We had not much cover, only some brush, and the Indians had driven us away from the cotton-

woods, many of which were two feet in diameter. If the Indians had guns they would have killed all five of us.

It was at this time I received an arrow in the back, close to my kidneys. It was a miracle I was not killed — I thought my time had come — but I pulled it out, an arrow head two and a half inches long and the head out of sight. The jagged edges caught the flesh as I pulled it out, and it gave me great pain.

I had a bottle of turpentine and, opening up the wound, one of my companions inserted the neck of the bottle and when I bent over about half a pint ran into the opening made by the arrow head. This was all the doctoring I ever got and in a few days I was well again.

We were using old muzzle loaders with balls and caps and we carried bullets in our pockets and in our mouths. Two Indians fell victims to our intermittent fire and the rest, after about twenty minutes fighting, rode to the river and jumping their horses into the stream, swam them across, taking one of my horses and another with them. . . .

Brown, in agony with the arrow wound, didn't take long to lose his famous temper. The result was what he later described as a "miniature civil war".

When the dust finally settled, the party had split up. Three of the men pushed on along their original route. Brown never heard of them again.

The fourth man, whose horse had been lost in the Indian raid, reluctantly decided to stay with Brown. No doubt the man, noting the fact that Brown still had two horses left, hoped that Brown would give him one. But Brown had all his worldly goods packed on the second animal and wasn't about to part with it under any circumstances.

Instead, he "helped" his companion by building him a bull

boat (a circle of willow covered with a green buffalo hide), packing him into it with a load of raw buffalo meat and shoving him off from the bank of the Saskatchewan River.

Brown's casual explanation of the act years later was that "I thought I might run across him at Fort Garry if the river flowed in that direction, but I was not sure."

(For the record, the man did survive. Brown met him again some time later — though not, it should be added, at Fort Garry.)

Now on his own, Brown struck out towards Edmonton. Or so he thought. The problem was that he had convinced himself that the Saskatchewan River would serve as the highway to his destination. "I reasoned that it must flow into the Atlantic Ocean or Hudson Bay and that it would eventually bring us to the fringe of civilization."

In fact, the river would bring him to Duck Lake and a new chapter in his life.

After several weeks of wandering along the twisting river, Brown came upon a small band of Cree Indians. From them, he learned that there was a "A-pit-hou-a-goo-es san", a "village of half-sons", nearby.

The "half-sons" were the Metis, and the village the Cree referred to was a settlement of 50 families of hunters who were preparing to winter at Duck Lake.

Brown pressed on to the settlement and was immediately accepted by the hunters. He spent the fall and winter living as part of one of the families, sharing the tasks of caring for the valuable buffalo ponies and of hunting for food. By the time spring came, Brown spoke the language and had learned the intricate social pattern of Metis life.

He spent several years with the Metis people, taking a Metis girl as his "wife" and building a reputation as one of the best buffalo hunters in a society that knew no peers as buffalo hunters.

In his later years, Brown made it plain that he could happily have spent the rest of his life as one of the Metis people.

But, sadly, by the time he met them history was already closing in on their way of life. The Metis had joined in the frenzied extermination of the buffalo, and when the buffalo disappeared so did the nomad hunters.

Brown had drifted far from the mountains, and he would drift further still in distance, in time and in feeling.

After he left the Metis, he joined in the life of the whiskey traders and wolfers who were streaming north across the International Boundary.

His recollections of this period are defiant, filled with a refusal to apologize for things of which he obviously felt deeply ashamed. One of Brown's anecdotes in particular catches the feeling of his life at the time.

Brown was engaged in the dubious pursuit of hunting wolves with poisoned bait, and on this particular day had brought in a load of pelts to a trader named Johnnie Gibbons.

He arrived at the post to find it crowded with about 30 Red Lake Indians. Gibbons had only two clerks and he persuaded Brown to help in the post for the day.

In those days — Brown explains — all traders sold rum and whiskey to the natives. Johnnie Gibbons was not any exception to the rule, and he put me in charge of dispensing the liquid. The Red Lakes would come in with a fur of some kind and hand it to me. It was my duty to give them as little whiskey as they would accept for it.

There were no bottles, cups or glasses in use in the west at the time, but the Hudson's Bay Company brought in thousands of little copper kettles and these soon came into common use.

It would be one of these kettles that an Indian would invariably push up to receive the whiskey in payment for his fur. Sometimes he would drink it where he stood and other times it was carried to his teepee.

On this day the Red Lakes had run out of fur before their thirst for whiskey had been quenched. Chief Starving Wolf had come in and asked for a drink free, gratis. By this time they were all very drunk and I didn't like to give them any more. So I said to him "My friend and brother, you know I am not a man of two tongues. I'll give you one drink and that's the last you'll get."

So he drank his drink and left.

With the Indians gone, Gibbons sent an old man, Jimmie Clewitt, out to a storehouse behind the post to bring in a fresh jug of rum.

Brown was uneasy about the Indians and he was standing at the window. He saw Clewitt enter the storehouse and, an instant later, saw Chief Starving Wolf jump through the door after him, gun in hand.

> I yelled that the Indians had gone into the storehouse. Instantly we heard the report of a gun and saw Clewitt running for his life to the store. We also saw the Indian emerge with a large copper pot which we assumed was full of rum, and it was. Clewitt made for the house and falling into the porch groaned "I'm done for."

One of the post's clerks, Billy Salmon, had been concerned about the old man going out to the storehouse alone and had followed. He was with him when the shot was fired. Like the old man, he had made a run for the porch, collapsing in front of the door. He had been badly wounded and later died.

Brown continues:

> The Indians immediately began peppering away at the store from their hiding places behind the store-

house. Odd bullets came through the chinking and there was rattling and clashing of all sorts of stuff on the shelves. We grabbed muzzle loaders and whenever the leg or wing of an Indian appeared around the corner he was nailed. Even Clewitt, who we expected was dead, jumped up, and, grabbing a rifle, began peppering through a window.

After several rounds had been fired, an Indian jumped out from behind the storehouse, probably to get a good aim, and Clewitt and myself both shot him. Another Red Laker ran out to pull in his dead body, but while getting over a fence he was shot in the leg and fled, dragging the broken member after him.

The other clerk, in the meantime, had managed to sneak away from the post and run for reinforcements. Just as the men in the post were running out of ammunition, the clerk returned with a party of 20 half-breeds and whites. The Red Lakers fled.

For a few years, Brown's life was a jumble of incidents like this. Finally he could stand it no longer.

Years earlier, when he had first come through the South Kootenai Pass to the prairies he had paused at a chain of lakes, the Kootenai Lakes (later to be known as the Waterton Lakes). At the time he had been struck by the beauty of the lakes and by the deep conviction that his place in life was on their shores. He vowed that someday he would return and make his home there.

Now, 12 years later, he remembered the vow. He was finally on his way back to the mountains and to the lakes that would make "Kootenai" his middle name.

Brown made a partner of a man named Fred Kanouse and the two opened a store on what later became Brown's homestead at Waterton.

The store attracted many Indian customers. Brown and Kanouse, despite the attraction of huge profits, avoided trading in whiskey. It wasn't a matter of morality. As Brown pointed out later they had both seen too many drunken Indians on the rampage to want to chance the consequences.

Despite the absence of whiskey, business boomed. It was as much a matter of gambling as good trading sense. Both Brown and Kanouse loved a bet, and they knew that some Indians would gamble on just about anything.

Brown explains:

> Someone taught the Flatheads and Kootenais to play poker and this became their great pastime when they visited the store. It took a card shark to beat them. Kanouse was an expert poker player so he attended to that part of the business.
>
> I was a foot-racer and a good shot, and in competition on the track or with the rifle I could always beat them.
>
> We had two good horses and in horse-racing we always got the best of them. In fact, we beat them at every turn.

Being a consistent winner is not without its risks and Brown, in his memoirs, tells of one incident where the partners showed a decided flare for diplomacy.

> I have a very distinct recollection of one very interesting race, not on account of the race so much as because of the big stakes we put up.
>
> We had just sold the Kootenais $500 worth of goods for furs they had delivered. They asked for a race and we asked "What stakes?"
>
> They had no furs and no money but they had the goods they just bought. So they took these goods — saddles, bridles, lasso ropes, blankets, dress lengths the women had bought for gaudy gowns — and piled them up in front of the store.
>
> Then they rounded up 40 head of Indian ponies

valued at about $20 apiece. They then asked what we would put up. Fred Kanouse had $500 in greenbacks and he told them we would put up this against their pile of goods and horses. And the race was on.

Kanouse rode Honest John and the Indians had two or three horses in the field. Honest John won easily and we carried the goods in and put them on the shelves again.

The Indian men took the loss quite philosophically but the women put up a howl. They said: "You are fools. You let these white dogs swindle you. It will soon be winter and we have no clothes, blankets or anything else."

There were only three white men of us . . . and there must have been nearly seventy full blooded Indians. So we had to go slow.

Kanouse suggested giving every squaw a blanket which we did, and every buck a knife or plug of tobacco or some small trinket he might ask for.

We also gave back the poorest of the horses we won, for some of the poor beggars were on foot and would have to double deck or walk back to the Flathead country. But we kept the best of the horses and all the saddles, bridles and other goods.

Every man, woman and child got some little present and away they went back to their stamping grounds quite happy.

Brown's most famous gambling story, of course, concerned the acquisition of his second wife, Nichamoose. Brown, a widower at this point, saw the girl when a band of her people came to trade at the store and he decided he would have her as his wife — at any price.

The price her family demanded was five horses and Brown paid cheerfully — which should have made them suspicious. No sooner was the transaction complete than Brown lured them into a bet and ended up with his five horses back and a new wife to boot.

Gambling and diplomacy notwithstanding, the store was a short-lived proposition for Brown and Kanouse. Most of the Indians who traded with them came from what was officially the United States side of the international line. As the border stiffened, more and more of the Indians traded in the United States.

Brown and Kanouse decided to close up shop. Kanouse bought out Brown's share of the goods and headed out to set up a general store in the town of Macleod. Brown stayed behind to homestead by the lakes he knew and loved.

Long before anyone else, Brown considered the Waterton Lakes area a national park. He became the area's protector, stamping out careless or abandoned campfires, doing what he could to control irresponsible hunting. When the area was finally made a national park, George "Kootenai" Brown was named its first superintendent.

Brown was aging and — very reluctantly — settling down. He had two homesteads on the go, and he was coming to uneasy grips with the bureaucracy of park administration. He had even made his marriage to Nichamoose legal, with the famous missionary, Father Lacombe, performing the ceremony.

Kootenai Brown was always enough of a visionary to know that civilization would come rushing into the west. But even he was bewildered by the speed with which what had been his way of life for so many years disappeared overnight.

It must have seemed ironic to him to write Ottawa for authority to control gambling among the tourists who were flocking to the park.

And for a man of the open range it must have taken a great deal of soul-searching to lead the way towards fencing off the ranch land around Pincher Creek. He did it only because, in the winter of 1911, 4,000 head of cattle had drifted into the park, and 2,000 head had died from cold and starvation.

In time, Brown would even have his famous, flowing hair cut. The job of park superintendent, he felt, demanded a certain dignity.

Brown was prepared to accept the need for civilization but, short hair or not, he just didn't have it in him to become a civilized man himself. Although he learned to control his temper, he never lost the wild, free feeling of the pioneer mountain man.

Perhaps no story sums up the older Kootenai Brown better than the one of how, in 1910, at an unmellowed 70 years of age, he took part in his last buffalo hunt.

Although the buffalo were basically exterminated during the era of the hide-hunter, a few did survive. These were eventually built into the famous Pablo herd (later to be moved to Wainwright).

It was the Pablo herd that gave Brown his chance at a final hunt.

A bunch (of buffalo from the herd) got away to the mountains — Brown writes — They belonged to Pablo and he got an idea that he would finish up the days of real buffalo hunting with a party of old-timers to go after these. He began looking over the country for a few real old buffalo hunters that were left.

One day I got a letter delivered to me by a long lanky half-breed cow-puncher. It was a letter someone had written for Pablo inviting me to be present at a buffalo hunt for a week.

The half-breed told me of the preparations Pablo was making and the amount of good whiskey he was putting in store.

I couldn't resist the invitation. The old instinct to ride after buffalo again came over me, and I have to admit I always have a keen appetite for any kind of good strong drink. We are not getting nearly as good whiskey as we used to. . . .

George "Kootenai" Brown   127

Anyway I accepted the invitation of Pablo and I rode my old buckskin over the border to Montana.

The most distinguished guest was Buffalo Bill, and to him fell the honor of killing three of the remaining buffalo. He was a great hunter. I have heard his wife tell of contests where he beat his opponents by killing nearly double the number of buffalo they could kill in the same time.

Pablo himself got two, I got one, and several others got one each. Pablo presented each of us with the hides we killed and with as much meat as we could pack home.

It was a tame meeting compared to the days when we hunted herds of thousands of animals. . . .

I have never seen a buffalo since, either wild or in captivity.

Ten years later George Kootenai Brown was dead. His grave is on a high point overlooking the park that is his legacy.

There has never been another man quite like him — "either wild or in captivity".

John Ware
A Living Legend
Andy Russell

One of the best known and best liked cowboys ever to live on the Alberta range was John Ware, a powerful black man who was a great bronc rider and cattleman. "Nigger" John, as he was called, was originally hired by Tom Lynch at Lost River, Idaho. Lynch was there in the spring of 1883 buying cattle for the Bar U Ranch. He was short of men to move several thousand head of cattle home, when big, soft-spoken John Ware showed up, without any saddle or horse but looking for a job. Lynch hired him and produced an old broken saddle and a gentle horse for him to ride.

Looking at this outfit, John remarked, "Ah say, boss, ef you'll jest gimme a little bettah saddle and a little wuss hoss, Ah think maybe Ah kin ride him."

The watching crew of cowboys broke into delighted grins at this opportunity for some hazing and promptly produced a good saddle and a much worse horse. John stepped up in the middle of him and put on a show like none of them had ever seen by riding the mean, snaky cayuse to a standstill. Then he went to work.

It didn't take Tom Lynch long to decide that John Ware was an outstanding stockman and he cut out a herd for him to take charge of on the trail to Canada. John and his crew were crossing Montana when a couple of hardcase ranchers showed up asking to cut out some cattle of theirs which they claimed had mixed with his herd. John knew they were lying, but agreed to let them look through the cattle, if they trailed along with the herd until it was time to bed it down for the night. This they angrily refused to do, but John was coolly unruffled though adamant. Then one of the ranchers moved for his gun and like a flash John jumped his horse between them and knocked them out of their saddles with the heavy butt of his quirt. As the herd moved on, the two claimers lay knocked out on the prairie. When they woke up it is likely their heads were sufficiently sore to remind them of the folly of trying any more shenanigans — anyway, they never showed up again.

John Ware's reputation for fairness and built-in fearlessness grew during the years he spent in Alberta. He was also a fun-loving man and nothing delighted him more than a good joke. One time he was working on a roundup in the High River Country and when he rode into camp for a fresh horse one day, he noticed the night herder getting some sleep in the bed tent with one of his feet sticking out from under the wall. John picked up a rope, put the loop over the sleeper's foot and tied the other end to a stout tent pin. Then he proceeded to pound on the tent roof with the flat of his hand while yelling as though the end of the world was at hand. The nighthawk woke up in the midst of this bedlam thinking he was about to be trampled flat in a stampede and came out of the tent taking steps ten feet long on the dead run. When he hit the end of the rope, he came down full length and upon rolling over he saw nothing but John and the cook doubled up with laughter.

John Ware was a living legend for years until he was killed by a falling horse. He left behind a wonderful family, who carved their own niches in the Alberta heritage. He will always be remembered for the part he played on the frontier — a generous, fun-loving, big-hearted rider who understood cattle and horses better than most.

Brother Jim
Robert W. Service

My brother Jim's a millionaire,
While I have scarce a penny;
His face is creased with lines of care,
While my mug hasn't any.
With inwardness his eyes are dim,
While mine laugh out in glee,
And though I ought to envy him,
I think he envies me.

He has a chateau, I a shack,
And humble I should be
To see his stately Cadillac
Beside my jalopy.
With chain of gold his belly's girt,
His beard is barber trim;
Yet bristle-chinned with ragged shirt,
I do not envy Jim.

My brother is a man of weight;
For every civic plum

He grabs within the pie of state,
While I am just a bum.
Last Winter he was near to croak
With gastric ulcers grim. . . .
Ah no! although I'm stony broke
I will not envy Jim.

He gets the work, I get the fun;
He has no time for play;
Whereas with paddle, rod and gun
My life's a holiday.
As over crabbed script he pores
I scan the sky's blue rim. . . .
Oh boy! While I have God's outdoors
I'll never envy Jim.

Caroline "Mother" Fulham
The Lady Kept Pigs
J. W. Grant MacEwan

When Mrs. Caroline Fulham — better known as Mother Fulham — left Calgary in 1904, members of the police department breathed sighs of relief and prepared to celebrate the great day. Most other citizens were secretly sorry to see her go because she was, in those years before radio, television and movies, the best source of local amusement. As the leading entertainer on Stephen Avenue, she needed no make-up, required no rehearsal and followed no script. Her charm was in being herself, rough as it might be.

With a sharp Irish tongue and a loud voice, she had the last word in almost every argument and when more was needed, she could draw upon the persuasiveness of two ready fists. Plump and powerful, she was a fair match for the best policeman on the beat. For one reason or another, the police officers saw much of her and knew that to escort her to a cell was normally a task requiring the chief and two constables — the entire Calgary force for some years.

The lady could neither read nor write but such circumstances were not to restrict her in gaining publicity. Between visits to the police court and her daily appearances guiding her horse-drawn democrat on Calgary streets, she became one of the best-known personalities in the community. And while police officers did their best to spare her from trouble, men and boys seeking fun delighted to tease and annoy her, knowing they would get instant and often exciting reaction.

Nor were those fellows above playing tricks on her, as on that day when she left her horse and democrat in the lane while she visited the long bar of the Alberta Hotel. In her absence, the pranksters unhitched the horse from the vehicle and then, after drawing the democrat shafts through the woven wire fence containing the railway right of way, rehitched with horse on one side of the fence and democrat on the other. In due course, the lady emerged from the hotel, feeling good enough to forgive all her enemies or make some new ones. Unsteadily, she walked to her democrat, mounted and clucked to her horse to move on before realizing that something was wrong and progress would be impossible. Sensing mischief, she seized her buggy whip and dismounted to search for the miscreants, all the while muttering threats of violence.

For most of her years in Calgary, Mother Fulham lived on 6th Avenue, just a short distance west of the site on which Knox United Church was built. Her occupation was that of keeping pigs. With no bylaws restricting livestock within the town, her pig feeding operations were entirely legal, even though they drew criticism from neighbors. To feed the swine, she gathered kitchen waste from Calgary's best hotels and restaurants. Here was good and economical raw material for pork production and she chose to believe that she had a monopoly on the contents of all garbage containers behind the Alberta, Queen's, Royal and Windsor hotels, and Criterion and New Brunswick restaurants. When other feeders of pigs threatened to encroach upon her garbage preserves, she was prepared to protect her interests with force if necessary.

With regularity befitting a town's bell-ringer, she made the rounds to gather the precious pig feed. Sitting squarely in the middle of the democrat seat, with barrel in the back for the transfer of the pig feed, she employed a willow switch to urge her aging horse to something faster than a walk and slower than a trot, muttering uncomplimentary epithets in reply to rude remarks from the sidewalk spectators. When somebody would shout "Hurray for Ireland," the speaker could expect to hear the rejoinder, "Sure, you'd like to be Irish too, ye pur fool."

Sometimes the mischief-makers visited her premises at night to carry out some nefarious trick. On a certain St. Patrick's night when the lady was celebrating, visitors painted her pigs a brilliant green, and on another occasion, according to *The Calgary Herald* (September 1, 1903): "Mrs. Fulham last night was awakened by hearing some men around her yard and saw them running away. This morning she got in her buckboard and the wheels came off after the horse had gone a few yards, so she knew the men had taken the nuts. She thinks she knows who the men were."

She kept her most outlandish green clothing for St. Patrick's day and began celebrating early. Her pigs might be neglected but a thoughtful neighbor was likely to give them feed and water. On that Day of Days, she took special licence to sing Irish songs from her throne on the democrat and, perchance, reach a state of intoxication long before it was time to attend the annual Firemen's Ball on that date.

Although uneducated, her wit was keen, as Dr. H. G. Mackid could testify. Meeting her on Stephen Avenue and seeing her walking with lameness, he inquired sympathetically if he could do anything for her. She replied that an ankle had been giving her trouble, to which the kindly doctor invited her to step inside Templeton's Drug Store where he could examine it. The doctor was, no doubt, aware that cleanliness was not one of the lady's obvious characteristics, but when she peeled down a stocking to expose the sore ankle, the doctor reeled at the sight of the unwashed limb and exclaimed impulsively, "By George, I'd bet a dollar there's not another leg in Calgary as dirty as that one."

Quick as a flash, the woman shouted back: "Put up your money, Doctor. I'm betting ye a dollar there is another and here's my money."

Before there was time for a retraction, Mother Fulham dropped her other stocking, thereby exposing another leg, just as dirty as the first one, and held out her hand to collect the doctor's dollar. (As told to the author by Dr. Mackid, May 3, 1956.)

There were altercations with police and neighbors that brought her name into the newspaper columns most often. And when she came to court, she would have nobody but the great Irish lawyer and personality, Paddy Nolan, to plead her case. Nolan may have enjoyed the assignments, even though he was never paid, because he was fascinated by the woman with the sharp tongue and was always assured of a big courtroom audience. When it was known on the streets that Mother Fulham and Paddy Nolan would appear together, everybody in the community wanted to be present. Sometimes the woman would be evicted from the court for reasons of undisciplined remarks and sometimes spectators had reason to wonder if the police were prosecuting the Fulham woman or if she was prosecuting the police.

Generally she was the defendant but in at least two instances she was the plaintiff. In April 1890 she was charging a Chinese employee of the Alberta Hotel with assault. As Paddy Nolan explained the circumstances, Mrs. Fulham caught the man bent over a garbage barrel at the rear of the hotel and administered a good Irish rebuke, either verbal or physical, and he struck her. But the evidence was confusing and there was reason to believe that the accused, instead of stealing garbage as alleged, was simply trying to recover a dressed chicken he had earlier stolen from the hotel kitchen and hidden temporarily in the barrel. The case was dismissed.

On the other occasion when Mrs. Fulham was charging rather than defending, she accused her neighbor, the Reverend Jacques, of insulting her with improper language. J. A. Lougheed acted for the reverend gentleman and Paddy Nolan, as usual, was on Mother Fulham's side. The evidence indicated that the woman had threatened to slaughter the minister's hens if they continued to wander onto her property and he replied by calling her a "blackguard". She admitted that she did not know what the work meant but was sure it was not a compliment. Paddy Nolan tried to take the argument from there, saying that his client was too often the object of barbs and insults. It was time the authorities took a stand against what looked like "a Fulham Extermination Society". The lawyer for the defense replied that Mrs. Fulham was "a notorious nuisance" in Calgary. Because of her presence and occupation, property in the neighborhood had fallen in value. To this the lady replied with some well-chosen abuse for the lawyer and was promptly ordered removed from the court. The defendant was fined one dollar and everybody present agreed that it was worth at least that much to be in attendance for the amusement.

For the next decade, she was one of the most frequent visitors at the police court, generally facing charges of disorderly conduct and generally ready to settle differences of opinion out of court by the expedient of a fight with the police. Editors knew that her story was always acceptable news and on October 21, 1901, she was reported as entering the *Herald* office and greeting the first man to face her with: "Good morning to you young man. An' it's an ill-used woman I am this day." While thus introducing the reason for her complaint, she placed a parcel on the desk, removed the wrappings and displayed a pile of dark-gray hair. Then, removing the ancient hat from her head and pointing to her uncombed locks, said, "The bastes of policemen tore that from me head."

Her complaint did not end there. A few days later, when city council met in regular session, the Fulham lady, carrying the same parcel of hair, made her way to the mayor's chair and insisted upon having the full attention of the City Fathers. Yes, she had a grievance. She'd been sitting peacefully in the kitchen of the New Brunswick Restaurant on a recent night when, according to her story, Constables Fraser and Walden entered, seized her by the hair and dragged or forced her into the police wagon and lodged her at the jail where she spent the night. In the morning she was brought to court, charged and fined the "usual fee for being arrested". She had had enough of this, especially when the police took to pulling hair. She wanted the aldermen to fire all the city cops.

The mayor promised to look into the complaint but the lady wanted immediate action and was still talking loudly when the aldermen were considering the next item of business. "Sure an' isn't mesiff that knows the wickedness of thim both. Those policemen are bad men. Sure gintlemen, this is my hair them bastes pulled out."

But the mayor, when he investigated, heard the other side of the story. The lady had been celebrating as she did rather often and when the police were called to the restaurant, she was in a fine fighting mood. As for the hair, it was found to match the mane and tail of the lady's horse and there was reason to believe it did not come from a human head.

Then there were the memorable negotiations about the Fulham cow, Nellie, which lost its life when hit by a CPR train. The owner made complaint, saying compensation would have to be high because Nellie was a very superior bovine. A hearing was convened and the railroad officials pointed out that "No

Trespassing" signs were posted prominently and neither cow nor person had any right to be on the railroad track.

But the cow's owner proceeded to nullify that point of argument, saying, "Ye pur fools, what makes ye think my pur old Nellie could read yer signs?" But failing to gain satisfaction from the company's minor officials, the lady wrote to Sir William Van Horne, president, and when he happened to be in Calgary, she forced her way into his private car and proceeded to hold him responsible for her loss. The president, with some feeling of sympathy, offered to find a replacement for the cow but that did not satisfy the woman because there was no other cow quite like Nellie. She contended it would take two cows to replace Nellie, but was obliged in the end to settle for one.

In any case, she exercised power and influence which might have brought envy to other citizens. And indirectly, she was the means of bringing a code of building restrictions to the city. Senator Lougheed, addressing the aldermen, said the time had come to bring in and enforce building regulations. "I for instance, have a number of lots in the vicinity of Mrs. Fulham's place and certainly no one would buy them when her pig ranch is taken into consideration. . . . Indeed, I had a sale balked just on that account."

Calgary obtained its building restrictions at about the time the city's celebrated lady specialist in pigs was departing. *The Calgary Herald* carried the disappointing news: "Mrs. Fulham, who has been a noted character in Calgary for many years, has sold out her business and property and gone to Vancouver to live."

The last news item to be found touching upon the lady was in the same paper about six months later: "Mrs. Fulham, who was without doubt the best known woman in Calgary, passed through the city on Monday night. She informed some of those at the station that she was coming back to live here in six weeks. This news will be received with mingled feelings."

Sure, she was often in trouble but deep in Calgary hearts

was affection for Mother Fulham. Her spontaneity and unvarnished personality were refreshing, even on a frontier. Calgarians would have been disappointed if she did not mark St. Patrick's Day by dressing in defiant green, or the twelfth of July by hurling shouts of derision at parading Orangemen.

But only those who watched her closely knew the generosity of her Irish heart. They alone knew the families she helped regularly with gifts of needed money, and the settler, Charlie Hawkes, who lost his three horses from glanders and had no money for replacements. The Sons of England presented him with twenty-five dollars but it was not enough. He met Mother Fulham on the street and told her of his predicament. Without comment, she pulled up her dress, exposing one of the perpetually dirty knees, took a roll of bills from a stocking and pressed forty dollars into the man's hand. "That'll help ye buy a horse," she said.

In spite of the remark made on the station platform, she did not return to take up residence in Calgary, but the memory of that great, roughcast keeper of pigs on Calgary's 6th Avenue lived on. If Calgarians did not actually love the Queen of Garbage Row, at least they missed her very much when she left.

C. W. Gordon (Ralph Connor)
Jacques Hamilton

It was the summer of 1917, near the end of a terrible war, and there were few tourists among the crowd that streamed out of Banff one Sunday to the foot of Mt. Rundle.

There, on a rock by a lake known — appropriately enough — as The Devil's Cauldron, a stocky dark-haired man in kilt and service jacket stood and began speaking.

He began hesitantly enough, as he always did, but as time passed his voice and words gained strength.

Rev. C. W. Gordon had just come back from the war in Europe. He had seen most of the men of his regiment perish in the horror that was France. At the Somme, he had said the funeral rites for his colonel and friend.

In all truth, many of those who had come to the foot of Mr. Rundle that day hadn't come to hear the strong, solemn words of this preacher. In all truth, to many of the people before him, Rev. C. W. Gordon wasn't even C. W. Gordon; he was the most famous Canadian writer of the day: Ralph Connor.

So popular were his books that it was estimated at the time that one of every sixty Canadians had a copy of the famous *The Man from Glengarry*.

In all, the novels he wrote sold a total of five million copies.

Even today, most people are familiar with such titles as *The Sky Pilot*, *Glengarry School Days* and *Black Rock*.

What those who listened to him that day at The Devil's Cauldron couldn't know was that the man facing them, the best and most successful Canadian writer of his day, was dead broke, ruined by the illegal acts of those he had entrusted with his wealth while he was away to war.

He said nothing of that in the sermon he preached. Instead he spoke of temperance, of courage and, above all, of forgiveness.

And, as was his habit, he spoke at great length. Those with Sunday roasts at home in the oven shifted uneasily before the vision of good roast beef shrivelling to charred leather.

Though much of his life was spent away from the mountains of Canada, Gordon was considered one of Banff's own sons.

What made this man, born in a small eastern town, a man of the Rockies? And what, even stranger, turned a committed missionary and minister into a popular novelist?

Gordon was born in Glengarry County in what was then Upper Canada in 1860, the same year his Presbyterian-minister father came to Canada from the Highlands of

Scotland to escape the confines of the established Church of Scotland.

The father was a fearsome, evangelical preacher and his influence on his son was enormous. The younger Gordon never gave serious thought to any other way of life than that of a churchman — despite the fact that his father's exhortations to the good life were often accompanied by the banshee wailing of a bagpipe with which he used to shake the walls of the house for hours on end.

Gordon was later to admit that he spent his life intensely disliking the instrument and would flee at the very thought of it being played.

Little is known of Gordon's relationship with his mother, but it is significant to note that he said the gentle, long-suffering heroines of his novels were all based on her.

The boy was taught to work for everything. Even as a child of ten he hired himself out as a laborer and he worked his way through the University of Toronto, paying every cent of his tuition and expenses from his own pocket.

He spent some time at the university after graduating, teaching classics, then put himself through Knox College Divinity School and through two years at Edinburgh University in Scotland.

He was ordained as a minister in 1890 and called to missionary service in the North-West Territories.

His first mission parish was Banff and he immediately fell in love with the mountain community.

Banff, in the 1890s, was far from being the pleasant tourist and resort town it is today. Rather it was a tough, hard-boozing settlement with more than its share of troublemakers.

A perfect town, as Gordon later noted tongue-in-cheek, "for an Evangelist".

A single man of 30, particularly one of such unquestionably sterling character, was an unusual attraction in a frontier town and Gordon was quickly drawn into the modest social life of the settlement.

Every evening, in one home or another, the young people of the settlement gathered to sing around a piano or to chat and sip tea. Gordon was one of the more faithful at these gatherings and, until recently, there were still old-timers in Banff who could recall that he would occasionally sing, in a fine tenor, for these parties.

Unfortunately, the old-timers pointed out, he usually accompanied himself on a guitar which he played exceptionally badly.

Ah well, a man can't be single, moral, a good singer and a good musician all at the same time. The girls of Banff took him to their hearts anyway and it looked for a long time as though he would find a bride among them.

But Gordon finally left Banff still a bachelor and it wasn't until he was 45 that a young Winnipeg girl, Helen King, won his heart and became his wife. He and Helen had 6 daughters and a son, King, who became a Rhodes Scholar and later an active figure in the United Nations.

In his long career with the church, Gordon would go on to become head of the Presbyterian Church in Canada and one of the leaders in the fight against booze, prostitution and conscription.

All this became overshadowed, however, by the emergence of his alter-ego.

Gordon was 36 and he had just made a futile trip to Toronto to try to get church officials to raise money for missionary work in the west.

He had come away empty-handed but with an incidental set of instructions from the editor of the church's weekly magazine to write a story "to illustrate the need" of mission work in the west.

At the time Gordon was the over-worked minister of a

run-down church on the outskirts of Winnipeg. Night after night, after prayer-meeting had ended, Gordon would go home and toil at the task of coming up with the required story.

The result, published first in 1896, was called "Christmas Eve in a Lumber Camp".

The story was a fictionalized sermon about how a Presbyterian minister moved a camp of hard-drinking lumbermen to prayer.

Its name would later be changed to "Black Rock" and it would become one of the main stories in the first anthology of Ralph Connor's work.

The first story behind him, Gordon began to write and write and write still more. Being a fiction writer was not a respectable occupation for a minister so he was asked to come up with a pen name. There was a sheet of mission letterhead on his desk when the request came and he compressed the first syllables in two of its words to come up with Cannor.

The publisher read Cannor as Connor and added Ralph because it seemed to go with the name. And so Ralph Conner — a non-existent being who Gordon would later say had grown to become a "second person inside me" — was casually born.

Ralph Connor was prolific, his books came out at a rate of one a year, and wildly popular.

By the time his second novel appeared public curiosity over his real identity had reached a fever pitch and Gordon came — briefly — from behind the mask.

Much of the clamor for his true identity came in the United States where his work was so popular that it was made part of many high school reading lists. "The world will insist on knowing it," the *St. Louis Democrat* editorialized in its plea for the true identity of the author.

Connor's work is "so intense that one grinds his teeth lest his sinews snap ere the strain is released", *The Chicago Tribune* added.

And "his passionate writing appeals to all that is best in human nature," summed up the *San Francisco Chronicle*.

His identity out in the open, Gordon made lecture tours and, in the United States, police had to be called out to hold back the crowds that gathered to hear and see him. President Woodrow Wilson was a well-publicized fan of Ralph Connor. And Henry Ford collected a complete set of autographed volumes of Ralph Connor's work.

In Detroit, when Gordon was asked to deliver a sermon in a church, he rose to begin a prayer and the congregation spontaneously broke in with the singing of "For He's a Jolly Good Fellow".

Few men could stand so startling a thrust into fame and fortune without changing. In Gordon's case, it is to his tribute that all the fuss did was heighten his affection for the simple life and increase his sense of humor.

His New York publisher once described a visit to Gordon. He arrived at the house to find Connor was out.

"I was guided through a trail in the woods," he recalled, "to where he stood, bareheaded and alone, in sweater and old clothes, whittling a cane from roots of trees."

Carving canes — walking sticks — from the roots of trees was one of Gordon's ways of staying in physical touch with nature. So were riding a horse and paddling a canoe.

"I should have been born an Indian," he once lamented.

As for his sense of humor, a long-time friend once wrote that: "He could unbend more completely than any man of his age that I have known."

His favorite practical joke was one he reserved for the first time a new guest sat down to the Gordon's dinner table.

The guest would be placed at the end of the table, opposite his host, and at a signal from Gordon the people on either side would lift the oilcloth table covering to form a trough down which Gordon would solemnly pour his drinking water and then howl with laughter as the astonished guest received the watery cargo right in the lap.

After the guest was wrung out, fed and installed in the drawing room, Gordon would entertain him by an evening of singing as badly as he could while accompanying himself on a banjo he proudly claimed he could play worse than anyone he knew.

In fact, though, despite the recollection of his early inability on the guitar, Gordon was an accomplished musician who could perform on the guitar, banjo or flute. Late in life he enhanced a natural singing voice by taking lessons.

He became so fussy on the subject of vocalizing that he thought nothing of stopping his congregation in mid-hymn to demonstrate how they could be singing better than they were.

By the time the First World War appeared on the horizon, Gordon's writing had made him a millionaire. He had built a large home for his family in Winnipeg and a summer home in the resort community of Kenora, Ontario.

When Canada entered the war he went overseas as a chaplain.

A careful man, he left his financial affairs in order before he left. There was a $100,000 insurance policy and all his cash assets were turned over to a lawyer-associate to invest in the booming Winnipeg real-estate market.

The real-estate boom never materialized and the market collapsed in 1915, but Gordon was assured by his friend that his money had been protected and was divided among eight land companies the lawyer had set up.

It was only with the death of the lawyer, while Gordon was still overseas, that it was learned that the money had been misused and that Gordon had been left virtually penniless.

Connor's publisher recalled that it was almost impossible to convince him that he had been the victim of a criminal; and that, when he was finally convinced, his decision was to forgive the act and to do everything in his power to have it forgotten.

Nor did he allow the loss of his wealth to influence a life-long habit of open-handed charity. He gave everything he could to those in need during the depression years that followed the war, even though he was often as badly off as those he aided.

His financial disaster, however, seemed to open the door to a host of other troubles. Although he would go on writing and writing, in retrospect, better than he ever had before, his work began to lose its popularity.

Unable to recover from the loss of his money, he gradually had to give up the life-insurance policy he had hoped would provide for his family after his death. The same was true of the taxes on his homes and these too had to be given up, finally.

The only thing that never failed was Gordon's determined Christianity. He worked on and on, creating hostels for the homeless, acting as an advocate for the working poor.

But all that was still ahead, unknown to any of those who sat on the grassy slope by The Devil's Cauldron and listened to Canada's most famous author and best-known churchman.

This man, after all, was a brave minister who had gone to a terrible war to ease the misery of their sons and brothers and husbands. That made him part of them all.

And this man, too, was Ralph Connor: the author who had thrilled them with his adventures and fanned their courage with the examples of the firm-hearted characters he created.

When all is said and done, what they felt, sitting on the grass by a mountain lake, was right. There were two men before them.

It is the same judgement that history wrote on his gravestone when he died in 1937:

GORDON AND CONNOR

MINISTER OF GOSPEL

C. W. Gordon   145

Goofy McMasters
Tony Cashman

In this age of mass mediocrity it's good to be able to recall Goofy McMasters. Goofy was never mediocre. Goofy was awful. As a boxer, as a soldier, as a bearer of sandwich-boards, Goofy was awful. He was awful at the Empire Theatre that night, when, as "Heartless Harold, the Alberta Assassin", he pranced up to the ring, made a nimble leap over the ring ropes, caught his foot in the tie rope, and plunged headfirst into the water bucket, knocking himself cold. Only Goofy McMasters could be so wonderfully awful. It was one of his ninety-six fights as a heavyweight boxer. He managed to lose, or at least failed to win, the ninety-five others. It was the pattern of his life, of all his endeavours.

In the nineteen-twenties, particularly in the thirties, and on into the forties, Goofy established criteria for ineptitude which will never be challenged. As boxer, soldier and advertising man, he was the worst — and yet he managed to be the worst with such abiding integrity, such earnest dedication, and such overriding dignity of spirit, that he is remembered not only with affection but admiration.

Goofy was a man. At the Salvation Army where he lived, and at the police station where he often recovered from parties, they recognized Goofy as a man. The people at the Salvation Army knew him as a man (even though he once demanded half the money on the drum for coming up to get saved at a side-walk service). So did the police, who would shoo him out of the cells when he was sober enough to find his way home. He was hardly ever charged and brought before the magistrates for the traditional five dollars or five days.

The police knew better than anybody how hard he worked to earn his money. He came by it slowly and honestly, losing fights, attending parades as a militiaman, skating erratically around the Gardens between periods at hockey games, lugging sandwich-boards, moving furniture, walking up and down Jasper Avenue with a tail and pitchfork to advertise the heat of a certain brand of coal, riding up and down in a bathtub to advertise a certain plumbing company, or dragging a cow up and down Jasper Avenue while dressed as a bullfighter to advertise that Eddie Cantor was appearing at the Capitol Theatre in *The Kid From Spain*. And he put on a funnier show than Eddie Cantor when Bossy got sore feet and lay down and refused to move.

Goofy never made any fast bucks. Except, perhaps, for the five he made for running in his stockinged feet — at ten below zero — from the St. Regis Hotel beer parlour to First and Jasper, and back again. You could always tell when Goofy was in training for one of his ninety-six fights. He'd trot along the street, instead of walking, and would stop for a fast foot shuffle and a couple of shadow punches at each lamppost en route.

In his role as a pugilist, Goofy generally referred to himself as "The Battler". He'd go in the ring with any man, and had the strength of six — or, at any rate, he could lift an army marquee tent, which according to regulations required six men to lift. The Battler was a spectacular puncher, executing monstrous uppercuts from the floor, which were so long in coming that his opponents were rarely in range when they arrived. But the crowd loved to see him throw those punches. Goofy knew they came to see him fight and so he figured he must be a better fighter than his record would indicate. And he was the only Alberta boxer ever to appear in the *Pathe Gazette*, one of the first movie newsreels. For his performance, he received a cheque for twenty-five cents, which he framed and hung in the many shoeshine parlours where he worked.

Goofy's pre-fight warm-ups were spectacular. He would flex his muscles by pulling on the ring ropes and making the gruesome sounds expected of the Alberta Assassin, (or of another of his aliases — the Unknown Undertaker). Once, in

Ponoka, when the Alberta Assassin was going through his warm-up, he flexed too hard for the temporary ring. He pulled the corner post right out, and the whole platform came down with a crash. One spectator threw a shoe. The Assassin was a bouncer as well as a boxer. In the confusion he forgot his assignment for the night, picked up a chair, and chased all the fans out of the arena.

At Brooks, the Battler scored the only knockout of his career — but it was on a spectator, a police magistrate. He was boxing a frightening heavyweight named Dan O'Dowd, who had once gone eight rounds with Gene Tunney. At one point, O'Dowd uncorked a ferocious swing that just missed the Battler's chin. It was so close a miss that the Battler decided he had better not be around when O'Dowd uncorked another one, so he dropped to the canvas expecting to be counted out. However, the referee would have none of this and he threatened to hold up the Battler's purse if he didn't get up and fight. So Goofy sprang up and made a gallant bid to K.O. his opponent. He backed up and charged across the ring with his fist coiled. But the blow never landed. Dan O'Dowd stepped aside, and the Battler went on out into the fourth row and K.O.'d the magistrate. Another time, at Stettler, the Battler contributed something new to the manly art of self-defence. A boxer named Billy Bonn was making a target of the McMaster countenance, so the Battler turned his back and waded in, in reverse, with fists flailing. Once again the referee foiled his plans.

Goofy turned promoter once. He promoted a fight at Tom O'Malley's barn near St. Albert, starring himself versus "Thrasher" Sam Logan. This was a draw, and so were two hilarious sequels fought at the Star Dairy on 102nd Avenue and 159th Street. Goofy's duels with the Thrasher got so much publicity that boxing fans in the Peace River country wanted to see the Alberta Assassin in combat with their pride, a very competent heavyweight named Jack Thibault. The Assassin's manager consented very reluctantly, but the Assassin was enthusiastic. Doing some roadwork on the south side, he had noticed a large tree blown part way over by the wind, so he had himself photographed leaning against it. When the picture reached Fairview in the Peace River, it showed the Alberta Assassin toning up his muscles by straightening up a tree. When they got to Fairview for the fight, Goofy's manager persuaded Thibault's manager that the fight would last longer if Thibault's arms were taped so that he couldn't bend his elbows too much. The Battler gave the fans a great fight, throwing punches all over the ring. Finally a long blow hit Thibault. He got mad, burst his bonds, and the battle ended abruptly.

One of Goofy McMaster's greatest fights was with himself. He was hard at work one morning, shining shoes at a stand where the Tip-Top Tailors shop is now. Jack Kelly, the sportswriter, came up behind him as Goofy perspired over a shoe. "Battler," he said, "there's a guy behind you wants to fight!" The Battler swung around, caught a fleeting glimpse of a man with his dukes up and swung from his heels. His fist connected with the mirror, a huge plate-glass mirror, and smashed it. Battling McMasters lost his shoeshine concession over the incident, but he wasn't worried or bitter. He knew there were plenty of other concessions and other jobs.

Goofy's military career was not so well known as his boxing and advertising careers, mainly because it was conducted out of sight — with the 19th Alberta Dragoons at Sarcee in peace time, and overseas with the Loyal Edmonton Regiment in wartime. His military career followed the inevitable pattern, because he didn't get into action. Perhaps the generals had heard that Battling McMasters never won any fight he was in; but he was a useful member of the regiment while it was in training. His superiors put him in charge of the grounds and barracks and as a badge of office found him two armbands of a particularly vile yellow, which pleased him tremendously.

When the regiment was on manoeuvres Goofy entertained each night with a wrestling act, teaming with an Edmonton shoemaker named Steve Jostle. Goofy had wrestled professionally as the Edmonton Bonecrusher. One night when he and Steve were performing on an estate in Hampshire, the rustic farm hands were so dismayed by the savagery that they phoned the lord of the manor to hurry over and avert the slaughter.

Goofy was left in England when the regiment sailed for Italy in 1943, and was back home before them. But on the night the Loyal Edmontons came home, the Battler put on his uniform and joined the parade as a sort of supernumerary, out of step as always, ready and willing, but unable.

In any case his military career did not have any effect on the conduct of the war. But it did have an effect on Goofy's sandwich-board technique, and also on the street-advertising technique of his spiritual descendant, the redoubtable Pete Jamieson. Goofy was already an established Jasper Avenue tradition that day in 1935 when Pete Jamieson was sent out on his first town-crier mission. Pete was an usher at the Dreamland Theatre. Patronage was slow at the third run of the Nelson Eddy and Jeanette MacDonald movie, and the manager sent Pete up the street to holler up some business.

At the sign-painter's shop, where they used to come to pick up jobs, Goofy would discuss with young Pete the application of military marching technique to the carrying of sandwich-boards. It was Goofy's opinion that when you came to a corner and wanted to make a turn, you should give a smart "hipe, one, two, three", then make a sharp turn as though on parade, and then step off — "hipe, one, two, three" — on the left foot. Thirty years later, Pete still marched in military style along Jasper. Although Pete marched like a general advancing at the head of a victorious column, Goofy, by tradition, marched like the sole survivor of some military disaster. But he was giving his best effort. He never gave less.

On his return from the actual war theatre, Goofy was rewarded with the shoeshine concession at the Memorial Hall. His great strength, bearing down on a shoe, could make it glisten, and if he can be said to have had a permanent occupation, this was it. However, he never had a permanent location. He had a knack of making each one temporary. The stand at the Memorial Hall, for example, was next door to the beer parlour, and he lost that location. But Goofy wasn't worried. He knew there were other locations and other jobs.

Harold McMasters, also known as Goofy, also known as Battling McMasters, also known as Heartless Harold the Alberta Assassin, lived as only he could live. And he died as only he could die. It was in 1950. He'd spent the day working at a carnival on 97th Street, and when the day was over he asked if he could have half a bucket of dill pickles which were left over at a hamburger concession. He wanted to take them to a party. No one could refuse Goofy a request like that. He took them to the party and ate them himself, and then fell asleep. The party went on, and the others paid no attention to him. They thought he was just asleep. But he had died, peacefully, as he had lived, no trouble to anybody. It was no mediocre soul which had slipped away.

The Greatest Rider in the World
Jacques Hamilton

Alberta is the unquestioned home of rodeo greats. Year after year, our cowboys and cowgirls bring home the top honors and the championship saddles.

With so many greats, it is easy to understand why today only a few people still remember a little cowboy from Pincher Creek who proved himself the greatest rider in the world and, in a few short minutes long ago, gave the sport of rodeo its greatest glory.

It was Winnipeg in 1913 and the announcement had just been made that Emery La Grandeur had won the title of World's Champion Bronco Rider, with a gold medal and a cash prize of $1,000.

As the crowd clapped and cheered, everyone thought the Winnipeg version of the late Guy Weadick's "Stampede" had come to an end. Only Emery La Grandeur knew different.

While the announcements regarding winners in other events were being made — Weadick recalled later — Emery La Grandeur approached me and asked me if I would do him a favor.

Sure, I'd be glad to do anything I could for him.

He then asked me if I would have the big sorrel bucking horse named Red Wings brought into the arena as he wanted to make an exhibition ride on him.

For my part I had seen about all the bronc riding I cared to during the past week, and told him so, also suggesting that considering he had ridden several top horses during the week — and had been fortunate enough to win the money, title, etc., — it was beyond me why he wanted to prolong the performance fooling around with this Red Wings which, by the way, was an outstanding bucking horse of the Ad Day string.

Never will I forget the earnestness in his voice nor the almost pleading look in his eyes as he replied, "Doggone it Guy, don't turn me down in this. I sure want to take a sittin' at that sorrel, and I know the audience will be glad to see one more final bronc ride after the last announcement has been made."

Then he continued, "Go ahead Guy, have them bring him in. You know old Joe La Mar was a friend of mine, and I'd hoped all week that I'd get to draw this Red Wings. Let me take a ride at him, Guy; I want to kinda square things up for old Joe."

His eyes sorta filled up as he looked at me — and I, I turned away feeling a little softened up myself. I ordered the sorrel to be brought into the arena at once.

Emery's eyes sparkled as he heard the order given. "I'll be right back," he called over his shoulder. "Goin' to get my saddle."

The attendants brought the big bronc into the arena and snubbed him up to a saddle horse. As Emery was saddling him, an announcement was made that turned the inside of the arena silent as a tomb. The new world champion bronc rider was going to give an exhibition ride on the noted outlaw Red Wings — the horse that had killed the champion's best friend, Joe La Mar, at Calgary the previous year.

In the stands, La Grandeur's wife Violet turned pale and held their infant son a little closer to her.

The area inside the arena fence was cleared, and every man who had competed in the week-long Stampede gathered at vantage points along the rail.

Picking up Guy Weadick's description again:

> The saddling finished, La Grandeur climbed up on the bronc, settling himself in the saddle with both feet set in his stirrups. He quietly told the man on the snubbing horse to take the dallies off his saddle horn and pass the halter rope over to him.
>
> When that had been quickly and quietly accomplished, Emery reached over and unbuckled the halter, stripping it off the horse's head.
>
> He straightened back up in the saddle and swung the halter in the air — bringing it down between the horse's ears with a resounding crack.
>
> As the snub man loped out of the way, La Grandeur tossed away both halter and shank and shouted: "Bow your head bronc, and do your best!"
>
> Raising both hands high in the air above his head, the reckless rider planted both spurs high in the horse's neck and raked him with both feet from there clear back to the cantleboard of his saddle.

As the big sorrel plunged forward he really turned on the juice. Not a sound was to be heard from the spectators in the seats nor the contestants encircling the arena, but gradually — it seemed almost unconsciously — all rose to their feet in spell-bound silence; everything forgotten but the drama that was being enacted out there in that long, tanbark-covered arena.

Red Wings had a reputation as a top bucking horse, and that August night in 1913 he sure lived up to every bit of it.

With his big head free and no restraining rein, either to hold him back or to assist the rider in steadying himself, the sorrel really demonstrated that his bucking propensities had not been over-estimated by the many who had touted him as a hard horse to ride.

He ducked, he plunged, reared, sunfished, leaped high in the air, swapped ends and hit the ground repeatedly like a ton of brick.

In fact he opened up his entire bag of tricks as he bucked this way and that, zig-zag across and down the long arena.

The sorrel did everything in his power to unseat the reckless, cool and calculating cowboy astride him — who was still holding both hands high in the air. . . .

And La Grandeur, instead of doing anything to restrain the bucking horse, urged him to still further "turn it on" by playing a spur tattoo, scratching him continuously high, wide and handsome from shoulders to flanks.

There was no time limit set to the ride. Nothing had been said as to when the horse was to be picked up, and after Red Wings had bucked the entire length of the arena he swapped ends and started his dizzy waltz back toward the upper end, seemingly getting tougher with every jump.

Emery still continued to work on him — all the time holding both hands high above his head.

Suddenly the horse threw up his head and his tail. He broke, and started to run like a race horse.

The pick-up men immediately started to close in on the fleeing animal and, as there was no halter or halter shank on the horse, they decided to crowd in on him from each side and pick off the daring rider.

Before these good intentions could be carried out La Grandeur nimbly quit the running horse and landed safely on both feet. The ride was over.

For almost a minute, there was nothing but stunned silence in the arena. Then, suddenly, the crowd went wild. They cheered and shouted in a non-stop tribute to Emery La Grandeur.

La Grandeur struggled through the crowd of contestants trying to congratulate him and made his way to his wife's side.

"You made a fine ride, Emery," she said with a quiet smile.

La Grandeur fumbled in his shirt pocket and pulled out the cheque for the $1,000 prize money and his gold medal.

He handed the cheque to his wife. "Violet, here's the money, it's yours, get what you want with it."

Then he pinned the championship medal on his shirt and commented softly: "It's a purty medal, ain't it?" Violet only nodded.

On the arena floor, one of the top riders in North America, Clay McGonagil of Texas, looked up at the still-cheering crowd.

"All these folks here," he said to a champion, "may live till they're old and greyheaded but they'll never see a bronc ride like that again. . . ."

With so many greats, it is easy to understand why today only a few people still remember a little cowboy from Pincher Creek. But it is a little sad, too.

Miss Tannahill

Joan Hanson

Miss Tannahill
wore 19th century greige dresses
with high necks and long sleeves
to hide her spare frame and limbs
had lived forever in Victoria
behind my grandparents' home
in gentle fearful spinster poverty
alone in an old skinny wooden house
with the shades always drawn

Miss Tannahill
wore gloves and high button shoes
kept her bunned hair tucked into a bonnet
tied properly beneath her chin
shading a softly glazed Belleek china face
with bright bird eyes ever watchful
lest a dog or cat venture into her yard
or a person

Miss Tannahill
age unknown
invited me age six to tea
and afterward everyone asked:
"What did you see?"
"What did you eat?"
"What did she say?"
 I didn't answer
 but Grandpa smiled and said:
"Miss Tannahill chose wisely,
 her secrets are safe with you."

The Informal Miss Rummel

Iris Fleming

Elizabeth Rummel was 73 years old when she gave up her camp at the 7,300-foot level below British Columbia's Mount Assiniboine. The decision was made because of arthritis. Age had nothing to do with it.

At 78 she is as vibrant a person as ever — this amazing woman, born to a wealthy and aristocratic family in Bavaria, who ran the Sunburst Lake camp for 20 years, cooking with supplies packed in on horseback (she used a snowbank as a refrigerator), hauling water from glacial streams, and guiding her guests through alpine meadows and up steep slopes.

Elizabeth Rummel has become a sort of legend in the Rockies. Professional mountaineers tell of her prowess as mountain climber and skier and of the help she gave them in their early climbing days. They tell of her strength and leadership as she rode horseback on the rugged trails.

People from all over the world who came to her camp keep in touch with her — an artist from Paris, an alpinist from Japan, a botanist from the United States. . . .

A Toronto doctor took a party of nine there year after year, almost filling the camp. Miss Rummel paid no attention to advice to enlarge the accommodation, though she made hardly any money. One of the things dear to her heart was the meeting of minds and fascinating conversation around the campfire at night. Too many people would spoil the magic of those moments.

Elizabeth von Rummel (she dropped the "von" as soon as she was old enough to decide for herself it sounded affected) came to Canada in 1911 in her early teens. Her mother, on a whim, had purchased a ranch in southern Alberta. Sight unseen. Her three daughters, she had decided, would benefit from the rugged life — no running water, no electricity — as a change from their 22-room, servant staffed (including a butler) home in Bavaria.

They stayed several weeks each summer and the girls were reluctant to leave. Then came the war. The von Rummels could not get passage back to Germany. The girls were delighted. But things were different. There was no money from the homeland to pay for hired help. Mrs. von Rummel and her daughters pitched in and ran the ranch themselves.

Elizabeth and her sisters loved it. To this day she clasps her hands in ecstasy as she thinks of it. Her eyes shine. "We took to it," she says, "like ducks to water."

As the years passed, she went into the mountains to work. She became a guide and at other times worked in mountain lodges. She managed some well-known ones. In 1950 she bought the camp at Assiniboine — the mountain known as "The Matterhorn of the Canadian Rockies", with an elevation of 11,870 feet.

There was a waiting list from the time she took over, though not a penny was spent on advertising. The trip into the camp was not for the weak of heart: a rugged 26-mile drive by truck from the highway and, after that, a horseback ride or hike 12 miles over Assiniboine Pass. Guests slept in canvas-topped cabins. In winter, the camp was open to skiers.

Elizabeth Rummel now lives in a cosy, white-fenced house in Canmore, near Banff, with the mountains all around. She sees Mount Assiniboine only when a friend, Jim Davies — a pilot well known in the mountains — phones to say he's taking off and has a vacant seat in his helicopter. She drops everything and goes. She loves flying.

She is a warm, fascinating woman, her eyes blue and steady, her handshake firm. Her voice is slightly German-accented. She rolls her own cigarettes — a habit she found convenient in the mountains and which she's kept up, she says with a smile, because it's cheaper. She reads a great deal — there are books everywhere in the house — and knits for her great-nephews and great-nieces while watching television. She works at a tumbler machine in the garage, polishing stones. And she spends many hours digging in her flower garden despite the arthritis.

Her love of the mountains is so great that since she gave up the camp she has spent hours and days taping the reminiscences of elderly mountaineers so that their stories will live. She has done research for the Archives of the Canadian Rockies.

She herself has always been shy of publicity. Most of the information about her comes from others; but it's a different matter when she begins talking about the lives and feats of other mountaineers. The hours pass.

She downplays her own incredible experiences, though people have said she's had enough of them to write a book. When it's mentioned, she shakes her head.

"Books," she says firmly, "are written by people who have something to say."

the witch
Terrence Heath

mrs. schmidt and the boy stepped down from the
backporch of the house onto the prairie.   they
followed two ruts toward the railroad yard.   grey
dust rose around their feet.   when they reached
the tracks they walked along the timbers and picked
up pieces of coal until her basket was almost full.
they turned towards her house again and walked
diagonally across the prairie.   every few steps she
pointed to the ground and the boy bent down and
found the plants she meant.   some of the plants he
dug out by the roots.   from some he picked the
leaves, from some the flowers.   the coal could no

longer be seen through the green plants in the basket.
they reached the framed rectangular screendoor at
the back of her house.

one moment.   i have something for you.   she went
into the house.   the coiled spring on the door
stretched open and closed again.   it had worn a
smooth groove in the side of the wood.   the boy
stood in the wild portulaca near the back door.   he
moved his feet; they raised dust in the air.   he could
not see into the house

she came to the door.   the coiled spring opened and
closed.   in her right hand was a black box.

here.   a camera.   for you.   now you can take pictures.

Tekahionwake
John W. Chalmers

What on earth was a nice Indian girl doing in Jerry Boyce's
High River saloon that spring evening in 1904? Didn't she
know that no self-respecting female would be found dead in
such an environment, and that any live registered Indian
discovered therein ran the risk of being incarcerated in the
nearest hoosegow? And why the outlandish costume with
human scalps dangling from her girdle?

Perhaps to describe her as a girl is to use a bit of literary
licence, for at that time Tekahionwake, better known as
Pauline Johnson, was over forty. She was in the saloon, not as
a customer, but because that was the only available room in
town large enough to accommodate her audience. For Pauline, poet and Indian princess, was primarily an entertainer.
Her act consisted mainly of readings from her own works,
many of which dealt with her own people.

And that was why she appeared in native costume, a

beautiful buckskin dress trimmed with ermine and adorned with ancient silver brooches hammered from coins by her own forebears. She wore a bear-claw necklace and bracelets of wampum, a red broadcloth blanket, and in her hair an eagle feather. Naturally she was shod in moccasins.

No, she hadn't lifted those scalps herself. One was Huron, perhaps inherited from her great-grandfather Jacob Teka-hionwake, who adopted the surname Johnson when he was baptised into the Anglican faith. According to Walter McRaye, her partner, the other hairpiece had once been worn by a Cree, and was dangling from the waist of a Blackfoot chief when the poet first saw it. She made the mistake of trying to buy it. The chief drew himself up and frowningly refused. Her interpreter explained that the lovely visitor was the daughter of fighting Mohawks, great warriors who had taken many scalps. The old man's eyes brightened. He untied the grisly trophy and handed it to Pauline's companion, saying, "Give this to the daughter of fighting men, whose eyes are like the dawn."

According to another biographer, Mrs. W. Garland Foster, the incident, which happened in 1895, occurred at Fort Macleod (or Medicine Hat), the chief was a Blood (or possibly Sarcee), the offer to purchase was made through Pauline's companion and not directly, the chief took an hour to consider it, and at the end of his long reply his punch line was, "I take no money from the daughter of fighting men." Finally, the original owner of the scalp was not Cree but Sioux.

Otherwise, the two accounts are identical.

It is unsurprising that the chief did not at first recognize Pauline as a fellow-Indian. Legally she was a registered Mohawk, descendant of a long line of famous warriors and wise counsellors, but genetically she was three-quarters white. Emotionally she identified with her father's people, and in her poetry, her prose, and her platform performances she exploited her native heritage.

But first of all, as evidenced by her poem "Canada", she

was a Canadian. In the days before radio and television, Air Canada and the Trans-Canada Highway, she travelled back and forth across the country, arousing in her audiences some appreciation of their great and wonderful land. She visited not only the lusty-growing cities but little farming communities, mining camps here today and gone tomorrow, tiny coastal fishing villages. She performed in schools and churches, pool rooms and saloons — as at High River. Incidentally, on her visit to that town, the "gate" amounted to $75, all of which the big-hearted innkeeper turned over to Pauline and her partner, Walter McRaye. Bob Edwards, then publishing his *Eye Opener* there, wrote up the affair, ending his story with, "Come again, Pauline, and bring the genial Mac with you."

Over the years, the poet princess visited many Alberta points, not only Calgary and Edmonton but such places as Lethbridge, Fort Macleod, Pincher Creek, Olds, Fort Saskatchewan, and other centres. The Alberta landscape and people were the inspiration for many of her poems, such as "Calgary of the Plains", "At Crow's Nest Pass", and "The Train Dogs".This last was so named because sleigh dogs were hitched and driven, not in teams but in trains.

It was written in Edmonton about the same time, probably on the same tour, as the High River bar-room performance. She and McRaye were standing on the corner of Jasper Avenue and First (now 101st) Street one late spring morning when a train of huskies came down the road dragging a sleigh loaded with furs. They had come from the north during the night, travelling on the nocturnal frost. "His dogs were skeletons, their ribs showing, and he himself weary and worn," McRaye relates, "but he cheerfully said, 'Good dogs, we beat um'." The piece was eventually published by a magazine which sent her a cheque for seventy-five cents. This she returned. The poem later appeared on the front page of another publication — over another writer's name.

During her lifetime and for awhile after her death in 1913,

Pauline Johnson was extravagantly praised for her poetry and her patriotism. Today, her *Legends of Vancouver* is increasingly esteemed, but her verse is seldom read. Her overly sentimental, romantic, and simplistic view of "the noble red man" is rather too naive for contemporary taste. In this day of free verse, her formal, rhymed, metrical stanzas, her inverted word orders and fanciful figures of speech, her "poetical" and archaic diction appear Victorian and dated. Her proud, even blatant nationalism now seems chauvinistic. Yet for the haunting beauty of her rhythms, as in "The Song My Paddle Sings" (she was an expert canoeist), and for the intensity and integrity of her feeling, Pauline Johnson deserves to be long remembered.

Suzuki
The Prime-Time Scientist
David Spurgeon

Prime time on CBC-TV is usually reserved for big draws like sports, sitcoms and crime shows — and here, in 1976, was a genetics professor pushing for a science show at an hour when most viewers hankered for the likes of Kojak and Mary Tyler Moore. But this professor was David Suzuki, no stranger to TV. His "Science Magazine" had been running for two years at off-peak hours.

With Suzuki's undoubted success over two seasons and the growing popularity of his 50-minute radio show, "Quirks and Quarks", CBC programmers gave in: "Science Magazine" went to 8 p.m. Wednesday on the national network. It was an immediate hit.

Last season, "Science Magazine" drew an average of 1.1 million viewers. That put it in the same league as "King of Kensington" (1.4 million), and ahead of many shows the public was presumed to prefer. "Quirks and Quarks", meanwhile, averaged 304,000 listeners. As a result, David Suzuki has become a public figure, enjoying the kind of recognition that few other Canadian scientists receive.

Although a distinguished scientist, Suzuki has built a reputation as our leading science communicator precisely because on air he does not act like a scientist at all. Alexander Ross wrote in *Maclean's:* "Because he is so articulate about his craft, it's possible to see him and every scientist for what they are — not as remote automatons in white lab coats, but as intelligent, anguished, noble, petty, screwed-up, talented, ordinary human beings."

Suzuki's taste runs to jeans, embroidered shirts and sandals. His hair is thick and wild, his manner completely casual. He has a rare faculty for putting science across. Explaining genetics at the University of New Brunswick, he said: "When sperm fertilizes an egg, an incredible thing happens. In that single cell is a complete blueprint telling the cell how to make an individual as complex as you and I. The information in the newly fertilized egg is the equivalent of 1000 volumes of the complete works of Shakespeare."

In demand as a speaker, he's been paid up to $3000 for a one-hour lecture, gets about six requests a week to speak and estimates he could easily earn $5000 a month from such activities. He is a member of the Science Council of Canada and an Officer of the Order of Canada. Last year, the Canada Council awarded him the equivalent of half his $34,000 salary at the University of British Columbia, plus traveling and research expenses, to promote better public understanding of science.

The scientific community's reaction to Suzuki turning the spotlight on science has been "schizophrenic", says Dr. Louis Siminovitch, chairman of the Department of Medical Genetics at the University of Toronto. "David Suzuki is doing something no other Canadian scientist does," says Siminovitch

"He is regularly bringing to mass audiences aspects of science and technology they need to be aware of and should be questioning — and he's doing it in a way that they can understand."

But, Siminovitch adds, scientists are suspicious of a colleague who gets into the media. "I'm dismissed," Suzuki has said, "as a man who's on his own power trip."

Still, he's after more than personal aggrandizement. He sets himself high standards. As a lively and controversial figure, he appeared a number of times on the late-night talk show, "90 Minutes Live", but became increasingly uncomfortable about what host Peter Gzowski wanted from him. "One night as we were talking about science, I saw on Gzowski's note pad, in great big letters, *Emphasize the scary stuff.* I didn't go back after that."

"Science Magazine" uses what TV calls a "magazine format" — two to four unrelated items in each half-hour program. Suzuki introduces each subject, shows film clips and interviews the experts, more like a journalist than a scientist. Says executive producer Jim Murray: "He isn't afraid to ask simple questions."

His show deals with everything from "black holes" in space (regions of intense gravity left after star collapse) to glass blowers in the laboratory (to show the importance of people who back up scientists). This year's programs included stories on a cure for stuttering; an improved bullock-drawn cart in India; the raising of an ancient Viking ship; a treatment for the disease of the central nervous system called Huntington's chorea; a study of hummingbirds . . . and shots of tsetse fly reproduction, showing the female giving birth.

Such subjects are presented with abundant showmanship, but an absence of show-biz hype. And the viewers love him for it. Last year the CBC sent out 20,000 copies of a brochure and reading list on the program's subject matter, and Suzuki sent handwritten answers to about 3500 viewers who wrote in.

"Almost all letters are addressed to David," says Murray. "People make a very strong identification with him. Their whole image of scientists has been changed because he's so direct and approachable."

David Takayoshi Suzuki is a third-generation Canadian, born in Vancouver in 1936. In 1942 when he was six, he and his family were sent to a detention camp where they spent four years for, as he put it, "having genes which were imported from Japan by my grandparents. Those four years shaped my whole personality and priorities, and fighting bigotry and racism became a preoccupation that has continued through my adult life."

His family settled in London, Ontario, after the war. He graduated from high school in 1954 and entered Amherst College in Massachusetts, where an introductory course in genetics convinced him this would be his lifework. From Amherst he moved to the University of Chicago and thence, with a doctorate, to the Oak Ridge National Laboratory in Tennessee, as a research associate in biology. He became the only non-black member of the local branch of the National Association for the Advancement of Colored People, sat in at whites-only restaurants and got deeply involved in the race problem. Eventually he found himself hating whites. "The moment you do that," he said later, "you're no better than the Ku Klux Klan." He decided to return to Canada.

He accepted a post with the University of Alberta in 1962 — and made his TV debut on an Edmonton show called "Your University Speaks". "I did eight programs for $50 each," he recalls, "with a blackboard and a projector. The show was on at eight on Sunday mornings, and it played to an audience of three — the producer, his wife and his mother. But I learned I could do it."

In 1963, Suzuki went to UBC as an assistant professor of zoology, and began to build his reputation as both brilliant lecturer and first-class researcher. The data he obtained had to do with the tiny flies that appear as if by magic when a plate of fruit is left on a table. Fruit flies have a particular attraction for the geneticist because, as Suzuki says, "they're small, they're cheap, they grow fast and they have lots of progeny." Science uses them to learn in detail how genes transmit hereditary qualities from one generation to the next. The advance for which Suzuki became most widely known was the adaptation to the fruit fly of a method formerly used with viruses and bacteria — introducing mutations in such a way that a given defect would appear or not, depending on temperature.

Suzuki and his co-workers bred fruit flies that would behave normally at 22 degrees but drop dead or become paralyzed as soon as the temperature was raised to 29 degrees. It was something no one had ever done with an organism as complex as a fruit fly, and it was a major advance because it permitted scientists to study how specific genes behave during a fly's life. It could lead them to learn, for example, how an organism gives itself the signal that starts and stops a limb growing. If they could learn how to switch such genes off and on, scientists could conceivably develop a method of inducing a new limb to grow where one had been amputated.

Suzuki's laboratory screened close to 1.8 million fruit flies and found a variety of mutants. Some were not tied to temperature changes. One fly was shocked into paralysis simply by someone banging the container in which it was kept. Another became easily exhausted. Still another staggered. With typical humor, Suzuki and his colleages named them Shudder, Wobbly and Stoned.

The importance of these findings was so great that Suzuki was showered with honors. His research grants were greatly increased, he was made a full professor, he represented Canada at international conferences and his research team grew to 20. But about the time his science was going best, Suzuki began to doubt the wisdom of it all. One day in 1968, surrounded by students in a UBC dormitory, he was asked: "Doesn't the potential of what you're doing worry you?"

Suzuki had long been concerned about attempts to use eugenics to "purify" races of people, ridding them of supposedly inferior qualities. Now his own science was beginning to show possibilities, through a process known as cloning, of asexually reproducing identical copies of a particular organism with specific desired qualities. He considered quitting science, but decided that to give up was no answer — scientists had a duty to tell others what they were doing, and its implications were. Thus began his career in broadcasting.

A low-budget television program in 1971-72 called "Suzuki on Science" appeared Sundays at 2 p.m. Three years later Jim Murray started "Science Magazine" with Suzuki as host. Says Murray: "He's one of the straightest, most direct and honest people I've met. I think his integrity really comes through."

What also comes through is his enthusiasm and commitment to science. He has increasingly become a sort of conscience of the Canadian science community.

Suzuki's quest for greater public understanding of science is something of a crusade this year as he travels across the country telling Canadians they need a national science association — so they can understand what tax-financed government science funds are being used for. Not only is it their money, he says, but the funds are often *misused*.

"Scientists," he says, "are just as human, fallible and full of self-interest, ambition and greed as any other group." Also, they have become increasingly specialized, communicate with fewer and fewer people and have grown enormously in numbers.

Until last spring, David Suzuki had not resolved what seemed the central question in his life: would he quit university life, stop being a practicing scientist and go full time into the media, or would he return to academe and settle down? An offer from the University of Toronto solved the problem: for one third of his time he teaches zoology; for another third he is free to talk, write and travel; and the other third is devoted to media work.

That's good news for his fans. Of David Suzuki's TV and

radio work, Dr. Louis Siminovitch has said: "Probably no other Canadian scientist has the combination of personal attributes and standing in the scientific community to do it as well as he can."

Twelve Foot Davis
Anonymous

High above the Peace near its junction with the Smoky stands the grave of Twelve Foot Davis. It is an apt resting place for that almost legendary figure of the Peace River country.

Henry Fuller Davis, who was born in Vermont about 1820, came to the Cariboo gold fields when he was twenty-nine years old. This adventurous young man who had previously gone to California in the gold rush had been lured further north by the thought of more gold. His nickname originated from a strip of land twelve feet wide that had inadvertently been left unclaimed by the people mining on either side of it. From this strip of land it has been said that Davis took gold worth twelve thousand dollars, and from that time on he was known as Twelve Foot Davis.

From the Cariboo gold field he moved on to Omineca diggings where he was amongst the first men to mine. However, Davis soon converted his newly acquired wealth into trade goods and had a chain of posts along the Peace from the canyon to Fort Vermilion. Before the railway reached Calgary in 1883 when Davis was able to bring in his goods from Edmonton, he brought them from Quesnel in British Columbia, overland and by canoe.

Davis became a well known figure in the district. His tombstone bears the inscription, "He was every man's friend and never locked his cabin door." His pumpkin pies were famous and Davis often practised the art he had learned as a pastry cook in Boston. The Indians called him "The Wolf" because of his endurance and strength, for on a portage he would carry two hundred pounds, which was twice as much as he would expect the members of his crew to carry.

Davis was illiterate and a story is told of how he once received a note from the Hudson's Bay Company, while his companions were absent from the post. Letters were fairly uncommon in the Peace River in those days, and Davis assumed that someone must be ill. Not daring to admit his ignorance to the messenger he sent over two bottles of whisky as a remedy, but it transpired that the note was a message with New Year Greetings and an invitation to supper!

As the years began to tell on him, he became more lined and began to stoop. For the last five years of his life he was totally blind, and his legs were affected too: he had to be carried from the post to the canoe. He was in this condition on his last visit to Edmonton, and on the way back he stopped at the Anglican mission on Buffalo Bay on Lesser Slave Lake and here he died on September 13, 1900. When asked by the Anglican sister at the mission if he was afraid of dying he answered, "No miss, why should I be afraid to die? I never killed nobody, I never stole from nobody, I never wilfully harmed nobody, and I always kept open house for all travellers all my life. No, miss, I ain't afraid to die." Thus he delivered what would have been an apt epitaph.

The $100,000 Dream
Jacques Hamilton

Around Stampede time in Calgary every year you can find a few sentimentally superstitious cowboys who'll claim they've seen a grey ghost prowling the grounds by dark of night.

It's not a frightening ghost, they'll assure you. Far from it. It's just Guy Weadick back to make sure his dream is still doing well.

The dream of the Calgary Stampede was born in 1908 when the young Wyoming cowboy pulled into Calgary as a performer with the 101 Ranch Show.

Guy Weadick took one look at the bustling frontier city and decided it would be the perfect place to stage the western show to end all western shows — the greatest rodeo and fair in the world.

Weadick managed to infect one of his fellow-performers — a young cowboy named Tom Mix — with the dream, but everyone else around seemed totally immune to Stampede fever.

Everywhere he turned, Weadick found his dream of a show offering unheard of prize money, a publicity campaign stretching to Mexico and brand-new facilities, rejected out of hand.

When he approached E. L. (Ernie) Richardson of the Calgary Exhibition, Richardson turned the mad young cowhand down with a flat "No thanks."

Harry McMullen, a former cowman who had taken over the job of general livestock agent for the CPR, was sympathetic to the idea, but he argued that Weadick was "premature" with his dream. Calgary just wasn't ready for the greatest outdoor show in the world.

Discouraged, Weadick left town. A few months later, his prospective partner Tom Mix abandoned the scheme and headed to Hollywood to become the greatest cowboy hero of silent films.

Weadick and his young wife turned to the vaudeville and rodeo circuits with a popular show of tricks and talk — "Wild West Stunts" or "Roping and Gab" or "Weadick and la Due" (Mrs. Weadick's stage name was Flores la Due) depending on where they were playing.

It was three years after his trip to Calgary, in 1911, and the Weadicks were playing the music halls in England when Guy received a letter from an almost-forgotten Harry McMullen.

The railroad agent's letter was a strong appeal to Weadick to bring his idea back to Calgary again. There was a land boom on and the city was bursting with money and enthusiasm for new ideas.

It was all the encouragement Weadick needed. In early 1912, he was back in Calgary again. On the way, he had stopped in Medicine Hat for a long talk with rancher Ad Day — who assured Weadick he had enough stock "to supply a hundred rodeos" and who hinted that Weadick should try to sell his idea to the "Big Four" of Alberta ranching: Pat Burns, A. E. Cross, George Lane and A. J. McLean.

Harry McMullen, whom Guy looked up as soon as he'd checked into Calgary's Alberta Hotel, shared Day's view that the Big Four were the logical backers of the show.

Weadick decided, however, to have one more try with the managers of the Calgary Exhibition. Again, however, he was turned down flat.

That interview over, Weadick was walking through the lobby of the Alberta when a man stepped forward to intercept him — Alec Fleming, foreman of George Lane's Bar-U Ranch. The message was simple and exciting. George Lane wanted to talk to him about this wild idea he had for the greatest outdoor show on earth.

When Weadick appeared for the interview, he found himself facing not just George Lane, but Pat Burns and A. E. Cross as well.

Weadick's enthusiasm was catching. Before he knew what had happened the three cattle kings were at the point where they were asking simply how much it was going to cost.

Guy, probably with an eye to dividing things by three, suggested $60,000. In a matter of minutes he was on his way to the bank with the trio, and listened amazed as they set up a credit of $100,000 for him. Archie McLean, the fourth of the Big Four, had simply been written in as a backer without his knowledge — a fact he accepted coolly when he heard about it.

What the Big Four realized, perhaps better than Weadick himself, was that they'd found the right man with the right idea at the right time.

Their judgment was sound. As it turned out Weadick did so well on advance ticket sales that he apparently never had to touch a cent of the $100,000 credit.

The name Weadick picked for the show was "Stampede"; chosen because it had never been used before, and because of its descriptive and publicity powers.

Weadick's only instruction from his backers was to make the show "the greatest thing of its kind in the world," and he set out to follow it.

The Stampede was scheduled for the week of September 2. At Weadick's instructions, Victoria Park was invaded by carpenters who constucted thousands of bleacher seats. Weadick, meanwhile, was busy recruiting riders and ropers from all over North America and building a publicity campaign to drag in visitors from thousands of miles away.

As Stampede time drew near, excitement in Calgary built to fever pitch. The city fathers suddenly realized that even if all the 40,000 people to fill the new seats in Victoria Park didn't show up, there were still going to be more visitors in town than could be handled.

With the show still more than two weeks away, *The Calgary Herald* reported:

> Mayor (John W.) Mitchell has sent all over the Dominion asking about tents in which to accommodate the Stampede crowd next month. He is now receiving wires and letters and expects to secure all he wants.
>
> It is proposed to make the tent city across the Elbow on the property which the Great Northern bought from Dr. Lindsay. It will be fitted up specially and those who secure accommodation there will be just as comfortable as they would be in hotels.

At the same time, *The Herald* noted an undesirable, if inevitable, result of the Weadick publicity campaign:

Warnings from an under-ground source which convey to the police inside information have been sounded. Reports from 2,000 miles away have reached Chief Cuddy regarding the advent of dangerous crooks who are coming for the Stampede. From all over Canada and the northern States talented pick-pockets and confidence men are planning a sortie.

The chief has been warned in time. When the Stampede opens half a dozen of the most astute sleuths in the employ of the Pinkerton Detective Bureau will be in Calgary to assist the local detectives in rounding up the bad men.

Not all press reports were so ominous. A few days later Harry McMullen, whom Weadick had recruited to help manage the Stampede, was quoted in *The Herald* as saying:

The pageant on opening day will be the biggest that was ever seen in Canada.

There are now in the city waiting for the competitions, cowboys and cowgirls from Texas, Colorado, Utah, Montana, Idaho, New Mexico, Washington and Oregon.

Then, on August 31, *The Herald* reported that:

One special train to the Calgary Stampede left Spokane today and a second will follow Sept. 2. The first started from Cheyenne and the second will be made up at Pendleton.

By Monday the heart of Calgary will be a blaze of brilliant colors, and when His Royal Highness, the Duke of Connaught, arrives the city will be in the vortex of the greatest celebration that has ever taken place in the West.

To open the Stampede, Weadick had hit upon the idea of a massive parade. And when that parade moved onto the streets of Calgary September 2, Weadick had immediately confirmation of the soundness of his dream.

In Calgary, a city with a population of 61,450, an estimated 75,000 people were packed along the parade route.

Mindful of his directive to create "the greatest thing of its kind in the world", Weadick had spent months of careful negotiation with every Indian tribe in Alberta. Those negotiations paid off in the parade as more than 2,000 painted and feathered Indians rode the streets of the city.

Moved almost to a literary frenzy, a *Herald* reporter wrote of:

> The wonder of the spectacle of 2,000 western Indians, smeared with paint and decked in the attire of ante-civilized years, who passed through the streets of Calgary yesterday morning.

> Authentic and seasoned opinions would have it that, never in all the world, since the red men became dominated instead of a dominant influence, has there been such a gathering of the picturesque aborigines who, a few short years ago, roamed these western foothills, unmolested by the white man.

> Verily, it was a spectacle that money could not present. Mayhap, never again will those who watched yesterday's procession have a similar opportunity afforded them.

When the parade was over, a crowd of more than 50,000 crushed into Victoria Park. Once he'd got them that far, Weadick could relax a little and leave the rest to the talent in the show. And what talent it was!

The first of the 2 special trains from the United States had brought in George Drumheller of the big Drumheller Ranch in Washington and 15 of his best riders — including 1910 world champion Bert Kelly.

Already on hand was virtually every top rider on the continent. There was Joe Gardner of Texas, Ed Echols of

Arizona, George Weir from New Mexico, Tex Macleod from San Antonio, Harry Webb from Wyoming, Art Acord of Portland, Otto Kline of Montana, Charlie Tipton from Denver, "Doc" Pardee and O. K. Lawrence from Oklahoma. There was also a large Mexican contingent headed by Señor Estevan Clemento.

Among the female competitors was the good Mrs. Weadick — registered under her professional name of Flores la Due — who was destined to win the trick and fancy roping crown.

In all, there were 150 competitors.

Ad Day, true to the promise he'd made to Guy Weadick in Medicine Hat months earlier, was on hand and determined to make the competitors work for their prize money. Ready to go into the chutes was the biggest herd of outlaws — from wild and rangy Texas long-horns to top bucking broncs — ever assembled in Canada. And to try the stuff of champions, Day had waiting the greatest bucking horse in the world; that jet-black terror called "Cyclone".

If Guy Weadick thought he had it made at the end of that first day, he learned differently the next morning when he woke up to meet the demon that has plagued so many Stampedes — bad weather.

Rain was falling in sheets, and so was attendance, as riders struggled in an infield that was a sea of mud. Wednesday, the third day of Stampede, was no better. Nor was Thursday when the Royal party arrived.

Also adding to Weadick's worries was the fact that Calgary's hotel and dining facilities just weren't up to the crowd.

Like many others, Weadick had seen the article in Tuesday's *Herald* noting:

It is estimated that up to 20,000 visitors are already in Calgary. Yesterday was the busiest day that restaurants and hotels have ever had.

From 6 until 9 o'clock last night it was impossible

to get into a restaurant and at 9 o'clock many of the waiting hundreds were saddened when the proprietors opened their doors and announced that every digestible had been consumed.

Nevertheless, the show went on.

Thursday, when the Duke of Connaught and Princess Patricia arrived, the Royal party had hardly settled in its box before the rain poured down again.

Weadick quickly decided to move the show into the Victoria Park arena, and soon thousands of people were inside, scrambling for seats.

Watching the show, the Duke was so delighted he decided to make an unscheduled return to the grounds the next day.

The decision seemed to mark a turning point for the show. By Friday morning, the rain had stopped and the crowd was swelling again.

By the time the Stampede ended, Weadick could justifiably claim it had been a success.

Thanks to bad weather and inadequate facilities, however, it wasn't an unqualified success.

In 1913, even though the show had made money, Calgary was unreceptive and Weadick had to take his Stampede to Winnipeg.

Then the war years came and put an end to any such shows in Canada. Weadick made one try to stage the Stampede in the United States in 1916, but it was a financial flop.

It wasn't until 1919, again with the backing of the Big Four, that Weadick and the Stampede returned to Calgary. That year the weather co-operated and the so-called "Victory" Stampede was an enormous success. Finally, in 1923, the Calgary Exhibition had a long-awaited change of heart about Weadick's show, and the amalgamation that followed made the Stampede a permanent part of the Calgary scene.

Weadick was the Stampede's master-mind until he retired as arena director in 1932.

The $100,000 Dream   177

In 1952, he was on hand to present the prizes to the victors in the 40th Calgary Stampede.

Then, the following year, Guy Weadick's career came to an end as a riderless horse, boots reversed in stirrups, led his body to a cemetery.

At least, it seemed to end. It remains a little hard to account for the grey ghost that wanders the Stampede grounds, smiling contentedly at a dream that came true. . . .

Frank Mewburn, Surgeon
Jacques Hamilton

Of all the great medical men who came to frontier Alberta, one is consistently singled out as "the Alberta doctor".

It's not that Dr. Frank Hamilton Mewburn was the best surgeon in the world, or that he headed off some grave epidemic.

It's just that, in this frail little doctor, strength, compassion and humor were blended in exactly the right proportions to let him face harsh and primitive conditions, and triumph.

The Lethbridge that Dr. Mewburn found in 1885 was about as primitive, in the medical sense, as he'd ever seen.

All medical care was being provided by the town druggist, who would examine patients, carefully write out a list of the symptoms, then mail the list to the NWMP doctor in Fort Macleod for a diagnosis!

Fortunately, as nearly as we can make out from history, all the patients were hardy enough to survive the wait.

Needless to say, everyone — particularly the druggist — was delighted to have Dr. Mewburn in town. The delight persisted even though the new doctor somehow managed to lose the first patient he treated.

The patient, a Swedish miner, had complained vaguely of some internal disorder which Dr. Mewburn couldn't pin down. The next morning, the miner was found dead in his bunk.

The man's superintendent tried to soothe Mewburn by pointing out that: "Well, doctor, we all must die sometime or another, and some pass away no matter how we may try to prevent it.

"It cannot, therefore, be avoided, so there is no use worrying over it."

To which Dr. Mewburn responded with an explosive "Doesn't that beat hell!"

The new doctor, people gathered, had a philosophical streak in him.

One of the biggest tests the pioneer doctor faced was the treatment of Indian patients. It wasn't just a problem of overcoming their primitive fears; it was also a problem of persuading them to part with a fee.

Dr. Mewburn met both problems almost right away, and solved both — with a little help — just as quickly.

The first Indian patient he treated was a man from the Blood reserve who arrived at his surgery surrounded by a flock of worried relatives.

Mewburn quickly diagnosed the man's condition as a severe goitre, and he knew he'd have to operate. He turned to face the Indian's relatives and delivered a solemn speech:

> I shall have to make a big cut. If you all do as I tell
> you after the big cut is made, this man may get well,
> but I cannot tell for sure until I have made the big cut,
> and then if he does not get well, and if he should die,
> you must not blame me.
>
> What do you say? Shall I make the big cut?

His audience — including the man who would have to undergo the "big cut" — all grunted eager agreement.

The operation was a success and the man recovered completely. From that point on, Mewburn had the total trust of the Indians and the Bloods, and every other tribe in the Blackfoot confederacy made a point of bringing all their seriously ill people to him for treatment.

Frank Mewburn   179

The second problem — that of collecting fees — was solved with the kind assistance of the Indian agents.

One day, an aged Indian woman appeared in Mewburn's office with a little girl — and a note which she handed to the doctor.

The note read: "Dear Dr. Mewburn; This old woman has a little girl with her who has a large lump on her neck, which she would like you to remove. Also, the old lady has in her pocket a lump of twenty-five dollars which she would like to have removed at the same time." The note was signed by an Indian agent.

Both operations were performed successfully.

Dr. Mewburn would treat any kind of ailment, but his real love was surgery. And it was in the operating theatre that he created his reputation as one of the west's most volatile characters.

Indeed, the only time he was ever known to take an operating-room incident calmly was a day when all the lights went out during an operation. As the nurses and assistants winced and braced themselves for the inevitable outburst, all they got was the gentle protest that "I can't do the subject justice."

That occasion, however, was the exception. Once, for example, Mrs. Mewburn tried to telephone him while he was in the operating room.

Mewburn stormed out, had a nurse hold up the receiver so he wouldn't have to touch it with his sterilized gloves, and yelled: "Is that you, Louise? Go to blazes!" He then returned to finish the operation.

Probably the most famous illustration of Mewburn temper is the one recorded by John Higinbotham in his book. *When the West Was Young:*

During a "Mission" at which a number of the Roman Catholic clergy, bishops and priests, from various parts of Alberta gathered at Macleod, one of the visiting fathers, who was over eighty years of age, was suddenly stricken with a strangulated hernia.

Dr. G. A. Kennedy was called in, but feared to operate owing to the patient's advanced age. He telephoned to Lethbridge for Dr. Mewburn and the latter immediately responded by Mounted Police conveyance.

He decided to operate at once by local anaesthetic and arranged that one of the bishops (Legal, I think it was) should read to the patient and thus divert his mind during the operation.

In the midst of the clinic a fly entered the room and buzzed so close to the operating table that it got on Dr. Mewburn's nerves. His lips began to move convulsively yet he continued with difficulty to work without exploding.

Finally, as the objectionable intruder persisted in annoying him, he looked at Dr. Kennedy, who shook his head as a warning to the "Chief" to contain himself, and said, "Kennedy, kill that fly or put the bishop out, I don't give a damn which, as I can't hold myself any longer."

I never learned whether the fly was swatted or the bishop made his exit.

Mewburn was a tireless worker. At no time in his life was he ever known to refuse an appeal for help, no matter what the weather or time of day. Nor was he ever known to make any distinction between rich and poor. He treated both alike, and never pressed a man for payment. When the Galt Hospital was opened in Lethbridge, Dr. Mewburn became its first superintendent.

And, for all his legendary temper, Mewburn was basically a gentle man. When, in 1929, he was in a hospital bed dying

of pneumonia, one of the last things he said to his nurse was:
"I hope my going won't give you too much trouble. . . ."

As we said at the beginning, it's not that Dr. Frank Hamilton Mewburn was the best surgeon in the world, or that he headed off some grave epidemic.

It's just that, well, he was "the Alberta doctor".

Emergency Operation!
John Braddock

April 22, 1977: 4 a.m. A car increases speed on a Vancouver street, misses a slight turn and hurtles into a concrete wall. The impact smashes the front end of the car, and lifts the rear 5 feet into the air. Within the tangled wreckage, screaming in pain for someone to pull him out, is B.C. Lions halfback Barry Houlihan, 23.

4:45 a.m. Dr. Mike Dettman is on duty at the Vancouver General Hospital. The ambulance has radioed ahead: "Multiple trauma on the way. Serious motor vehicle accident." One of the five beds in the emergency room's resuscitation unit is ready when Barry is rushed in.

Nurses ask routine but important questions of the ambulance crew. What happened? How was he found? State of the vehicle? Was he belted in? Approximate amount of blood lost at the scene? Limbs deranged at the scene? Movement of arms and legs since?

Dr. Dettman orders an intravenous (IV) and a saline solution of sodium chloride. The fluid is a "volume expander", essential in keeping the circulatory system operating. Then Dettman and a resident work on clearing Barry's airway. He has a broken jaw. Since the tongue is connected to the jaw, there's a danger that it will fall backward and he'll choke to death. So tubes are inserted to keep the airways clear.

Next, Dettman checks vital signs — pulse, blood pressure, breathing — and inserts a large-bore intravenous tube to allow a rapid transfusion of blood. A portable X-ray machine confirms no breaks in the skull, neck or backbone. Here's one piece of luck at least.

Meanwhile, Barry is semi-conscious, shouting and screaming with pain. Doctors cannot give him an anesthetic yet. "At this stage our most valuable monitor is the patient's consciousness," explains Dr. Ken Kristjanson, chief of emergency room physicians.

4:55 a.m. By now Dettman has a pretty good idea of the extent of the injuries. They make a formidable list: excessive blood loss; weak pulse; severe shock; fractured jaw; something ruptured in the abdomen; deep laceration of left hand showing tendons; fractured pelvis; compound fractures of left thigh, left kneecap and right ankle. Large tear in perineum (floor of pelvis); dislocated right hip; compound fracture of the right elbow.

The internal ruptures are worrying. An immediate operation is necessary.

6:45 a.m. The operations — several of them — start. A team of 15 or so skilled staff is in attendance; each specialist has 1 or 2 residents assisting him.

The abdominal surgeons start their exploratory incisions, although there's a fair guess that the most life-threatening situation is the ruptured bladder.

Dr. A. D. Forward (general surgery) and Dr. Don MacDonald (urology) are exploring the open abdominal cavity. "There was a slight crack in the liver," says Dr. MacDonald. "We knew beforehand that there was also a rupture in the bladder but when we opened him up, the tear was much larger than expected." Dr. Forward places a packing against the torn liver, and Dr. MacDonald inserts a small tube, a catheter, into the urinary tract and begins to sew up the bladder. A few feet away, Dr. Robert Meek and his orthopedic surgical residents pull out and reposition Houlihan's dislocated hipbones.

The bone surgeons now investigate the legs. The force of

the impact on Barry's knee has shattered the strong thighbone, the femur, and pieces of bone have come through the skin. His left ankle caught on something and the joint is exposed.

Dr. Meek cleans out the original wound in the thigh and leaves it to drain. He makes another incision the length of the thigh and exposes the shattered, dislodged femur. He removes some pieces of bone from the pelvis and grafts them onto the femur. Then he tidies up the ends and clamps them together with a metal plate.

9 a.m. The abdominal team is now closing up. The orthopedic surgeons finish on the legs and begin work on Barry's right elbow. They are joined by plastic surgeon Dr. A. D. Courtemanche who comes to repair the partly severed thumb, exposed tendons of the left hand and fractured jaw.

Dr. Courtemanche takes a fragment of bone from Barry's pelvis, and with chisels and a small power tool similar to a dentist's, he shapes it into the form of the distal phalanx — the top bone of the thumb. The joint is lost so he grafts new bone onto the middle section. The thumb will be rigid, but it can move from the bottom joint. Then he moves to fix the broken jaw. This means opening up the jaw to wire the broken ends together, then also wiring the bottom teeth tight to the upper ones to insure the jaw sets in the right position.

3 p.m. Suddenly Dr. Meek swears. The intravenous tube inserted in the collarbone vein has become dislodged. It's tricky to insert. There is a danger that if the catheter misses its target it will penetrate the lung area, sending fluid around the lung. An X-ray is taken just in case, and the film shows a slightly larger than normal cavity between the lungs, which contains the heart, great blood vessels, esophagus and windpipe.

At this moment the enlargement is enough to cause comment but not alarm. The immediate task is to finish the operations.

4 p.m. Time now for a double check on that enlarged cavity. Another X-ray. The gap has widened. Diagnosis: ruptured aorta.

Barry, still anesthetized, knows nothing of the catheter pushed up his arteries almost the length of his body into the aorta. A dye is injected and clearly picked up on the X-ray. Thanks to the slipped IV-tube, the ruptured aorta has been discovered early.

6 p.m. So after twelve hours on the operating table, Barry Houlihan faces the most serious operation of all — open heart surgery. The first part of the operation is to make a curving incision between two of Barry's ribs, about three-quarters of the way down the chest wall. Next, the muscles are sliced and the rib bones separated. The job is much tougher than usual because Barry's chest muscles are three times the size of the average person's.

The surgeon, Dr. Larry Burr, tries to see where the aorta has ruptured. It's not easy. The artery is a mass of swollen blood-soaked tissue. The doctors have to be cautious because blood obscures nerves that go up to the throat in this area, and down to the stomach. "It's like trying to find a thread in a raw steak," says Dr. Burr.

10:45 p.m. The idea now is to bypass the break in the aorta by shunting blood from the heart through an artificial pump and back into the body. Dr. Burr deftly opens the sack around the heart and puts a drainage catheter into the left atrium. He then connects that to the oxygenator of the heart-lung machine and returns the blood through a line into the aorta below the break. Then he cuts out the damaged piece of aorta and inserts a short section of dacron graft, sewing it at both ends.

April 23: 12:03 a.m. The insertion is now complete, and the clamps are released. Barry can come out of the heart-lung machine. Burr and his assistants carefully check that the graft is holding and all bleeding has stopped. Then they start closing up the chest. The dacron tube will stay in place permanently. In about four to six weeks, the body will form a new lining of tissue both inside and outside the tube.

2:15 a.m. At last, Barry's marathon series of operations end. He's moved to the intensive-care unit.

April 24. Barry is given morphine to reduce pain. He is strung about with intravenous and nasal tubes to help his breathing. However, the nasal tube is inadequate for full venting of his lungs, so Dr. Burr performs a tracheotomy and inserts a specially shaped tube connected to the ventilator to help his breathing.

But now a more serious situation has developed. Barry's kidneys have "shut down". It's been expected, a predictable delayed reaction from the great loss of blood at the time of the accident two days ago. So, tubes are inserted into an artery and vein at the bottom of his right leg, and the blood is circulated through an artificial kidney machine. He will be hooked up to the machine six hours a day, every second day, for six weeks.

April 30. Barry shows distinct signs that he will make it. The basic job of the doctors and nurses now is to keep his spirits up and to maintain normal chemical balance in his body.

May 21. Barry's birthday. He's 24. Family and friends come to visit in such numbers that it is difficult for the hospital staff to regulate them.

May 25. Barry is taken off the artificial kidney machine. Up to now he's been kept alive on liquids. He's lost 40 pounds. "For three weeks I've been dreaming," Barry says. "All this is a miracle. I should have been dead."

June 25. Barry Houlihan, one of the most smashed up car accident victims that the hospital staff had ever seen, goes home. He'll need some time to get in shape for just a quiet walk, but he vows that "I'm going to be running by next January. By June I'll be back on the football field."

Alberta Pearl
Cliff Faulknor

Alberta Pearl was her name and bronco busting was her game, but she didn't know it was her game yet. All the slim, fourteen-year-old in the faded middy blouse, short skirt, and outsize sheepskin chaps could see was the six-dollar prize which awaited her if she could stay on the hurricane deck of the bronc for eight seconds. And six dollars was a mighty big sum to the Cardston youngster in 1921.

As she took up her position above the chute, the crowd gasped and leaned for a closer look. A young girl as a bronco buster? What was the world coming to? Pearl's teacher, who never missed a rodeo or ended a sentence with a preposition, wondered to what was the world coming. Even Old Chief Mountain, peering grandly down on the scene through a fleece of summer clouds must have stood aghast at this brash intrusion into the male domain.

But Pearl was more worried about the floppy hat anchored tightly under her determined chin by a broad ribbon, than about the surcingle-rigged outlaw that snorted and fidgeted below her. Another concern was the crowd itself from whom she kept her face averted, until she had to concentrate all her attention on the bronc.

Outwardly calm, she waited for just the right moment to slip down onto the squirming back. This would be her first ride in a rodeo contest, but not her first time on the back of a bucking horse — not by a long shot. She had been riding buckers since she was twelve years old.

The right moment came and she slipped easily down. The bronc gave a heave as it felt her weight then became strangely quiet as if saving its strength for the contest to come. Suddenly she heard the announcer's voice, bellowing her chute number, her name, and the name of her horse. She didn't even notice that his announcement ended with a chuckle.

Pearl felt the bronc's muscles starting to bunch under her as she cried "Turn him loose!" to the chute gateman. On protesting hinges, the gate swung open and with one jump the bronc was out into the arena. He squealed and jumped again, and daylight showed under the woolly chaps as Pearl rose briefly skyward. But she was still on when those hooves returned to Mother Earth.

The crowd roared its appreciation.

Then the bronc headed off across the infield like an arthritic jackrabbit, squealing and grunting its anger at every hop. Every time those hooves hit the dirt, Pearl felt the contact all the way to her teeth, but she increased the pressure of her legs against the sweaty flanks and stayed with him.

The horse sunfished a couple of times and the roar of the crowd deepened. Pearl wasn't sure whether they were cheering for her or the bronc.

She had become attuned to the outlaw's plunges now and could feel that six-dollar prize almost within her grasp. Then all at once it changed tactics and began to whirl around and around in a tight circle. Pearl felt herself getting a little dizzy, but she hung in there grimly. She had come too far to give in now.

Suddenly the horn blared and she knew she had made it. She heard the thunder of hooves and pick-up man Dud Leavitt rode up beside the plunging bronc and reached out a helping hand. As Pearl swung up behind him, another rider chased the bronc off to a corral gate at the end of the field.

"Hey, where are you going?" Pearl cried in alarm as Leavitt headed towards the grandstand instead of back to the chutes.

"I'm going to show you off to the crowd," he grinned. "Not often they get a chance to see a girl bronc rider!"

"In a pig's eye!" snorted Pearl, attempting to slip off the saddle horse and gain the safety of the ground.

Every time Leavitt swung his horse around so the crowd could get a look at her face, Pearl would turn her face the other way.

"She sure is a bashful one," she heard somebody shout from the grandstand.

Finally, Leavitt rode back to the chutes in disgust. Pearl slid gratefully to the ground and ran behind the chutes to change.

"I just couldn't get those clothes off fast enough," Herman Linder laughed as he recalled his first rodeo performance. "That was the first and last time I ever dressed up as a girl. It was a stunt, you see. The people running the Cardston Rodeo figured the crowd wouldn't recognize me dressed as a girl and they knew I could handle myself on a bucking horse."

Many years later when Herman had become an established rider, rodeo buffs would come up to him and ask if he recalled a famous girl bronc rider named "Alberta Pearl" and how well she could ride, little realizing they were talking to "Pearl" in the flesh.

"Sure, she could ride well," chuckled Warner Linder, Herman's older brother. "When we were kids, Herman and I lived to ride. We started riding yearling steers when we were ten to eleven years old. By the time we were twelve, we were trying our hand at bucking horses."

"That's a long time ago," Herman nodded, "over fifty years, in fact. I suppose that first bronc had a name, but I don't remember what it was.

"In those days, they didn't have strings of horses that went around the rodeo circuit like they do today," he explained. "They'd bring in these horses — wild horses, I guess you'd call them — right off the range, although, at that time, they did have local horses with a great reputation without being what you'd call top bucking horses. If they had names they were probably made-up names for each particular rodeo."

Later on, when he had become a big name on the North American circuit, Herman was to meet and conquer bucking horses that had become famous in their own rights with colorful names such as: Broomtail, Liberty Blond, Blondie, Black Cat, Miss Meeks, Old Man of the Mountain, Too Bad, and Easy Money. And, to this day, he swears they made so little impression on him he cannot remember one from the other.

There are always exceptions, of course, and two come readily to mind. For instance, old Pardner almost nipped Herman's career in the bud by bucking him off so easily and often he began to despair of ever being a bronc rider. Then there was Rimrock, who threw rodeo promoter Linder for a financial loss and bucked him all the way to B.C.'s Supreme Court. A man isn't likely to forget a pair of horses like that.

Two years after "Alberta Pearl's" first encounter with rodeo, Herman entered a professional rodeo contest in his own right and won it. For ten years the 145-pound champion strode across the rodeo scene like a giant with seven-league boots. He travelled to Australia to display his skills at the Royal Agricultural Fair at a huge arena in Sydney, winning silver cups both times for the individual top score in saddle bronc riding. He went to England and won right up until the penultimate day when he stepped off a non-bucker and turned his ankle which put him out of the finals.

Despite the protests of promoters and fellow riders alike, Herman decided to hang up his competition saddle in 1938. He was thirty-one years old, and in his opinion, he had been sitting the hurricane deck long enough. He made his last ride in Madison Square Garden that year to the roar of thousands of fans and came off with top money. They liked him so well they asked him back the next year to judge the big event. His final competition ride came that same year.

Herman Linder wasn't just a bronco rider. In addition to saddle bronc and bareback titles, he won honors in bull riding, wild steer riding, and calf roping. Although he never won what is officially known as a World Title, he was Canadian All-Around Champion seven times and North American All-Around Champion five times and the latter event was open to anyone in the world.

He first sprang into prominence at the Calgary Stampede in 1929 when he took the Canadian championship away from all-time great Pete Knight. In nine years of competition at Calgary, Herman won an incredible total of twenty-two championships. Little wonder that headlines in Canadian newspapers of those days ran stories that proclaimed him "The Cowboy Supreme" and "King of the Cowboys".

Said *The Calgary Herald,* Saturday, July 14, 1934: "Turning in one of the greatest individual performances in the history of the Calgary Stampede, Herman Linder, youthful cowboy from Cardston, Alberta, won the Canadian Bronc Riding Championship with Saddle, the Bareback Bucking Horse Riding Championship, the Wild Steer Riding Championship, in addition to placing himself second in the North American Bronc Riding Championship with Saddle in the finals Saturday afternoon. . . . Linder was declared Best All-Around Cowboy for the fourth Consecutive year."

When the big rodeo show at Sidney, Iowa, celebrated its Fiftieth Anniversary in 1973, the American Legion post which sponsored it put out a book describing how the show got started and naming the big-time rodeo stars who had competed there over the years. In the history of their event, said the book, two cowboys had dominated the competitions: before World War II, it was Herman Linder of Cardston, Alberta, and afterwards it was Jim Shoulders of Henrietta, Oklahoma.

As Herman's fame grew, so did the headlines. Screamed a big heading in an American paper, "Linder Man of the Year At National Cowboy Hall of Fame!" Shouted another:

"Herman Linder Crowned Rodeo King!" And yet another: "Cardston Rodeo Hero Invited to World's Fair!"

Years later, after he had quit riding and become a rodeo promoter, Herman Linder made headlines in the big dailies of Vancouver, B.C. for the better part of a year, more often than not in two-inch type. These screamers were of a radically different flavor, but that is a story in itself.

Persuasions & Power

Bobby Clarke

Fred McFadden

An Important Victory

No one expected Philadelphia to win the Stanley Cup in 1974, but now they were in the finals against Boston. Since they had entered the National Hockey League as an expansion team in 1967, they had played the Bruins in Boston nineteen times — losing seventeen games and tying two.

In the first game of the finals, Bobby Orr led the Bruins to an easy victory over the Flyers. Most fans expected them to sweep the series.

Before the second game, the Flyer's captain Bobby Clarke quietly spoke to the players in the dressing room. He didn't usually speak to the players, but this game was special.

"Alright, guys, tonight we give it a little extra. If we're going to win, everybody has to work harder."

The players all knew that Bobby would work twice as hard as anyone else.

For this game he seemed to be more tireless than ever. He was the centre on the top line; he led the powerplay; he helped kill off Philadelphia penalties; he seemed to have the puck most of the time. He scored the first Philadelphia goal. With 50 seconds to go in the third period, and Boston leading 2-1, he assisted "Moose" Dupont on the tying goal.

In overtime, although dead tired, Clarke inspired the Flyers to forget their fatigue. After twelve minutes, he broke in and fired a backhander at the Boston goal. Gilles Gilbert flopped to the ice and blocked the shot. Bobby dashed in, picked up the rebound, and flipped the puck over the sprawling Gilbert to score the winner.

The Flyers went on to do the impossible. For the first time, an expansion team won the Stanley Cup. The sports writers had a difficult choice to select the outstanding player in the series for the Conn Smythe trophy — Bernie Parent or Bobby Clarke. They selected Bernie Parent for his excellent net-minding.

Bep Guidolin, the Boston coach, disagreed.

"They're nuts. Clarke's the guts of the Philadelphia team. He's the guy that chased us out of the rink."

For Bobby Clarke, it was a fantastic feeling. "They said we couldn't beat the old teams like Boston Bruins or New York Rangers or Montreal Canadiens. They said we didn't have the class to win the Stanley Cup. But we showed them. It was a great team victory, and the biggest thrill of my life."

Growing up in Flin Flon

Eight hundred kilometres north of Winnipeg is the small town of Flin Flon. It is an isolated community of about 12,000 people, built on the bare rock of the Canadian Shield. The Hudson Bay Mining and Smelting Company, which mines copper, zinc, gold and silver, is the only industry in town.

In 1913, pioneer and prospector Tom Creighton discovered gold near a lake in Northern Manitoba. The place reminded him of a story that he had once read, in which the hero, Josiah Flintabbatey Flonatin, explored a bottomless lake and discovered a city of gold. So Creighton named the site Flin

Flon after the hero of the story, and it has been called that ever since.

It was here, on August 13, 1949, that Bobby Clarke was born. His father had lived near Prince Albert, Saskatchewan, but had moved to Flin Flon to get a job in the mines in the 1930s. Bobby and his younger sister Roxanne grew up in this small northern town.

Mrs. Clarke says, "It was a good community for kids. There was little opportunity for them to get into trouble. They were kept busy all of the time with school and sports, but mainly sports."

Like most fathers, Cliff Clarke encouraged his children to play hockey. He built a small rink in the backyard. It was here that Bobby started to skate and play hockey at the age of four.

Flin Flon is so far north that the temperature is below freezing from October to April. Bobby and Roxanne and the older boys and girls could skate almost every day during this time. Sometimes the temperature dropped to -40 degrees, but they still played hockey and skated most of their spare time.

The outdoor ponds and rinks of Western Canada have produced many outstanding hockey stars — Max and Doug Bentley, Gordie Howe, Johnny Bucyk, Norm Ullman, Garry Unger and Bryan Trottier, to name only a few. In these communities, the hockey season lasts over six months; the outdoor rinks are free and always available; and there are not many other activities to take you away from hockey.

Bobby Clarke played hockey every day after school, and for hours every weekend. It was here that he developed the skating skills that helped to make him an NHL allstar.

But Bobby was not always a star. His parents remember that when he started skating, he was very awkward and went over on his ankles.

When Bobby was 8, he started playing on his first organized team. "When I started, I was just an average player. I used to score 2 or 3 goals a year. But our coaches told us to just play and have fun, and we sure did." His first coach remembers, "Bobby was a small, quiet, shy kid, without special ability. But he listened carefully, and he tried hard. He was a great young kid to coach."

Most young Canadian boys watch "Hockey Night in Canada" on TV every Saturday night. This is part of growing up. Many dream of being another Orr or Dryden or Howe or Hull. But when Bobby Clarke was growing up, Flin Flon was so far north that it was out of the range of TV signals. Bobby never saw television until he was about 11. Even then, the local station only got films of the previous week's hockey game.

"When I was a kid, I hardly knew about the NHL. I had heard of Rocket Richard and Gordie Howe and some of those stars, but I didn't think about playing for a professional team. Hockey was just fun. I think that's the way it should be for kids today. There's too much emphasis on winning, and getting ready for the pros. Kids should have more chance just to play the game. That's the way we did it in Flin Flon."

Bobby was active in most sports. He was a good catcher on the local baseball team. He liked to go swimming, and obtained several Red Cross badges. He also enjoyed cubs and scouts.

Unfortunately, Bobby began to lose interest in school when he got to high school. "A few times, I skipped class to play hockey. Sometimes, if I was sent home from school for misbehaving, I went to play hockey instead. My parents were not very happy with that, as they wanted me to do well in school. But school was never very interesting to me."

Mrs. Clarke says, "Bobby liked to play hockey more than anything else. He was happy playing hockey any time or any place. I don't think that he could have survived without it."

Minor Hockey
"Bobby, You'd Better Give Up Hockey"

When Bobby was fifteen, he began to feel unusually tired. His mother warned him, "Bobby, you need more rest. Why don't you stay inside, instead of playing hockey all the time?"

"But the other guys aren't tired, Mom. I'll be O.K."

But Bobby was thirsty most of the time, and he began to have double vision. When he started to lose weight, his parents knew that something was wrong. They took him to the doctor, who examined him carefully. The doctor told Bobby that he had diabetes.

The doctor sat down with Bobby and his parents. "Bobby, this means that you won't have the energy to play sports like other boys your age. You'd better give up hockey. Or if you want to play, why don't you become a goalie?"

Bobby was very upset. He wanted to do things like other kids his age, and they all enjoyed the skating and fast action of hockey. He asked the doctor, "Couldn't I try to play hockey? I'll take care of myself — and I know that I can do it."

"Well, you can play, but you must take special care of your diet. You will have to take an insulin injection every day for the rest of your life, and get lots of sleep. If you do that, we'll give it a try."

Bobby was relieved. He knew that he would take care of himself. Even if it meant that he had to work harder than others, he was determined to do his best.

The Desire To Win

Bobby had developed into a good hockey player even before he had diabetes. But the disease created a new situation.

"I was determined that if I was going to be as good a hockey player as the others, I would never use my diabetes as a crutch." About the time he was sixteen, his coaches and other players recognized Bobby's fiery desire to play and to win. He did not fool around in practices.

"Smarten up, you guys," Bobby yelled at some teammates. "You don't win games by horsing around in practice." His coach noticed when Bobby spoke, the others responded. He gradually became the natural leader of his team. He also developed into the best player in Flin Flon.

Flin Flon Junior Bombers

The Flin Flon hockey games were the most important events in town. Most of the players worked in the mine for four hours and practised two hours every day. Road trips went to cities like Winnipeg, Saskatoon and Regina, sometimes over 1500 km away, and often lasted two or three weeks at a time. The nearest game involved a ten-hour bus ride to Winnipeg. The local high school discouraged junior hockey players from staying in school, since most found it difficult to keep up their school work. Bobby's parents tried to encourage him to stay in school, but he decided to quit.

"I sometimes wish that I had stayed in school. It would have helped me when I finish playing hockey," says Bobby. "Young players today have a better chance to go to school while playing hockey."

For Bobby, his future was a choice between being a hockey player, or working in the mines in Flin Flon for the rest of his life. Bobby was determined to do his best in junior hockey, and hope for a professional career.

The Road to the NHL

When Bobby started playing junior hockey in 1966, he was quite small. But as always he hustled and worked hard. His coach Pat Ginnell recalls, "Bobby was a quiet, thin young kid, who wore glasses. He was not spectacular, and he didn't look like a future star. But he was a hard skater, and worked like a demon. I knew that he was going to be one of the best kids I ever coached."

Bobby played for the Flin Flon Bombers for three years. He was the scoring leader for his team each year. In his second season, he scored 51 goals and had 117 assists, to lead the Western Junior League in scoring. He teamed with his winger, Reggie Leach, to be the best scoring pair in the league. The next year he scored 51 goals and 86 assists and was again the scoring champion. He worked so hard that other players were bound to follow him, and so he was made team captain. In 1969 he won the award as the best junior hockey player in Western Canada. The people of Flin Flon thought so much of him that his number 11 sweater was retired, never to be used by another player.

His coach knew that Bobby could be a star in the pro leagues. But hockey scouts always raised the question, "What about his diabetes? Could he handle the long schedules and rough play of the NHL?"

The Flin Flon team arranged for Bobby to go to the Mayo Clinic in Rochester, Minnesota, to have a complete medical check-up. The doctors reported that Bobby's diabetes should not hinder his ability to play hockey if he continued to take good care of himself.

The NHL Draft, 1969

Each June, the NHL teams draft some of the bright young amateur hockey players. The best players are usually picked first. In 1969 many thought that Bobby would be an early selection. But the coaches were still afraid to gamble on Bobby's diabetes.

Gerry Meinyk, the scout for the Philadelphia Flyers in Western Canada, had carefully read the report from the Mayo Clinic. He knew how good a hockey player Bobby was, and he knew how disciplined Bobby was about his diet and rest. He insisted that Bobby have a chance to prove himself.

However, in the first round Philadelphia drafted Bob Currier. Other teams drafted such players as Ernie Moser and Frank Spring, and others who failed to really make it in the NHL. Jim Skinner, the chief scout for Detroit, had lived in Flin Flon and knew Bobby was talented. But Detroit was looking for a goalie and skipped Clarke. In the second round when Bobby was still available, Philadelphia picked him — the seventeenth player picked.

The Training Camp Scare

In September 1969, Bobby arrived at the Philadelphia training camp in Quebec City.

"I was very nervous. I didn't know how I would do against the pros. I had only seen two NHL games in my life. I only knew one player on the team, Lew Morrison, who had played in Flin Flon. I was just a young kid, lost in the big city."

Bobby had to take an injection of insulin every morning, and eat regular meals. One morning, in a rush to get to practice on time, Bobby skipped his breakfast. At the workout, he almost passed out. Some people feared that this proved that Bobby was not strong enough to stand up to the strain of playing in the NHL.

But this warning made Bobby realize that he would simply have to follow the doctor's instructions exactly — regular meals, lots of rest and his injection of insulin every day. Since then, Bobby has never had another insulin scare. He eats regular foods and watches his diet carefully. He takes a soft drink with a cube of sugar before each game, and some orange juice between periods.

He is about 175 cm in height and weighs about 80 kg, which is not big compared to other players in the NHL. He plays a robust, checking style of play, which means that he has to be in excellent shape. He works out in the gym regularly during the season and in the summer. He is in excellent health, and has never missed an NHL game because of illness.

The Rookie Becomes Team Leader

When Bobby moved to Philadelphia, it was the first time he had ever lived in a big city.

"I was scared stiff in Philadelphia. Flin Flon has only a couple of main streets, and I knew everybody. But Philadelphia is a huge city, with so many people, and all in a hurry to go somewhere. Even though I had driven cars and trucks in Flin Flon, I was afraid to drive in Philadelphia traffic. But after a couple of months I got used to it."

Bobby was nervous playing his first game, which was against Minnesota. The first time he got the puck, he was checked by Bill Goldsworthy, who went in and scored.

"That was a great start," said a disgusted Bobby. But he soon settled down, and has been one of the leaders of the Flyers ever since.

In his first season, he scored 15 goals and had 31 assists. He finished second to Tony Esposito for the Calder trophy as the Rookie of the Year. The next season he had 63 points, and in 1971-1972 he had 35 goals and 46 assists for 81 points. Since then he has always been among the leading scorers.

In 1973, at the age 23, he was selected to be the captain of the Flyers, the youngest captain in the history of the NHL. He was not picked just for his ability to score goals. Bobby is the team leader on and off the ice. In practices, he listens carefully to coaches Fred Shero and Mike Nykoluk. When he skates, he digs hard all the time. He always gives one hundred per cent.

Vic Stasiuk was Bobby's first NHL coach. "Bobby just gives and gives and gives. He loves the challenge of playing. He is a great competitor, and he hates to lose."

All of Bobby's coaches have noted how Bobby's play fires up the other players.

"Clarke is the perfect captain," says Fred Shero. "I never had a team with so much courage and discipline and spirit. And most of it comes from Clarke."

Bobby is the team leader in many ways. In 1972-73, when teammates Simon Nolet and Bill Flett were in a scoring slump, Bobby asked to have them as his wingers. They practised together after the other players left the ice. With Clarke as his centre, Flett scored 43 goals. "Having Bobby as your centre is worth an extra 20 goals to any winger," Flett claims.

When players are having other problems, Bobby will take them aside to help them out. If the players have a complaint against the Philadelphia management, Bobby speaks for the team — and management listens.

Canada — Russia, 1972

In the summer of 1972, it was announced that at long last a Canadian professional hockey team would play against a Russian team. Coach Harry Sinden selected the best players in the league to make up a super all-star team. Bobby Clarke was one of the last players selected. Sinden picked six centres — Phil Esposito, Stan Mikita, Gil Perreault, Red Berenson, Jean Ratelle and Walter Tkaczuk. When Tkaczuk couldn't get away from his hockey school, Bobby Clarke was picked as his replacement.

"When I went to the Team Canada training camp, I didn't expect to play much. They had Esposito, Mikita and all those other stars. But I was thrilled to be even picked, so I decided to give it a try and hope for the best."

Bobby was placed at centre on a line between Paul Henderson and Ron Ellis of the Toronto Maple Leafs. Clarke was the persistent checker and playmaker, and Ron Ellis was a solid defensive player. Paul Henderson, a fast-skating winger, rose to great heights as one of the top scorers in the whole series. The trio was the most consistent Canadian line. Much of the success of the line was due to the leadership of Bobby Clarke.

Boris Kulagin, the Russian coach, recognized Bobby's abilities. "Not only is he an excellent skater and checker, but he is completely unselfish. He makes every move count for the team, not just for show. Bobby Clarke is the best all-round player on the Canadian team."

"I really enjoyed playing against the Russians," says Bobby. "There is something special about playing for your country. It's different than just playing for the money. I would like to play for Canada against Russia again. It's a fantastic experience and I would like to have another chance."

The Red Army Team

In January 1976 the touring Red Army team met the Flyers in Philadelphia. Fred Shero and the Philadelphia players had carefully studied films of the Russian team to see their style of play. They had practised how to forecheck the Russians in their own zone, to break up their careful patterned plays.

Before the game, Bobby Clarke got together with the Flyer forwards for one last chalk talk. "Guys, if we play our style and check their forwards we can take them."

Some other teams playing against the Russians had been anxious and tense before the game. Somehow, when Bobby spoke in his quiet manner, the players were reassured. When they went out on the ice, they were calm, and confident that if they followed their game plan, they would win.

As the players were individually introduced, the Flyers' fans cheered enthusiastically. Finally, the announcer called, "Number 16, Bobby Clarke," and a tremendous ovation greeted the hero of Philadelphia.

The Flyers played their usual robust, aggressive style of

play, and decisively defeated the Red Army 4 to 1. As usual, Bobby Clarke set the pace for this victory with his solid checking, accurate passing, tireless skating and plain hard work.

Pursuit of the Stanley Cup

Bobby has continued to improve each year in the NHL. In 1972-73, he scored 37 goals and had 67 assists. He was second in scoring to Phil Esposito, and was picked to the second all-star team. He was honoured that year by winning the Hart Memorial trophy as the "player judged to be the most valuable to his team."

But Bobby was still not satisfied. "Hockey is a team game. The goal is to win the Stanley Cup. Until we do that, I won't be satisfied."

Philadelphia gradually was recognized as the best of the expansion teams, and the one most likely to win the Stanley Cup. They played a bruising, aggressive style of play. Because of their willingness to start fights at any time, they were called the roughest team in hockey. Many hockey fans felt that their style of play was unnecessarily violent.

Bobby Clarke was not often involved in fights. However, he has been accused of hooking, and slashing and using his stick against other players, and has been called a dirty hockey player. In the 1972 Team Canada series, Valery Kharlamov was one of the stars of the Russian team. In a famous incident, Bobby slashed at Kharlamov's ankles, and injured him.

"I am not proud of what I did; I did it during the heat of the game," said Bobby. "But I'd do it again if I felt that I had to." It is this desire to win at any cost, even when it breaks the rules, that has led some people to question Bobby's sportsmanship.

Like many other players in the NHL, Bobby felt that he had to prove that he could not be pushed around in the NHL. This led him to get an unusual number of penalties (he is sarcastically called "Mr. Clean" by some other players). But like Stan Mikita and Gordie Howe who started off with a lot of penalties, he has become less chippy in the last few seasons.

Bobby does not consider himself a dirty player. "I'm not even an aggressive player. I'm just a little guy compared to most players in the league. If I were dirty, I wouldn't last. I get knocked around by other players, and you should see the bruises I get. I just like to win, and to do that, I have to work hard all the time."

Bobby has always inspired his teammates. Bernie Parent says, "Clarke is our leader. He works so hard himself, that the other guys just have to work to keep up. He is the guy who makes us go."

And in 1974, Bobby's hard work and determination paid off — Philadelphia won the Stanley Cup.

A Super Player

The Philadelphia team did not have many star players. They did have coach Fred Shero, who carefully studied hockey, and provided the team with an excellent system. They had exceptional goaltending from Bernie Parent, one of the best goalies in the world.

Most of all, they were led by Bobby Clarke. He centred their first line, he killed penalties and directed the power play, he scored goals and set up plays for his wingers.

Coach Mike Nykoluk sees Clarke play every game. "Bobby is the star in 90 per cent of the games he plays. He has never played a bad game for us. But one game stands out in my mind.

"We were playing in Montreal. It was a tough game, with both teams going all out. By the third period, the score was tied 5-5. Bobby had scored two of our goals, and he had dominated the play every time he was on the ice. We knew he was tired but with one minute to go, he went over the boards for the final shift.

"He grabbed the puck at the blue line, and swept in towards

the goal. Larry Robinson was draped all over him, and Lapointe was hooking at his stick. But somehow Bobby carried Robinson, veered towards the net, and flicked a backhander up over Dryden's shoulder. We won the game, and Bobby got the hat trick.

"I have never seen anyone play a better game in my life than Bobby did that night."

A Super Person

Bobby is a different person off the ice. In the game, he is all over the ice like an angry hornet. He is tireless in his skating, checking and digging in the corners. He plays a tough game.

Off the ice, he is quiet and very modest about his achievements. When it was suggested that he worked harder than other players, Bobby replied, "There are lots of guys on other teams who work as hard as me. It's just that I'm on a winning team, and it's easier to see the results of my efforts."

Bobby won the Lou Marsh trophy, as the outstanding athlete in Canada in 1975. When told that only three other hockey players had ever won that award — Maurice Richard, Phil Esposito and Bobby Orr — Clarke said, "I'm not in their class. But I'm thrilled and honoured to receive the award."

Bobby often visits sick kids in hospitals and is especially interested in helping out diabetic organizations. He is very sensitive to the needs of others who have problems or face handicaps.

In Philadelphia, a "Player of the Month" award is presented which includes a cash prize. More than once when Bobby has won this, he has turned over the money to other team members who have had emergencies in their families.

Warren Elliott, the assistant team trainer, received a cheque from Bobby to help pay for a heart operation needed by his wife.

"Bobby is just that kind of person," said Elliott. "He is interested in others, and completely unselfish. He's a great guy."

In the Off-Season

Bobby now lives in Philadelphia with his wife Sandra, son Wade and daughter Jodie. Sandra was his girlfriend in high school in Flin Flon. They now have a beautiful house in New Jersey.

After the long, gruelling hockey season, Bobby and his family usually take a vacation in the islands of the West Indies for a complete rest. They come back home to relax, golf and enjoy life in their backyard swimming pool.

Every summer, Bobby and the family return to Canada.

"We like to go back home to Flin Flon. My parents are still there. We really enjoyed growing up in a small town. I'll never forget the people that I grew up with."

In 1973, a special Bobby Clarke Day was held to honour Flin Flon's most famous son. A hockey game was played and many old-timers came back to Flin Flon for the occasion. At Bobby's request all of the profits from the game went to help local hockey.

The Future

Bobby is now a superstar in the NHL. With him as team leader it is likely that Philadelphia will continue to be a strong contender for the Stanley Cup.

Bobby is not sure what he will do when he finishes his hockey career. "I would like to stay in hockey some way. I like working with other players and helping them out. I think that I'd like to coach at some level, either in junior hockey or in the NHL."

Bobby is already moving in this direction. He analyzes the style and weaknesses of other teams, and explains this to his team. He helps rookies break into the Philadelphia line-up by showing them how to win face-offs, or how to pass the puck to a winger on the fly, or how best to dig the puck out of the corner. He is admired and respected by all of the Flyers, not only because he is the finest player on the team, but because he sets a standard of excellence in everything he does.

Jim Proudfoot, a Toronto writer, summed it up: "Bobby Clarke is more than their captain, more than their best player. He is their conscience."

Bobby has made a good living out of hockey. Like most hockey stars in recent years, he has been paid a high salary. Some young hockey players have been spoiled by the big money and have lost the desire to play as well as they can.

Bobby Clarke has never lost his desire. He has pride in being a hockey player, and in playing up to the best of his ability. This pride in excellence, which has always inspired Bobby and his teammates, will guarantee him success in whatever he does.

The Swimming Smiths
Helen FitzPatrick

SMITHS HONOUR DAD AS GAMES POOL OPENS

The headline appeared on the front page of *The Edmonton Journal*. The dateline was December 3, 1977.

Everyone immediately knew that the Smith children — affectionately known as "The Swimming Smiths" — must somehow be involved in the official opening of the Commonwealth Aquatic Centre in Edmonton.

All eight children of the late Dr. Don Smith gathered in Edmonton to swim a dedication lap in the competition pool which he helped to plan, and which is named for him. All the children had distinguished themselves in swimming competitions.

The eldest son, twenty-eight-year-old George, who came in from Lacombe for the event, swam to a fifth place finish at the 1968 Munich Olympics, and won four medals at the 1970 Commonwealth Games in Edinburgh.

Susan, twenty-seven, married to Terry Halak, also won a medal at the 1970 Commonwealth Games, and competed in the 1971 Pan Am Games in Cali, Columbia, and the 1972 Olympics in Munich.

Sandra, twenty-five, now Mrs. Gordon Osborne, made the Canadian team for the 1967 and 1971 Pan Am Games, and the 1970 Commonwealth and World Student Games.

Twenty-four-year-old Lewis, a promising swimmer and one-time provincial champion, dropped out of swimming at eighteen to turn to wrestling.

Alison, twenty, married to Manel Carriga of Spain, flew in for the pool opening. A brilliant swimmer as a youngster, she broke every ten and under age group Canadian record, but retired from competition at fourteen.

Nineteen-year-old Graham came in from the University of California for the event. Canada's high point athlete at the Montreal Olympics, he has had an astonishing swimming career. His world-record swim earlier that year was just a forecast of the headline performances he would accomplish on the 1978 world swimming scene.

Becky, eighteen, is a legendary figure in swimming circles. The darling of the world media, she brought medals home from the 1975 Commonwealth Games and the Montreal Olympics.

The youngest Smith, Scott, sixteen, follows the Smith family tradition of swimming excellence. Named the outstanding male swimmer in Alberta in 1976, he competed in the British Nationals in London and won a medal in the 1977 Canada Summer Games.

The pool-side appearance of the eight Smith children

stirred the emotions of the crowd in the bleachers. Aware of Dr. Smith's death from cancer a little over a year before, they watched in silence as the youngsters, clad in red and white swim suits, stood at the starting blocks at one end of the Dr. Don Smith Memorial Pool.

According to all reports, as the young swimmers finished their lap, there wasn't a dry eye in the centre. When the crowd rose to give the young people a standing ovation, Dr. Smith's widow, Gwen, was overwhelmed.

"To see my eight children swimming in this pool," she told the crowd, "is a realization of the dreams of many years."

The dreams began on the University of Toronto campus, when physical education students Gwen Lewis of Toronto, and Don Smith of Port Colborne, met as partners in a first aid class. It was a case of love at first sight. After graduation, Gwen left for McMaster University, where she became swim coach and the first Director of Women's Athletics. Don stayed on as instructor at the University of Toronto but they managed to see each other during Toronto-McMaster swim meets.

It was Don's idea to move west. "The hunting is superb out there," he told Gwen. He accepted a post at the University of Alberta, and they were married a year later, in 1948.

Gwen laughs as she talks about the years that followed.

"Even before we had the children, we got a house with seven bedrooms, because we planned on having twelve, and we didn't want to be moving all the time. We rattled and echoed around the house for about two years. Then we decided — okay — we're going to fill this place up."

As the Smith family grew in number, a love for swimming came about quite naturally.

As Gwen tells it: "They put a sign up right in front of our place, even before we arrived, that said: *Caution Watch For Children.* We discovered that there was a municipal pool right across the road.

"We had no summer cottage and every year we had another child. The pool was a great place for kids." Season tickets were only $2 for each child. "We used to say that swimming was the cheapest sport there was — all you had to do was buy each one a bathing suit."

She chuckles about that now in the light of later travel expenses to send the children to national and international swim meets.

According to pool regulations, a child had to be accompanied by an adult until he could swim one length of the pool. Each spring one more Smith arrived at the pool, and the busy young mother devised a plan.

"You know how it is when you have a lot of children around the house. It's nice for them to have somewhere to go so you can get a little work done once in a while. I'd work like crazy to teach each one to swim" Gwen remembers," so that he could go to the pool on his own. I'd watch them cross the road with their towel and suit. They'd be there all day. They'd just love it . . . and were as safe as could be."

Swimming wasn't the only preoccupation of the Smith children. The newsletter which went out every Christmas to distant relatives and friends offers an interesting peek inside the cheerful white house on Saskatchewan Drive.

There were pleasant entries:

The entire family had their first camping trip together in the foothills of the Rockies.

Sue and Sandra sang a duet called "My Task" in church.

Susan's ninth birthday was a success. The game of fish (down the clothes chute for favours) is still enjoyed by all.

George joined Wolf Cubs and Don is helping as assistant cubmaster.

Don hunted at Nordegg and Edson. The trip was not wasted as he brought home a king-size Christmas tree.

Babies were loved in the Smith household, according to the following items:

Alison Grace was christened on December 8th, with interested little Smiths watching from the church balcony.

No baby has ever had a warmer homecoming than did our wee Scott after his lengthy hospital visit.

Sometimes things got a bit hectic:

The four children had chicken pox during the Christmas holidays.

Lewis managed to toss a rock through the windshield of an unfortunate motorist, which will limit his allowance somewhat (for the next forty years).

Sports held a high priority for the Smiths. With numerous backyard skating parties, Gwen was kept busy "lacing and unlacing skates in her spare time".

One May, "everything revolved around little league baseball practices," and one October day, "George shot his first pheasant." A significant September item noted: "It was a sad day when the pool closed." For as the years went by, the Smith children became more and more interested in swimming.

George was the first to join the South Side Swim Club, which offered training at the Strathcona Composite High School pool. Later, one by one, the other children followed his example.

Predictably, Don and Gwen were totally involved in the swimming programs.

Gwen says of those early days: "I coached the little kids until they learned their four strokes: free-style, backstroke, breast stroke, and butterfly. When they learned to do those properly, I would shift them up to Don, who would coach them."

Don looked after the morning training. The youngsters got up at five, and while they dressed he played a recording of "The Impossible Dream" to inspire them.

When they headed home from the pool, Gwen remembers, he'd play the record again while they ate breakfast. They were always ravenous after training.

"I learned how to be a great short-order cook," Gwen says. "I got pretty speedy at getting eight different flavoured omelettes cooking."

During training the children lived by a strict schedule. It was Gwen's job to keep them in line. "I'd feed them right after school and save the meat and potatoes meal for after training," Gwen says. "I had to have it ready so they could get at their books, or they'd fall asleep over them."

There was training on land too for the youngsters, with cross-country runs in the park, "bunny hops" up the 106 stairs between the local pool and the Smith home, and workouts in the gym and at home."

Soon they were headline news:

SMITH FAMILY BEST AT MEET; SMITH KIDS DOMINATE MANITOBA SWIM MEET; RECORDS CONTINUE TO FALL AS SMITHS RIDE THE WAVES.

Toppling existing records became a habit for the Smith family. At one stage, Sandra told a reporter: "We just don't know how many records we currently hold."

The children were taught to compete against the clock rather than against other swimmers. Becky explained this philosophy: "If one of us wins some events, that's good. But the one who improves his time the most gets the attention, even if he finishes fifth."

They were also trained to be tough.

Graham remembers, "When we were little kids at the supper table, we'd all pick on one person . . . just pick on them until they'd cry. The idea was to be so tough you wouldn't cry. After you lose a race, you can't lie down and say, 'O well, that's it!' That's weak! What you do is get ready for the next one."

George proved his stamina when, at the height of a brilliant swimming career, a near-fatal motorcycle accident ended his dream of competing in the 1972 Olympics. His recovery was painful and slow, but he stoically returned to university, at U.B.C. With a nine-inch pin in his leg, he competed in and won — the Canadian Intercollegiate Athletic Union Finals.

The family were to face an even greater test of their courage. In early spring 1976 they learned that their father had cancer and less than a year to live. The sad news came to Becky and Graham while they trained at Thunder Bay for the 1976 Montreal Olympics. Becky, whom her father always called "the shy one", wanted to come home.

In an emotional phone call, her father talked her out of it.

"In this family you don't quit in the middle of a year," he told her. "We don't believe in quitting."

At his insistence the illness did not alter the family's plans. Becky and Graham continued their intensive training with coach Don Talbot at Thunder Bay; Susan married Terry Halak in March; and Scott went to England for the British Nationals.

The following June, at the Olympic trials in Toronto, the world watched in admiration as Becky and Graham broke Commonwealth records within five minutes of each other.

They swam their hearts out that day, in the knowledge that their father, ill and very thin, watched proudly from the stands.

"I wanted to do my very best," Graham told reporters. "I wanted to show my parents that I've matured, that I can be independent, that I can look after myself. I wanted to prove to them I had reached a point in swimming where I'm not doing it only for myself, but also for to others. For my family, my club, my country. And I've done it for my dad. His illness wasn't an added pressure for me. It was an added inspiration."

In turn, Don talked to a Toronto reporter about his kids.

"It's funny," he said. "You worry about them for years, wondering how they're going to turn out, and then they're suddenly very mature and understanding. They're good kids; we're a pretty close family, I guess."

He was able to watch on TV as Graham received his silver medal, and later Becky her two bronzes, as they took turns standing on the medal podium in the Olympic swimming hall.

"It's the greatest feeling I've ever had," he told reporters. "It makes all those years of working with the kids worthwhile. It's a terrific moment in my life."

He succumbed to the cruel disease a little over a month later.

Becky and Graham went on to compete in the XI Commonwealth Games in Edmonton, where she won a silver and a bronze medal, while her brother pocketed a spectacular six golds. A few weeks later, at the World Aquatic Championships in West Berlin, Graham became a world champion as he set a new swim record and won both a gold and a silver medal.

Gwen Smith is now facing the toughest challenge of her life with traditional Smith courage and style. She can speak without bitterness of her husband's death.

"If it had to happen, we were glad of the time to prepare. We had time to talk about things, time to spend with each other."

Her husband's acceptance at the end is an inspiration.

"He didn't really feel cheated," she says. "He felt he had lived a full life. He did a tremendous amount in fifty-five years. "He lived every day. He never put off things. He didn't miss a moment."

Accolades from colleagues and sports writers across the country testify to his contributions to the national sports scene. Though Red Cross water-safety programs and learn-to-swim classes for kids of all ages were his main interests, he also loved to coach a variety of sports.

His real legacy is his family.

There are four more children in the family now. George and his wife Lorraine have two sons; Alison and Manel have a boy; and Lewis and his wife Kathy have a baby girl.

Gwen continues to be busy with amateur sport and swimming commitments. In the 1976 Christmas newsletter, she told her friends: "I am fortunate to have most of my family close by and so many happy memories."

The letter closed with a couplet:

True love's the gift which God has given
To man alone beneath the heaven.

Vancouver Speed Boy
Helen Palk

The idol of sports fans of 1948 was a twenty-year-old Canadian girl who brought to Canada its first Olympic skating championship.

Twenty years earlier a slim Canadian boy just out of high school became the hero of the sports world of that day. His achievement was the capture of two sprinting titles at the Olympic Games in 1928. It was Percy Williams, the speed boy from Vancouver, who won these amazing victories.

Not for many years had Canada produced a sprinter capable of matching strides with front-ranking athletes of the world. Many had tried and failed. Then in 1928 Percy Williams triumphed over them all, achieving the best showing the Dominion had ever made in the famous Games.

Unlike the noted athletic stars with whom he was matched that summer, the slight, boyish sprinter from Canada was not known as a champion nor did he look like one. But he had sporting blood in his veins. When he was a small boy three of his uncles played on a lacrosse team which for six years had never been defeated. They were proud of that record, and even more proud when their little nephew was chosen as the team's mascot.

Percy actually took his first lessons in running from his dog

Sport, a fox terrier that kept his little master's legs on the run most of the day. But his real career as a runner began when at the age of twelve he broke a school record by running one hundred yards in twelve and four-fifths seconds. During his first year in high school he made an outstanding showing in track and field events on Sports Day. His unusual ability was recognized by Bob Granger, a local athlete who later became Percy's coach. His faith in the boy's skill had much to do with his future achievements.

Bob Granger loved games for their own sake, and he saw in Percy Williams an athlete after his own heart. He knew that the boy had been advised by his doctor not to overdo the strenuous sports. Granger persuaded him to spend long hours during the summer vacation in the fields at Brockton Point taking sun baths, doing some practice, and incidentally, learning many fine points of the art of sprinting.

This became Percy's summer vacation programme while he was in high school. His winters included rest from the strenuous sports he loved. Much against his will he turned his back on rugby and basketball so that he might be ready for the summer track and field events.

When spring came Granger was always on hand to encourage and help him as he prepared to enter not only the high school sports, but much more ambitious competitions. Granger watched his protégé break record after record in school and provincial events. He was particularly delighted when Percy entered the Caledonian Games and beat the best collegiate runners on the Pacific coast.

After such a triumph the enthusiastic coach would urge more and more practice. Percy was often lukewarm about spending the time such a programme took from other things, especially when Bob insisted that swimming also must be sacrificed.

Although there was never any talk between the two friends of world competitions, Bob Granger had ambitious plans in mind for his pupil. Each season saw Percy's speed increased, his stride lengthened and his arm action perfected. His spectacular record made him the idol of his schoolmates, and the pride of all British Columbia amateur sportsmen.

Interest and zest were added to the nerve-racking drudgery of practice by the time-trials that Bob Granger arranged just for fun. In one of these tests over a rough track of 175 yards Percy made a record of two seconds ahead of the one held by the world champion of the day. It was an unofficial performance, but from that day Bob Granger began to talk openly of the 1928 Olympics.

The Canadian championships came before the Olympic try-outs, and it took money to travel from Vancouver to the East. Neither Percy nor his coach could afford to pay for the trip, and the funds of the local Amateur Athletic Association were very low. But Bob Granger was not daunted. He seized what he considered a golden opportunity to press for Percy Williams to be sent to Toronto.

A crowd of Vancouver citizens had gathered to watch the Caledonian games of the season. It was a tensely exciting occasion for their local speed boy was facing three crack sprinters from the University of Washington. When he beat them all with ease, the crowd went wild. It was Bob Granger's opportunity. That afternoon enough money was raised to send the victorious sprinter East, but not enough to send his coach with him. Bob Granger was determined to go, so he managed to obtain a job on the Eastbound dining car and paid the rest of his expenses out of his own savings.

Everything seemed to go wrong on that trip from its late start to its disappointing finish. Restful sleep was impossible in an upper berth in midsummer. The train-tired boy and his coach arrived in Toronto just in time to get to the field for the 100-metre race. The young athlete from the West, unknown and unheralded, quietly took his place to qualify to race for the championship. With a supreme effort he reached the semifinals. Then at the last minute it was discovered that there was not enough lanes to accommodate all the finalists. In a toss for place Percy Williams was declared out of the running. It was a heart-breaking disappointment, but never did he show finer sportsmanship. Without protest or argument he prepared to enter the 220-yard race. Though he won the first heat he was unplaced by three famous sprinters in the finals. It was his first great defeat, but it was not unexpected by either Percy or his coach. Both realized that conditons had been against them. Next year, Bob Granger declared, things would be different.

Next year was 1928, the year of the much talked-of Olympic Games at Amsterdam. But first the British Columbia and Dominion Olympic try-outs had to be faced. Though spring was late that year Percy chalked up some overwhelming sprinting victories for himself, and made some brilliant new records. There was no doubt that he was the West's outstanding candidate for Olympic honours.

At the British Columbia try-outs he raced over a rough grass track that had a noticeable incline against the runner. Even with this handicap he equalled the Olympic record of ten and three-fifths seconds for 100 metres.

The Dominion Olympic try-outs were to be held in Hamilton, and again the question of funds for the journey arose. Enough money was raised by public subscription to send Percy East, but again the fund was short of the amount required for two tickets. This time, as before, lack of funds did not alter Bob Granger's determination to see his pupil through this last Canadian trial. Again he worked his way East. Again he paid his own expenses in Hamilton as he put the last-minute touches to Percy's training.

It was difficult for Easterners to believe that this was the same Williams who had failed to reach the championship finals the year before. By winning decisive victories in both sprinting events he earned his place on Canada's Olympic team. His brilliant performance helped to erase the disappointing experience of 1927 from his memory. But best of all, it fully justified Bob Granger's faith in him.

It is impossible to write of the achievements of Percy Williams without referring continually to his debt to his loyal coach. Bob Granger was more than an interested and skilful coach. He was a devoted friend. No sacrifice on his part was too great to further the interests of his clever young protégé. This was never more clearly demonstrated than at the time of the departure of the Olympic team for Amsterdam. The ship was almost due to sail when Bob Granger was shocked to learn that the Olympic Committee did not provide passage for private coaches. Bob was a private coach, and though he was assured of free entertainment overseas, he did not have the money to pay his passage.

This disturbing news caused great consternation in Vancouver. No one knew better than Percy Williams's mother and his close friends what such a separation would mean to him. A few hundred dollars were hurriedly gathered and rushed to Montreal to help Bob out, but the gift arrived after the Olympic ship had sailed. The desperate efforts Bob Granger put forth to follow can be imagined when it is known that he arrived in Amsterdam just three days after the Canadian team.

Whatever he missed of the stirring Olympic ceremonies of torch-bearing, parade of nations and speech-making, Bob Granger was there in time to cheer and support his protégé before the races, and he was there to witness the dazzling performance that electrified the sports world. From the Canadian section of the observing stand he watched the finals of the 100-metre race. He saw Percy's slight, composed figure lined up with the giants of the sprinting world from England, America and Germany. He was one of the frenzied crowd that seemed to live a lifetime in the last seconds before Williams of Canada flashed into first place.

The Canadians cheered themselves hoarse. The band

played "The Maple Leaf for Ever" as Canada's flag rose to the mast head. Interested friends finally took their eyes off the new champion standing at attention in centre field to search for his coach. They discovered Bob Granger standing alone in the Canadian enclosure. Tears were streaming from his eyes. His hand was bruised and bloody from pounding the barbed wire in front as he had joined in the thundering "Come on Williams" of the Canadians.

It was a glorious victory for the twenty-year-old Vancouver boy, but the next day he faced a far greater test of endurance and skill. It was the day of the first of the 200-metre heats. Though the young Canadian was matched with fresh champions who had not run the 100-metre race, the events finished with him still in the competition.

On the day of the 200-metre final the spirits of the Canadians matched the leaden skies overhead. After the tough going of the day before did their hero have a chance? The champions were on the track early, nervously warming up for the great event, but there was no Percy Williams. Buried under a pile of blankets in the dressing-room he was quietly submitting to Bob Granger's special method of warming up. He was in his lane, however, calmly waiting at starting time but looking so frail that few believed he could finish the terrific 200 metres. The race started with others in the lead. Until the last forty yards Percy Williams was still behind. Then with unbelievable swiftness he seemed to shoot forward and, as if borne on the wave of the deafening cheers of the spectators, he finished first.

For the second time in four days the flag of Canada rose to proclaim a Canadian victory. The Dutch police were powerless to keep the jubilant Canadians off the track. They draped the victorious champion with the Canadian ensign, raised him high above their shoulders and cheered. Before the young hero was finally rescued, one of the Canadians, who was himself a former Olympic champion, heard Percy Williams gasp, "Well, won't Granger be pleased! Golly, I owe most of this to him."

It was true that Bob Granger had given him much, but not the high fortitude that enabled him to endure to the finish when others failed to stand the strain. Nor was any coach responsible for the qualities of mind and heart that made him the likeable fellow he was. With charming, boyish modesty he marvelled at the deluge of cables that greeted his spectacular victory. And he was amazed that he should be receiving the acclaim of the whole world. It was, in fact, his unaffected desire to avoid the limelight that made him finally decide to give up exhibition running and settle down to a normal life.

Percy Williams is a citizen of Vancouver living with his mother on the edge of Stanley Park. Instead of sprinting his outdoor sports now are flying, golf, and photography. But whenever sportsmen recall the feats of Canadian athletic heroes of yesterday, Percy Williams's achievement takes first place.

The Gold Medal
Nancy Greene

The first time I saw the courses at Grenoble came the day I arrived there in early February to practise for the Games. I think I was lucky that they were new to me. Some of the other skiers on the team had skied in Grenoble earlier in the year, at a time when I'd been sick, and they came away moaning. Brother, they kept telling me, those runs are so hard, they're so steep, so icy, those kids had already created a tremendous obstacle in their own minds, but I was spared the advance fears. I guess I had it both ways — I had no basis for building up my hopes and at the same time I hadn't psyched myself out with needless worrying.

The Team went through all the familiar arriving rituals

when we reached Olympic Village. There was the usual unpacking, touring the area, greeting our fellow racers and all the other first-day business. Maybe the whole thing was *too* familiar to me. It was my third Olympics and some things struck me as being a little corny. Opening the boxes of clothes, was hardly the thrill it had been at my first Olympics in 1960. This time, the clothing seemed intended for school girls, not for someone like me, in her mid-twenties. There was a suit made of white Orlon pile that made you look like a snow ball when you put it on, and the Hudson's Bay blanket coats, which were by tradition a regular part of the Canadian uniform, didn't seem nearly as smart in 1968. But it was the after-ski boots that really took the cake — they were actually Ernie Richardson Official Curling Boots. Apart from looking terribly homely, they were totally impractical for wear around the ski area because they let in the snow. Dressed up in all our garb, I thought we Canadians looked kind of dowdy, just about on a par with the Russians.

The opening ceremonies were as impressive as ever. I had the honour of carrying the Canadian flag, and along with the other flag bearers, I watched the ceremonies from a higher vantage point than the other competitors. Everything looked twice as thrilling. There were fireworks and music and marching and jet planes dipping overhead, a couple of speeches and a torch-lighting ceremony. Nothing was missing from the spectacle. There was even a tiny bit of humour when Leo Lacroix, a skier on the French team, took the Olympic Oath. That was pretty funny, or at least ironic, since Leo and his cousin happened to be in the ski manufacturing business, making money out of skiing at the very moment that Leo was swearing under the Olympic Oath that he was an amateur.

We had about a week at Grenoble to train on the courses and to tune up our technique before the races began. I didn't feel much pressure during this period. I knew that everybody, the press, my fellow racers, a lot of people back in Canada, expected me to really shine in the '68 Games, and I suppose the knowledge of their anticipation should have heaped some pressure on me. It didn't. The simple fact was that no one expected anything more of me than I expected of myself.

I was especially anxious, *very* anxious, to win the downhill. It's funny, I've always liked the downhill the best of all the events, but people have never believed me, largely because I made my reputation in 1967 and after as a winner in the slalom and giant slalom. I wanted to prove that I was a winning downhill racer as well, and I was determined to prove it in the Olympics. And the downhill course at Grenoble encouraged me to think I *could* win on it. I liked the course. It just seemed to suit me in practice, and I didn't see why it shouldn't suit me on the day of the race.

But I blew it.

My troubles began with the wax, an old familiar story with me. Usually on the day of a race, after we'd waxed our skis, we would take one short trial run. That seemed to work the wax into the best texture for racing. It was the practice everyone followed. But on the morning of the Olympic downhill, for some reason, perhaps because of the excitement of the day, we didn't take that first short spin. Instead, without any preliminary testing, I moved up to the starting point, which at Grenoble happened to be surrounded on three sides, on all but the side that opened on to the course, by a crude little hut. The hut was designed to protect the starters and other officials from the cold and wind, and while it may have been a comfort to them, it constituted a special hazard to all the racers. And it was a positive booby trap for me.

The trouble was the dirt. Inside the hut, the snow was covered with mud, dust and all sorts of dirty residue from the officials' boots. The snow was black with filth, and, as I later figured out, my skis picked up acres of the stuff. Well, it *seemed* like acres. My wax was, of course, still fresh, as fresh as the moment I'd put it on, without even the benefit of one short practice run. Worse, it was a soft wax, and it couldn't help soaking up all the dirt in the vicinity of that hut.

I knew the moment I pushed off and started down the course, that I wasn't making time, and I learned from the official course timers after the race that I lost at least two seconds to the other racers in the top part of the course. My skis just wouldn't go. They weren't running. The course was fairly slow anyway, slow for everyone, but it was twice as bad for me. And everything else seemed to go wrong. I steered wide on turns when I should have cut the gates closely, and, generally, I skied the course the way I had always skied it in practice, instead of making allowances for the changed conditions.

At the bottom I felt washed out. I went numb. I knew I'd failed and so did everyone else. Skiers and officials rushed over asking me what had happened. Why was I so slow? I couldn't answer. I could hardly bear to wait around the course. But I stood there and watched the rest of the skiers run the hill. Olga Pall of Austria won the race, ahead of Isabelle Mir of France in second place and Christl Haas, making her comeback, in third. I finished tenth, and I went back to my room and just bawled my eyes out.

It was the worst disappointment of my career, the absolute rock bottom. Portillo may have been bad, but Grenoble was far worse. I felt disgusted, disturbed, sorry for myself, desperate. That afternoon, after the tears, I went out on the hills and skied slalom as recklessly as I could. I kept falling and crashing all over the place, but I didn't care whether I hurt myself or anything. I just didn't care.

The next race, the slalom, was only a couple of days away, and I approached it with a minimum of confidence. I hadn't been sharp in the slalom races in the early part of the 1968 season. I'd raced beautifully in slaloms in 1967, but in '68, out of two competitive slaloms prior to the Games, I'd finished third in one and I'd missed a gate, disqualifying myself, in the other. With that record, and with my downhill failure, I went into the Olympic slalom radiating pessimism.

Given the situation, given my mood, I positively stunned myself, when I wound up close to the top at the end of the first run. I didn't ski a great race, but I was steady and in control, and I managed to take the course as it came. I stood fifth, with the American girl, Judy Nagle, in first place. She was the sixteen-year-old who had pushed Penny McCoy off the U.S. Olympic Team, and she skied an even more surprising slalom than I did to lead the field by two full seconds.

But Judy met her Waterloo in the second run and I could almost have predicted her fate. After the first run, Judy and I climbed back up the hill together, heading for our second slalom runs, and all the way up, fans along the side of the course, especially American fans, kept calling out to her, stopping her to chat and offer a few words of encouragement. People like that turn up at all the meets, and unless you want to lose your concentration altogether, you have to learn to ignore them and blot their voices out of your consciousness. But Judy was very nervous and she didn't have the experience to cut off her friends. There was one fellow in particular who bugged her that day. I recognized him. He hung around all the ski meets, talking to the racers, usually bothering them, and as I passed him on the hill, I told him to leave Judy alone. But he couldn't resist and I could hear him blabbing away at her. By the time Judy reached the starting gate her concentration had vanished and she was a nervous wreck. I felt so sorry for her — she wasn't used to the pressure. And she'd only skied through a couple of gates on her second run when she fell and couldn't finish the race.

I felt loose and free as I waited for my second run. I guess my showing in the first run had boosted my confidence and I made an even better run the second time down the hill. A lot of other girls, like Judy, fell or missed gates or skied poorly. Marielle Goitschel was the one exception and she finished first.

My two good runs, combined with the other girls' poor runs, boosted me into second place, with Annie Famose third. I'd won a silver medal, my first in the Olympics and I was extremely proud, but I still wanted a gold, and after the slalom, I was sure I'd get one in the giant slalom.

My whole attitude changed with the silver medal. From the depressed, desperate skier I'd been after the downhill, I turned into a matter-of-fact confident racer. I studied the giant slalom course very coolly and I found it ideal for my technique — long and smooth, the kind of course where you had to really work. I knew I could win on it, and approaching the race I expected nothing less, nothing more, than a first place finish.

The night before the race I had waxed my two pair of giant slalom skis. Very deliberately I prepared them in exactly the same way, and next morning I put on one pair while I inspected the course. I skied down the side of the run once and then once more, until I was certain I had memorized every bump, every gate, every turn, practically every snow flake on the thing. I had that course down cold. I was certain of it.

The second pair of skis were, of course, for the race, the skis I expected to wear while I *won* the race. I took them up to the top of the course and sat down with John Platt, the National Team head coach, and Verne Anderson, my coach, and we talked for awhile. We talked deeply and seriously and even philosophically. We talked about a lot of things, about everything *except* the day's giant slalom. I guess their idea was to keep my mind from brooding on the race, and they were so successful that we were almost late for the start. I'd become too engrossed to notice that it was time for my run.

I stood up, put on my skis and pushed down to the starting gate. I saw the Annie Famose was leading the field up to that point. I knew that Annie had a cold, and I thought to myself, as I waited, that if she could lead in her sick condition, then surely I could win.

I came out of the starting gate very quickly and took off

from there. I'd really have to say with unblushing immodesty, that I skied just about a perfect run. A couple of months later, I saw films of that race on television and, watching my run, I realized that there wasn't a move I made that I would change if I had to ski the giant slalom again. I skated furiously on the flat part of the course where I had to work to gain acceleration, and I shot down the bottom part of the course, which was steep and icy, with absolute freedom. I let my skis run for me, the way a racer does when he's travelling with all the stops out, and when I whipped across the finish line, I knew I had what I wanted.

I was, I must say, surprised that I won by such a wide margin. I finished almost three seconds ahead of Annie Famose who was in second place, and that's remarkable for an Olympic competition. Marielle Goitschel came down the hill after me, but I knew she wouldn't beat my time and she didn't. She finished far back. She'd won her gold medal. Now it was my turn.

An Olympic Gold Medal! All mine!

I honestly could hardly believe it once it had finally happened. But it was true, all true.

To a Woman
Alexander M. Stephen

Who are you?
To one, you were a daughter
in whom he saw his own sunshine refracted —
an image in a drop of dew.

To one, you were a sister,
a weaker self.
Thinking of you,
he was a little contemptuous,
and a little proud.

To one, you were a sweetheart —
beauty incarnate to him —
a star that, following,
he became a hero and a poet.

To one, you were a wife.
Careful of his health,
prudent, useful,
you meant home to him.

To one, you were a mother.
He leaned upon you,
neglected you,
resented your vigilance,
and knew
that your love would not fail.

Yet,
these were but facets of you,
fragmentary gleams through windows
of the house which held your soul.

Teacher, artist, warrior,
ruler, merchant prince, and laborer,
a superb animal,
a strong and beautiful god —
these, too, you were —
a human being —
Man — the microcosm!

But we,
who saw only your sex,
passed you by,
blinded by the illusion
of separateness.

Nellie McClung
Loved and Remembered
J. W. Grant MacEwan

Every time a woman casts a ballot, she should pause to breathe a prayer of gratitude for the pioneer efforts of Nellie McClung, the unrelenting western crusader for women's rights and a score of other worthy causes. Her zeal was the main reason for Manitoba women being the first in Canada to have the right to vote and the women of the three Midwestern Provinces being the first in the world to gain the same.

The lovable rebel, to whom Manitoba, Alberta and British Columbia had the strongest claims, was in the front line of battle for social reforms for about fifty years, never lacking a good cause. If it wasn't prohibition or votes for women, it could be better working conditions for girls, minimum wages for all workers, women's property rights, mothers' pensions, public health nursing services, free medical care for school children or something else of importance to Canadian homes and homemakers.

She saw so much to do, and with only one lifetime in which to do it, she knew she had to hurry. But with extraordinary energy and imagination, she succeeded in having a succession of careers; at one time or another she was a schoolteacher, homemaker, author, crusader, social worker and politician, all of which she did with distinction. How could one person accomplish so much? Determination and tirelessness explained it in large part. She demanded some useful accomplishment from every day. One of her friends said she wrote her books while waiting to have her babies, but there was a disparity of numbers requiring explanation because she had five babies and fifteen books. As a mother who loved her home and family, she once said it could have been better if she had reversed a few things in her life: instead of producing fifteen books and five babies, she might have had fifteen babies and five books.

As Nellie Mooney, the youngest of six children from an Irish-Canadian father and a Scottish-Canadian mother, she was born on a Grey County farm in Ontario, October 20, 1873. The first contingent of North-West Mounted Police had just completed its arduous journey by way of the Dawson Route to Fort Garry and the new province of Manitoba was only three years old.

When the little girl reached the age of seven years, the family moved to a homestead community in the Souris Valley. Until ten years of age she had no opportunity to attend school but thereafter, she made good use of her time and at sixteen was enrolled at the Manitoba Normal School in Winnipeg, preparing for a teaching career. Then, having qualified for a teacher's certificate, Nellie Mooney obtained an appointment at a school near Manitou. More than anybody could have guessed, the years in the district proved important in shaping the girl's entire life. The strongest single influence was that of the local church minister's wife, a woman of fine character, an ardent supporter of the Women's Christian Temperance Union and an advocate of equal rights for women.

Miss Nellie admired the lady and grew to share her convictions. Admitting the attraction, the girl told friends that the minister's wife was the only woman she had known whom she believed she would like to have as a mother-in-law. Whether the comment was intended to be taken seriously or not, the indicated wish was one to be realized. When the lady's son, Robert Wesley McClung, returned home from college, the two young people stared at each other with a fascination neither had known before. He was a fun-loving youth with good features and a ready smile. She was a beautiful girl of medium height and with precision in her speech. They enjoyed being together and before long they were married and Nellie McClung got the mother-in-law of her choice.

She took to writing. It was a most unusual pastime on the western frontier but rather logical for a girl who was bursting with ideas she wanted to share. Her first book, *Sowing Seeds*

In Danny, appeared in 1911, the refreshing story of a small-town family struggling to survive. Danny was the youngest of nine Watson children whose father worked as a section hand on the railroad and whose mother augmented her grocery money by washing clothes for the neighbors. The first Watson home was a Canadian Pacific Railway boxcar, but as children were born, the quarters had to be enlarged, one shanty-like addition after another until the home "looked like a section of a wrecked train".

Canadians were surprised to find an author living on the Western Prairies, of all places, and bought books to satisfy a curiosity and learn something about this Danny fellow. Sales soared and the publisher rejoiced at having a book of Western Canadian origin which had to be reprinted again and again. Nothing like that had happened before. With sales reaching close to 25,000 copies, the book was profitable to the author, and naturally, she wanted to continue with her writing.

Through her books and magazine articles, Nellie McClung was becoming known far beyond the Manitoba community. Thousands of people who never saw her came to know her as the woman with strong opinions about prohibition and social reform. "Sure," she was saying, "women belong in the home, but not for twenty-four hours a day. They should have exactly the same freedoms as their men."

With a family of four sons and one daughter, the McClungs, in 1911, moved to live in Winnipeg where the father had been appointed to a new position in insurance. For Mrs. McClung, the big city offered big opportunities for study and big challenges for service. Here was poverty more pronounced than anything she had seen in the farming districts and here were men and women working under conditions that shocked her.

Almost at once she was engrossed in social work and seizing public platforms to speak out against the injustices she saw. And coinciding precisely with her arrival was the rejuvenation of the earlier campaign to obtain voting rights for the women of Manitoba. As early as 1893, there had been an Equal Suffrage Society in Winnipeg, of which Dr. Amelia Yeomans was the prime mover, but with her departure and lack of continuing leadership, the movement failed and disappeared. The most effective continuing force was the Women's Christian Temperance Union, of which Nellie McClung's mother-in-law was for a long time provincial leader. In the year in which Wesley McClung brought his family to Winnipeg, however, the Political Equality League of Manitoba was formed, with Mrs. A. V. Thomas as the first president.

Members of the new organization were deadly serious and their program was carefully prepared. Among other things, a speakers' committee was formed to train and direct young people to take and address meetings in various parts of the province. Although those who volunteered were predominantly young women, some young men offered their services and were accepted. The Provincial Government was not sympathetic but support was coming from some unexpected places. The WCTU had the longest record of support but now the Grain Growers' Association was giving endorsation and scattered editors — including Bob Edwards of the *Calgary Eye Opener* — were doing the same.

With other members of the League, Nellie McClung was more convinced than ever that to be effective in correcting social injustices, women had to have the instrument of the franchise. At once she was a leader, the League's most popular public speaker.

Came 1914. Nowhere in Canada and nowhere in the world had women been granted full voting rights in provincial, state and national elections. British women were gaining notoriety for their belligerence in the struggle; Emmeline Pankhurst and her colleagues had effected considerable destructiveness. Mrs. McClung, with no less zeal, believed it was not necessary to go on window-breaking sprees in order to gain attention. Her oratory and logic were the best of all instruments and she and her friends resolved to carry their cause directly to the Premier of Manitoba with an orderly show of strength.

On the afternoon of January 27, 1914, several hundred women and a few men representing the Political Equality League of Manitoba, the WCTU, the pioneer Icelandic Women's Suffrage Association, the Women's Civic League, the Mothers' Association, the Manitoba Grain Growers' Association and the Trades and Labor Council streamed into the Legislative Building in Winnipeg. They filled the halls, filled the Chamber, filled the galleries and confronted the uneasy Premier, Sir Rodmond Roblin, while Mrs. McClung, as leader and spokesman, skillfully delivered the main message: If democracy was to be more than a sham, women had to be permitted to share to the full and Manitoba should be the first place to provide the necessary legislation.

> We are not here to ask for a reform or a gift or a favor, but for a right — not for mercy but for justice. Have we not the brains to think, the hands to work, hearts to feel and lives to live? Do we not bear our part in citizenship? Do we not help to build the empire? And in addition to all this we pay the life tax on existence. No man can know as a woman does the cost of human life.
>
> Perhaps you will tell me that politics are too corrupt for women. I've never heard a satisfactory explanation of why politics should be corrupt. There is nothing inherently vicious about politics and the politician who says politics are corrupt is admitting one of two things — that he is party to that corruption or that he is unable to prevent it. In either case we take it that he is flying the white flag of distress and we are willing and ever anxious to come over to help him. . . . How would you, Sir Rodmond, like to be governed by a parliament of women?

The Premier, who had been in power for almost fourteen years, listened attentively and a little nervously. He was polite but at the end of the submission, when he was expected to reply, he confessed that he was not convinced by the argument from the ladies. He conceded that "this is a large, respectable, very intellectual delegation," but he could not get away from the view that the extension of the franchise would be a backward step.

"There is the question of conditions in the Motherland," he said gravely. "There the women are appealing to the authorities for the suffrage. As you know, we all draw our inspiration in legislation, theology, art, science and other subjects from the Motherland. Now, that being a fact that none will dispute, can you, can anyone, in confidence say that the manifestations that have been made by the women there constitute a guarantee that if the franchise is extended, what we have today will be preserved and not destroyed."

It was a horrible thought but "if a few short days of disappointment as in England, caused such hysteria as to endanger human life and result in the destruction of millions of dollars worth of property, is that not cause for the authorities to hesitate in extending the suffrage to women?"

His convictions were clear. If it was not safe for the Mother of Parliaments to trust women with the vote, it would be a mistake for Manitoba to rush into such a program. He had "great respect for women" but he would have to vote against any measure for the extension of the franchise.

Perhaps Nellie McClung did not expect any more in encouragement at that stage in the campaign but her determination was unshaken and she had a final comment: "Sir Rodmond, we have come to the last ditch in our onward march towards freedom and usefulness and we are stretching out our hands to you to help us over. It is now your move."

The Winnipeg women were making history and this was one of Nellie McClung's finest hours.

Convinced that a subtle approach would be more effective than violence, the women rehearsed for the famous Mock Parliament which was held in Walker Theatre in Winnipeg on January 29, 1914, just two days after their appearance at the Legislative Building. Humor and laughter might win where anger would fail. The Mock Parliament, a clever satire on the Roblin Government, was an overwhelming success. Winnipeg people laughed heartily and told their friends to be sure to see the show on the second evening. The star performer was Nellie McClung who played the part of Premier as the women in power rejected the request for Votes For Men. Playing with her were some well-known Manitoba personalities: Mrs. Francis Graham as Speaker; Dr. Mary E. Crawford as Minister of Education; Miss Kenneth Haig as Attorney General; Mrs. Genevieve Lipsett Skinner as Minister of Agriculture; Miss Clendennan as Provincial Secretary; Miss Alma Graham as Clerk; Mrs. Crossley Greenwood as Sergeant-At-Arms; Misses Florence McClung and Ruth Walker as pages, and Mrs. A. A. Perry as Leader of the Opposition.

Three gentlemen in the cast, R. C. Skinner, A. V. Thomas and Percy Anderson, were there as a delegation requesting Votes For Men, and seeing their petition sadly rejected. Men, it was argued, were not qualified. The Premier delivered the decision: men could not be trusted with ballots. "Men's place is on the farm."

The audience howled with laughter and friends of the government were embarrassed. Requests to repeat the performance at outside points came quickly. Nellie McClung and her friends were capturing Manitoba imagination and doing further injury to the aging and scandal-ridden Roblin Government which was to lose seats later in 1914 and go down to defeat in 1915. The new Premier, Liberal T. C. Norris, came to power with a promise that Manitoba women would be given the vote. Good as his word, the necessary legislation was introduced at the first session and on January 27, 1916 — two years to the day after Nellie McClung and her orderly army of women marched upon the Capital — the desired amendment to the Manitoba Election Act was given third reading. At the instant the Bill passed that final stage, eager women and a few male supporters crowding the galleries, stood and sang "O Canada", then took up the strain of "For They Are Jolly Good Fellows". What under ordinary circumstances would have been regarded as a serious breach of parliamentary conduct seemed to disturb nobody and pandemonium reigned for some minutes. The Manitoba women were the first in Canada to gain voting privileges although similar legislation was passed in Saskatchewan and then in Alberta just days later. In the final legislative vote in Manitoba, there was only one dissenting voice, that of the member for Ste. Rose, but the women were in a forgiving mood and invited him to their victory banquet to propose a toast to their success and he accepted.

But by this time of triumph in Manitoba, the McClung home was in Edmonton; Wesley McClung had been transferred and his loving wife accompanied him, even though she was in the best possible position for a political career in the province where her campaigning had been so effective. The Manitoba women, however, did not overlook the unparalleled part rendered by Nellie McClung.

It did not matter, however, where the lady lived; she would see plenty to do wherever she was and in Alberta she was involved at once in prohibition work and the local battle to gain voting rights for members of her sex. She rejoiced to see two Alberta women, Mrs. Louise McKinney and Miss Roberta McAdams, elected in 1917 to the legislature. Miss McAdams was elected while serving overseas but when Mrs. McKinney took her seat in the Alberta Legislature, she was the first woman in the British Empire to do so.

Nellie McClung was elected as a Liberal member of the legislature in 1921, the year in which the Farmers' party was swept into power in Alberta. Miriam Green Ellis said that men in the Press Gallery at Edmonton "adjudged her about the best student of legislation in the entire group." Of course, her quick wit stood her in good stead. Those in the Press Gallery remembered when a young member with a reputation for giving his opinion on every question, complained about missing a certain opportunity to speak. Nellie McClung followed, "regretting" that proceedings were moving too fast for him, causing him to break a record, for, as far as she could recall, "the honorable member has never had an unuttered thought in this House."

Ever a forceful personality with unyielding views of right and wrong, she was a good member of the legislature but not a good party woman. She favored free medical and dental treatment for school children, mother's allowances, better property rights for women and she was not opposed to divorce and birth control. Her opposition to liquor never changed but prohibition was losing its former strength as a popular cause, and in the provincial election of 1926, she suffered defeat. But she was as busy as ever. Joining forces with Emily Murphy, Canada's first woman magistrate, she helped in the fight for the female right to sit in the Senate, taking the matter through the Supreme Court to the Privy Council to establish the fact under the British North America Act that women are indeed "persons" and must be eligible to sit as Senators.

Mrs. McClung did not escape criticism from those people who chose to believe that women should stay at home and give full time to families. But nobody could ever say that her family had been neglected. One son was a Rhodes scholar, one became a deputy minister and all five children did well and were justifiably proud of their mother.

Again the McClungs moved, this time, in 1933, to British Columbia, where the distinguished wife and mother died in

1951. Miriam Green Ellis reminded friends that "the last few years were not easy for Nellie M." She suffered a lot but never lost her sense of humor. "Toward the end she was lying very still. Wes wondered if she had gone. But with a little twitch she opened her eyes. 'Oh, I'm still here. I'll never believe I'm dead till I see it in the paper,' and she closed her eyes again."

Who among Canadian women had more to show for a lifetime of service? In addition to careers in writing, teaching, homemaking, politics and crusading, she served as the only woman on the Dominion War Council in 1918, the only member of her sex to represent Canada at the Ecumenical Council of the Methodist Church in 1921, first woman on the Canadian Broadcasting Corporation Board of Governors, Canada's only woman representative at the League of Nations in 1918. If Canada had a superwoman, she had to be Nellie McClung, for whose memory the Women's Institute of Grey County, Ontario, erected a beautiful cairn on the property on which she was born, unveiling it with proper dignity in 1957.

Her tombstone in a Victoria, British Columbia, cemetery displays the simple epitaph: "Loved and Remembered". Nobody can know the political and social history of Canada — Western Canada in particular — without some knowledge of the life and contributions of Nellie McClung, the idealist, the one who insisted that "Nothing is too good to be true."

Emily Murphy
Byrne Hope Sanders

On a bleak afternoon about fifty years ago, a woman tapped at the back door of a prairie farm. When there was no answer, she knocked louder, then pushed the door open, calling out cheerily, "Anybody home?"

The farmer's wife was sitting by the kitchen table crying bitterly, her head buried in her arms. The visitor, whose name was Emily Murphy, was swift to comfort the weeping woman. She lifted the woman's head to her shoulder and held her close. Presently Emily heard what had happened.

For eighteen years the farmer's wife had toiled beside her husband to develop the farm from unbroken prairie. Then suddenly, without warning, the farmer had sold the land, taken the money, and gone off to the United States with another woman, leaving his wife penniless, homeless, and utterly alone.

This was a common story in western Canada at the beginning of the present century. Fifty years ago a woman had no rights in her husband's property. She could spend her life, working side by side with her husband through the hard, long hours that pioneer farming demanded, yet, if he wished, he could sell the land without her consent, and without giving her a cent.

Emily Murphy, who, with her husband, had just come west from Ontario, could not believe such an unjust situation existed. "We can surely do something about it!" she insisted. "It's shocking that a woman's home can be taken away from her like that — and by a no-good man who runs off and leaves her. After she's worked as hard as you have!"

"But it's the law," sighed the farmer's wife, sipping the hot tea Emily had made for her.

"Then we'll have to change the law," said Emily.

Her encounter with the farm woman was to change the course of Emily Murphy's life. Seven years later, as a result of an active campaign led and directed by Mrs. Murphy, the provincial legislature of Alberta passed the Dower Act, designed to remedy the unjust situation which had so shocked her. Securing the passage of this Act was only one of the many crusades in which the indomitable little woman was to engage, and which were to make her one of the best known and most widely respected women in western Canada.

As a child, Emily Ferguson had been one of a family of four brothers and a sister, growing up in Cookstown, Ontario. The

Fergusons were of Irish origin, well-to-do, high-spirited, and devoted to one another. Emily's childhood was a happy one in every way. Part of the tenderness and the strength that were so characteristic of her came from the happy home surroundings in which she grew up.

Her father was a man of strong convictions. Among them was his belief that boys and girls should share responsibilities equally. The young Fergusons all had their assigned tasks, whether it was weeding the garden, piling wood, or caring for the lawns and shrubberies. Each child must ride well, and learn to take care of the horses. Mr. Ferguson taught his daughters, as well as his sons, to ride, play cricket, hoe the garden, and carve the Sunday roast.

It became, then, a part of Emily's life to enjoy work shared between boys and girls, and to take it as a matter of course. If there was a job to be done, and it was her turn, she went to work and finished it. But if she were to share the family responsibilities she felt that she should also share the rewards for duties well done. With just as much energy and confidence as she put into her work, she went after any privilege her brothers had, that she felt the girls of the family should also enjoy. The idea that she was "just a girl", and therefore, for some reason, less capable than the boys, never entered her head.

When Emily was about fifteen, she met Arthur Murphy at a friend's home. He was a student for the ministry, and twelve years older than Emily. Writing about it afterwards, Emily recalled:

> There was this sweetheart with whom I had my picture taken, the very tall one with the fair hair, who said he was going to marry me when I grew up. . . .
>
> On Sunday afternoons, one of my brothers, who were then at Upper Canada College, would call and take me out [from Bishop Strachan School], promptly transferring me to the custody of this young divinity

student, whom I shamelessly mulcted for teas, chocolate éclairs, rides on ice-boats, sail-boats, or any kind of boat. He brought me Valentines too, and books of poetry, in which he wrote things in Latin or Hebrew, so that my schoolmates might not read them, but which he translated accurately for me.

Did I marry him when I grew up?

Of course I did.

Since then I have lived so much, and have been so happy, that possibilities for a future life have never disturbed my days. It would be asking too much of the Deity to expect another period like it. Truly it would!

When Emily was nineteen she and Arthur were married. For the first years of her marriage she channelled all her energies and interests into her life as the wife of a minister and the mother of three little girls, Kathleen, Evelyn, and Doris.

She worked with Arthur, helping him to prepare his sermons. Even as a young girl she had loved quotations, particularly those which expressed noble thoughts. Now she copied inspirational ideas into old ledger books for his reference. She indexed her husband's library. She liked to memorize passages from his books, and it became one of their amusements in the long winter evenings to have her give, without reference to a book, the volume and the page in which some quotation occurred that Arthur needed. Developed in this way, Emily's memory became remarkable.

Arthur became a missioner and travelled for a time with his wife and family through Ontario, holding mission services. Emily missed the pleasant home life she had known. Now they lived in small hotels or boarding-houses. She was very much alone, too, as Arthur was preaching or visiting the parishioners almost every evening.

It was typical of Emily that instead of feeling sorry for herself she found a new outlet for her energies. On those lonely evenings, with the children tucked in bed, and no household duties to occupy her, Emily began to write down her impressions of what she saw about her. She and Arthur were sent to England for a short period; on their return her first book was published. It was an account of what she had seen in England and what she had thought about the country and its people.

Then calamity struck the happy little family. A case of diphtheria is rarely encountered today; it is one of the many diseases that modern science has conquered. In the early years of this century, however, diphtheria epidemics were common. This disease attacked the Murphy family. Both Emily and Arthur were seriously ill, and the youngest daughter, Doris, who was only seven, died from it. Arthur Murphy found it very difficult to regain his strength after his illness. His doctors advised a change of climate for him, and suggested that he go to western Canada. Emily and her husband decided to go to Swan River, Manitoba, where Arthur had purchased a small piece of land some years previously.

It was a sad break-up of the life Emily had known. She was leaving her own closely-knit family and the people she knew so well to travel into a new world and a strange way of life. On her last night in Toronto, Emily wrote in her diary:

> To move means a review of your whole life. Inside one little hour you laugh, swell with pride, cry, grovel with humility, and burn with indignation as the fingers of still-born projects, dead joys, or foolish frolics reach out and touch you from the past. . . . There are compensations, though. Things get cleaned up. You lose fifteen pounds of absolutely useless flesh. There is the secret and blissful consciousness of removing mountains and making things happen.

Removing mountains and making things happen. As she left her old life, this idea was born in Emily's mind, and she wrote down these words which summarized, in part, her philosophy of life and set the pattern which the activities of her new life were to follow, activities which would bring her so much pleasure and satisfaction.

After a few years in Manitoba the Murphy family moved to Edmonton. When she arrived in Alberta, Emily was almost forty. She was a small woman, just over five feet, with merry, blue-grey eyes, thick, dark hair, and a quick smile. Under her pen-name, "Janey Canuck", she had published a number of delightful books which had proved very popular. She was eager now to write more, and the new life in the new land, upon which she entered with lively satisfaction, was to provide her with a theme. From her very first days there she loved western Canada. "Surely the West is golden," she wrote. "The sky, flowers, wheat, hearts".

Edmonton was an exciting city, with thousands of people pouring into it from every part of the world. "It's a great place, this Canadian West," she wrote. "It's a country of strong men, straight living, and hard riding. Tut, who wants to go to Heaven? . . . We're very socially inclined with teas, tennis, 'mobiling, dancing, dining, and wild riding across the hills. When people are healthy and prosperous, they are instinctively hospitable and always in a big-handed, big-hearted way."

One of her pleasures was to ride over prairie trails where, she said, "nothing met but the four winds, nothing passed but the clouds." Often she accompanied Arthur on his journeys through the countryside. Temporarily he had not taken on the responsibilities of a church, and was engaged in the flourishing real estate business. He travelled about the country a great deal, checking on the values of land in which he was interested, and it was Emily's pleasure to join him in his travels.

"I tell you there is magic in this land," wrote Emily in one of her books, *Open Trails*, "and you can hear unsung things. My heart is on tip-toe for the reach of them."

This, then, was the Emily Murphy who on a bleak

afternoon entered the kitchen of a prairie farm, and found there a weeping and deserted woman.

When Emily heard the tragedy of the farmer's wife, left penniless by her husband, she made the cause her own. She determined that a law must be passed to protect the property rights of the women of Alberta. It was typical of Emily that, having decided to take up the cause, she plunged headlong into a crusade with boundless energy.

She began by learning the facts; to do this she spent many days studying law books and references. She interested all her friends in the cause and also the members of the various women's organizations to which she belonged. She became a familiar figure in the gallery at the provincial legislature, learning how legislation was passed, finding out the routine for getting a Bill accepted.

When she felt there was enough public interest in the subject, she went to a young lawyer in Calgary, Mr. R. B. Bennett, a member of the legislature, who later became Prime Minister of Canada. He introduced a Bill to make it law that a woman should have some part of her husband's property, so that he could not sell it and leave her destitute. The Bill failed to pass. It was brought up again and again and voted down each time. Many of the Members vowed they would never let it become law. One of the officials snorted, "Why should women worry about possessing some of their husband's property during his life? Time enough after he's dead!"

When Emily heard this kind of comment she reminded herself, "Whenever I don't know whether to fight or not — I fight!" So, remembering the heart-broken, poverty-stricken prairie wife, and all others in the same situation, Emily continued to fight.

The battle lasted seven years, and resulted in a final victory for Emily's cause. In 1911 the Dower Act was passed by the legislature of Alberta. It provided that every wife had a right to a one-third share of her husband's property. If he sold his farm, or his business, his wife's share must go to her.

Just before the Bill was passed, a reporter on *The Edmonton Journal*, who had watched Emily Murphy's crusade, wrote:

> Mrs. Murphy is so much in earnest over the Bill, that its success is as good as accomplished. It may not be this year, nor the next, but this leader of women will keep hammering away until even the most obstinate man will be convinced that it is best to withdraw quietly and, without further ado, let down the bars.

The experience gained in securing passage of the Dower Act had taught Emily much, and had brought her into prominence throughout the province. Earlier she had written in one of her delightful books, "Oho! and oho! Why should I stay in town, I who know the songs of the country? Why should anyone stay in a town which puts lines in her face; hardens her eyes; which spurs her feet and bridles her tongue?" But Emily was destined to spend the rest of her life in the city. Gradually she became more and more involved in social service, and accepted more and more responsibilities in the community. Whatever her own wishes might have been, her life was spent in helping the downtrodden, punishing the vicious, and crusading against evil.

An incident with important implications for Emily occurred on a spring morning in 1916, when a group of girls were brought into a police court. There were rumours that some of the arrests were illegal and that an injustice was being done. A committee of members of the Local Council of Women went to court to observe the case, and to see if they could help any of the girls.

The prosecuting lawyer said, "This is a very delicate case. I don't think it is fit to be heard before a mixed audience."

A spokesman for the women explained that they were

members of a committee on laws which had to do with the protection of women and children, and they felt they should remain. But the judge said, "No decent women would want to sit through this case. Please retire." The ladies left, embarrassed and angry. They went straight to Emily.

"Should we go back into court?" they asked her.

"Definitely," said Emily. "Go back and agree with the magistrate. Such cases should *not* be heard before a mixed audience. Then we shall go to the government and ask that a court be set up for the City of Edmonton in which women offenders may be tried by a woman, in the presence of women."

Here was another crusade; the women turned to Emily to lead it. She went to the Attorney General and talked to him about her idea for a woman magistrate.

"An excellent suggestion," he said thoughtfully. "When are you ready to be sworn in, Mrs. Murphy?"

"Oh no! That is to say, I'm not ready at all," cried Emily in astonishment. "I never thought of this. I don't know anything. I have too much work at home — and my people wouldn't let me!"

Later, telling about the interview she said, "All the excuses slackers ever use, came tumbling from my lips." But the Attorney General paid no attention to them. "Let me know next week," he said firmly.

Emily's family was enthusiastic over the idea. "Presiding over a court," they said, "is not essentially a man's job. It is a job for whoever can do it best." They had no doubt that Emily would make an excellent judge.

She asked a close friend whether she thought a woman should be a magistrate. The woman, a mother of six children, said, "A woman with a family can keep court better than a man, because she has done such work for years in the management of her family. In training her boys and girls, she has had to do with false pretenses, assault incitement, breach of peace, cruelty to animals, cheating at play, loitering, appropriation, false evidence, trespass, idle and disorderly persons, and many other offences!"

Shortly afterwards, Emily Murphy was sworn in as police magistrate in and for the Province of Alberta. She was the first woman in the British Empire to be appointed to such a position.

Her brothers, who were now distinguished lawyers in the East, were delighted. On the first day she sat in court, she received telegrams from them. One said: "Let me offer my congratulations to Your Worship. Try to temper your decisions with mercy, and do not hand out too much of your own medicine, namely, hard labour."

Another wrote: "Well done. In fact, I say 'Shake, Judge!' . . . You beat your brothers to it. . . . And while I am at it, Emily, be easy on 'them wimmin'. That is the one thing I am afraid of — that you may not possess sufficient gallantry to pass over many things."

Emily herself has written of that first day in court:

> It was as pleasant an experience as running a rapids without a guide. Besides, the lawyers and police officials looked so accustomed and so terribly sophisticated. Indeed, I have never seen brass buttons so bright and menacing as on this particular day. All the men became embarrassed and started to stammer over their manner of addressing me. One said "Your Worship" and another "Your Honour". A negro said "Your Majesty" and the rest said "Sir".

It was on that first day in the court that the need for another crusade was first foreshadowed. One of the lawyers objected to Emily's presence in the court as magistrate, on the grounds that she had no right to sit in judgment.

"Why?" asked Emily in surprise.

"Because," said the lawyer, "the law has it that a magistrate must be a person duly sworn and duly qualified."

"I have been sworn, and I am duly qualified, you will find," said Emily gently. She did not want trouble on her first day.

"I'm sure you are, Your Honour," said the lawyer. "But are you a 'person'?"

Emily stared at him. "Nothing has been done," the lawyer went on smoothly, "to establish that a woman is a 'person' in the eyes of the law. And therefore I challenge your appointment as a magistrate."

Emily thought for a moment, then noted his objection and went on with the next case. The incident was repeated in the weeks that followed. Every time the same lawyer was in court, very politely but very positively he made the objection that a woman was not a "person" in law. On each occasion Emily noted the objection and went on with her work. But the injustice of the idea that a woman was not a "person" in the eyes of the law was deeply impressed on her mind. Years later she was to take a leading part in remedying that injustice.

Emily Murphy proved to be a good judge; she was well liked by lawyers and other magistrates, feared by some criminals, admired and even loved by others who were brought before her.

Through her court work a new Edmonton was brought before Emily's eyes. She who had known the city as a friendly place of tea-parties, dances, and sports, now saw it as a cruel and relentless world. Before her came a steady procession of tragic figures deep in wretchedness and despair. Her woman's sympathies were aroused, day by day, as she listened to the stories behind a young girl's downfall, a family break-up, an old man's fear. She knew her law thoroughly, through careful study, and came fully prepared for every case.

Many a time when a girl was brought into court for the first time, Emily's motherly heart was stirred. Sometimes she would take the girl to her own home until she could find a job for her. "Let's give her a chance to forget the past, and begin life again," she said to friends who she thought might employ the girl. "What chance had she with the curse of that pretty face? Life is a conspiracy against a girl like that. But she's going to be all right now. She has had a hard lesson, and I could not let her go to jail."

The Murphy family became accustomed to wedding parties in their home, following the marriage of some girl who had appeared in Emily's court. The ceremony was often performed with Emily's own wedding ring. The boy and girl, their marriage given dignity by Emily's kindness, started on their life together with hope for a happy future.

At the same time she could be cold and strict with those she believed to be vicious, or those who defiantly broke the law. Many women objected to being tried in Emily's court, saying that she was hard. Emily knew instinctively when they were lying, and paid no attention to easy tears. She could become very stern on occasion. When she sensed that a woman was trying to fool her, she would listen very quietly for some moments, then snap her lorgnette open and gaze very steadily at the woman as she talked. Suddenly she would rap out three words, "Stop your lying!" and pass sentence.

Many of the life-stories she heard told in the dock haunted Emily. The energy which she had formerly poured into writing her books, now went into writing letters to the family of some prisoner whose story appealed to her, or writing to the prisoners themselves.

A friend of Emily's who accompanied her on a jail inspection vividly recalls the visit:

We walked together down the corridors of the jail. Emily darted from side to side calling to the women by name. "Hello, Pearl! I saw your husband last week. He's looking well — and said the children were fine." Or, "Anything I can do for you, Maisie? Things are going to be better when you're through here, aren't they?" Most of the prisoners were happy to see her, and sent messages back home, but some of them sat in stony silence. Emily's eyes were sad as she passed these hardened women, with no hope, and no future.

Threats on her life were common. Drug addicts, to whom she had given heavy sentences, vowed they would shoot her on their release. A number of women criminals threatened to have her officially disqualified because they maintained that she gave unduly harsh sentences. She became used to anonymous letters promising revenge.

"There is one distinct benefit, however, to being a police magistrate in a woman's court," she wrote, "You are saved from the risk of stagnancy. You will have the distinction, too, of having persecuted more perfectly pure, unoffending ladies than any other woman in your city."

As she worked in court, Emily began to make plans for reforms to cure some of the terrible situations she found. She wrote many magazine articles trying to arouse the public to existing situations. One of her most impressive campaigns was the one she waged against the narcotic traffic. She saw the dreadful results of the drugs in many of her cases, and set out to discover for herself how the traffic was developed. Driven by compassion, and longing to awaken people to the threat of drugs, she followed the police fearlessly into terrifying situations. She recorded her findings and experiences in a book on the drug menace, *The Black Candle*.

Through these difficult years, Emily's home and family were comfort, joy, and balance to her. She and Arthur, whom she always referred to as "the Padre", were always devoted to one another; he was a gentle soul with a delightful sense of humour. And the two girls were her pride and joy. Kathleen was married in 1916, but Evelyn always lived at home and was her constant companion and helper. They were all of the deepest importance to her throughout her life. "What is good enough for 'company'," she liked to say, "is not too good for your family, be it courtesy or the silver teapot."

Whenever she felt overtired or worried by the problems of the day, she turned to solitaire for relaxation, slapping down the cards rhythmically, while she thought out some principle in a judgment she had reserved. At other times she put on an old flowered house-coat, grabbed a can of paint, and went to work on a garden chair, or some kitchen shelves. The family became used to a brilliant splash of colour, "something bright and cheerful", Emily called it, added to a corner of the house. She enjoyed playing rollicking old tunes on the piano: "I'm Captain Jinks of the Horse Marines", or "I'm Gonna Dance Wid de Guy What Brung Me!"

She had not forgotten the objection to her appointment raised on her first day in court, on the grounds that, as a woman, she was not a "person" within the meaning of the law. Emily had asked the courts in Alberta to give a judgment on the matter, as far as it concerned her appointment as magistrate, and had cleared up the question there. The first round was won.

But did Canada as a whole consider women as "persons" before the law? This was what Emily intended to find out. She began by writing to a magazine in the East and suggested that it launch a campaign to get women appointed to the Senate of the Canadian Parliament. "I am sure," she wrote, "that you will find a woman in the East who will be the ideal appointee." But nothing came of her suggestion.

One morning in 1921, Emily opened a letter from the Montreal Women's Club, asking if they might put her name forward for an appointment as senator. The idea came from a western woman, now living in Montreal, who knew of Emily's work, and of her campaign to have the word "person" interpreted as including women when it concerned the appointments of magistrates.

Emily had no personal ambition to become a senator. But the campaign was being waged to have a woman appointed to the Senate not simply because she was a woman, but on the grounds that a woman was capable of doing as good or better work in many fields as a man. If it needed proof, Emily had proved this point in her police court and juvenile court work, in her writing, and in her many activities on behalf of women's rights. She was well known in every part of Canada and rightly deserved the honour of being appointed to the Senate. On behalf of the women of Canada, all of whom suffered by not being considered "persons" in law, Emily agreed to the plan of the Montreal Women's Club, and her name was formally passed on to the Prime Minister, Sir Robert Borden. He wrote in reply a polite but firm letter. Women, he said, could not be appointed to the Senate, because they were not "persons" within the meaning of the British North America Act. This Act stated that only "persons" could be summoned to the Senate.

There it was again, the same objection that had been made on Emily's first day in court. Emily began to gird herself for battle in earnest.

Another Prime Minister came into power; again the Montreal Women's Club asked that Emily be appointed to the Senate. This time, the answer was that a woman could not be appointed without an amendment to the British North America Act, which would make it clear that the word "persons", as used in the Act, could apply to women as well as to men. An amendment, however, was an impossibility. To obtain it would mean, to begin with, securing the agreement of all the provinces and endless argument lasting over many years. Women did not even have the right to vote in some provinces. What hope was there of having these provinces agree to allow the appointment of women senators?

The idea of Emily as a woman senator, however, caught on throughout Canada. She was well known for her writing, for her work as a magistrate, for her many crusades. She had been president of several important and influential women's organizations, and had spoken from platforms in many cities. Thousands of petitions urging her appointment were sent to the government from these organizations. Editorial writers endorsed the idea, and the press of Canada published many comments and letters suggesting that Mrs. Murphy be made a senator, so that the Senate might be better qualified to deal with matters that affected the women and children of Canada.

There was another change of government, and the Rt. Hon. Mackenzie King became Prime Minister: fresh hope stirred in Emily's heart that he would agree to the appointment of a woman as senator. But nothing happened. No one in the Government paid any attention to the matter.

Then one of Emily's brothers had an idea for a new plan of attack. He wrote to Emily to tell her about Section 60 of the Supreme Court Act. In simple words, this Section said that any citizen could ask a question of the King about the meaning of the British North America Act. If the Department of Justice felt the question was an important one, and in the general interest of the Canadian people, it could ask for a ruling on it from the Supreme Court. The question had to be submitted, not by an individual, but by a group of citizens.

Here was a plan which suited Emily perfectly. Without delay, she asked four leading women of the West to join her in asking the question: "Does the word 'persons' include women, within the meaning of the British North America Act?"

In the Red Room of the Senate hangs a plaque honouring the five women who joined together to force an answer to this question. Because they always signed their petitions in alphabetical order, their names are listed like this:

Henrietta Muir Edwards
Nellie McClung
Louise C. McKinney
Emily F. Murphy
Irene Parlby

Each of the women, in turn, signed the petition, before sending it on to the next one. Nellie McClung, who, like Emily, was a well-known author, wrote to her: "I have just sent the petition on with my blessing wrapping it around. God Bless our Cause, and confound our enemies."

The petition was forwarded to the Minister of Justice, who ruled that it should be submitted to the Supreme Court. All the provinces were invited to send lawyers to argue the case before the Court. Two responded. Alberta thought the answer should be "yes". Quebec believed that it should be "no".

The argument was a lively one. "What an absurd thing to say! Of course women are 'persons'," said some. "If senator is a masculine term only, what about chairman, president, journalist, doctor, dentist, lawyer? If these terms can be used of women, why can't senator?" Others were equally vehement, though less logical, in opposition. "A woman in the Senate? The idea is ridiculous!"

Cried Emily's supporters, "Why does a woman, Agnes MacPhail, sit in the House of Commons where laws are made, and yet none is allowed to sit in the Senate where the laws are only approved? To say a thing is right in one House and wrong in the other is nonsense!"

Lawyers had expected the hearing to take only an hour; to their astonishment, it lasted all day. Judgment was reserved, and Emily had to wait five weeks for the verdict. Then the Supreme Court of Canada decided against the women. In the minds of learned judges, women were not "persons" within the meaning of the Act, and therefore could not be summoned to the Senate. Their decision was based, in the main, on the fact that when the British North America Act was drawn up in 1867, the position of women was a restricted one. They did not vote, they could not hold public office. The Fathers of Confederation had no conception that this situation might change and so had made no provision for a change. In their minds, when they drew up the Act, clearly the word "person" referred to men only.

The women of Canda were sorely disappointed by the decision. One noted woman, in a newspaper interview, said bitterly, "The iron dropped into the souls of Canadian women when we heard that it took a man to decree that his mother was not a person." But Emily and her allies did not hesitate a moment before taking their next step. Even before the case had gone to Supreme Court, they had decided that if the verdict went against them, they would appeal it. Within a week another petition was being prepared and circulated to the five women for signature. It asked that the case be taken to the highest Court available, the Privy Council in London, England. This, in effect, was asking the King himself to rule on the question.

Lawyers who had argued the case in Canada went to London to appear before the Privy Council. The province of Quebec withdrew its objections and sent an encouraging message to the five women. There were invitations to Emily to go over to London as the guest of honour of some of the women's organizations there. But she refused, feeling it was wiser to wait at home for the verdict.

The case was argued in a quiet room at Number One Downing Street, that famous street where Britain's Prime Ministers have lived for many years. Five distinguished judges, with the Lord Chancellor of England at their head, and a battery of lawyers, wrestled with the question put to them by five Alberta women, on behalf of all Canadian women. A newspaper man present wrote: "At the end of all these endless speeches and debates, it will be decided, if one may hazard a guess, that women are Persons. Which one may say, without exaggeration, most of us know already!"

The Privy Council, too, reserved judgment. Some weeks later, in the middle of the night of October 18th, 1929, the telephone shrilled in Emily's home. The family was awakened by the joyous shouts of Judge Emily Murphy. In a white flannelette night-gown, her hair tousled, her cheeks flushed, she was dancing with delight in the living-room, crying, "We've won! We've won!"

Congratulations poured in from every province and from hundreds of friends and well-wishers. It was confidently expected that Emily herself would become the first woman senator. Most people felt the way one writer put it in her letter to Emily:

> It was a famous victory and you will go down in history. Now we are praying that you will be made the first woman senator. How proud we would be to see our "little general" there, taking her seat. How you would wake up that dull assemblage!

People on the street stopped Emily again and again to cry, "You've done it again, Mrs. Murphy! You showed 'em." Newspapers across the country congratulated her. Again the women's organizations got busy. Petitions, letters, newspaper editorials poured in on the Government, urging Emily's appointment as Canada's first woman senator.

One woman said to Emily, "But wouldn't you be afraid of sixty-two men?"

"Afraid?" Emily exclaimed, "Why should I be afraid? I am used to co-operating with them. You see, my father was a man. I have four brothers, and I married a man. Indeed, and I've been obliged to send scores of men to jail!"

She was happy about the victory, happy, too, that so many people believed that the first appointment to the Senate should be hers. She read many letters in this vein:

> I want you to be Canada's first choice not because I like you — a woman's usual reason. Not because you're a success. Not because you're a "Who's Who" lady — but because I know you are honest of purpose, level of head, and because you're big enough to do for East and West. Just think of what you can do for Canada!

But the honour of being Canada's first woman senator was not to be hers. About a year after the winning of the case, the Government appointed Cairine Wilson, an eastern woman, to the Senate.

If Emily was disappointed, she showed no sign of it. When

asked to comment on Mrs. Wilson's appointment, her reply was characteristic. It was that all women should rejoice because, at last, a woman had been appointed to the Senate.

Emily was now sixty-two, and the years had lessened her tremendous energy. She resigned as magistrate in the fall of 1930, keeping only her responsibilities in the juvenile court. There was a great deal that she wanted to put down on paper, and she turned back to the writing she had left so long ago. She wrote in bed in the morning, using a large green wicker bed-table that a friend had sent her. Her walls were lined with deep shelves, jammed with her books and papers, including sheets of notes for unfinished books and articles. "I've so many bones in my back-yard to dig up!" she told a friend.

This was really the life she liked best, in her own family circle, reading, writing, thinking, sharing ideas with those she loved. In her early writing she had put on paper what was always her secret dream. It was the other side of Judge Emily Murphy's crusading public life. She wrote:

> The small, small house in the woods, and the black and white cow, and my churn that will go round and round and make little rolls of butter like to August corn in the ear . . . My four white hens that will plump out their feathers and scold at me, and a pontifically-mannered cockerel, like to flame colour . . .
>
> There will be a stream where I may fish for hours, and bathe on warm days. There will be no wires, or post office, or any church, but the Padre will say to me every day, "The Lord be with You;" whereupon I shall bow to him and make reply, "And with thy spirit."
>
> We shall have books a-plenty, and a fireplace. My pans will hang on the ends of book-cases, so that when I cook cakes or mix other things that are good for us to eat, the Padre may read to me. I will halt him and say: "Ho! Ho! Not so fast, sir! Just see what the brown book on the top shelf says about that."

How we will argue and laugh! Oh! we'll be great laughers, I can tell you. And of night the wind will make plaint in the trees and cry, so that we may be glad for the shelter and for the feel of the heat from the fire.

I shall one day find it, for so it is written; and may it happen, my gentle friend, that you may find one too.

Emily never found that life in its entirety, but during the last two years of her life she came close to it.

One day, having followed her customary habit of writing all morning in bed, she went to the library in the afternoon, where she wrote an article denouncing the CCF. At four o'clock, Evelyn drove her to visit Kathleen and her daughter, Emily Doris, of whom Emily was especially fond. On the way, she bought some raisin buns to share with her family and with some workmen who were renovating Kathleen's house. In her sleep that night, she sighed deeply, and was dead.

The Edmonton Journal, next day, published a poem by one of its young reporters, Lotta C. Dempsey, who had known and loved Emily Murphy since childhood:

TO A GREAT WOMAN

Paeons of praise they sing, because you stood
High in the world, and raised one steady hand
Against the wrongs that women suffer most . . .
And they shall call your name, because your pen
Was mighty as the sword, and followed swift
Upon long, deep injustice, and laid bare
The jagged danger of some hidden rift.
And we, who saw you far from lines of battle,
And knew the gentle tenor of your wit,
Who felt your quick response to all earth's beauty
And this great-heart that would be sharing it,
Who knew the quick forgiving of your spirit,
The tender sympathy for those who wait
Without the temple, and your quiet mercy —
Shall silent be, before one very great.

Ranch Wife

James M. Moir

All day she has followed
the solitary road
of her work and her thoughts
and now in the early evening
she opens the door
and looks out to the west
where a low sun touches grass tops
on the far side of the valley.
In the distance, a rider
moves across tawny fields.
A saddle horse, alone in the pasture,
flings up his head
and sends out a wild whinny
across the hills
as he sees loaded hay wagons
coming toward home.
A crow flaps heavily away
and there is a feeling in the air
that summer is fading
and change is near.
The woman's eyes brood.
She dreams of an English past;
she dreads the long winter
which shall imprison her.
The veery, that lost spirit,
calls from the trees.
Night, like a great river,
flows through the hills.

Not a Penny in the World

Barry Broadfoot

We come to Calgary in 1898 and then we moved out of there
about 10 miles and then my father died, so my mother she took
a homestead. Oh yes, a woman could take up land then, but
not many did. Not many. I don't know how she did it or how
she ever got the idea she could do it. A wonderful woman, my
mother, wonderful woman. Even today I don't know how she
managed.

See, she had no experience. We weren't farm people. We'd
come from the Falkland Islands, and if you know them there's
nothing there to farm.

I don't know how in the world she ever got along. Three
children, two sisters, and myself and not a penny in the world.
Somehow she got a roof over our heads. A neighbor or two
helped but she did it all, mostly. That's the kind of women there
were then. I wish I had a picture of her to show you. Not a big
woman but all this spirit. She knew she had to provide a home
for the three of us and that's how she did it, right out on the
prairie. She would work 18 hours a day. Absolutely.

At first she'd hire to get a little bit of plowing done when
she could get a dollar or two. She'd sell eggs in High River, and
sometimes women in the town would hire her for a day. She'd
walk in to town, work all day, walk back. For just a few cents.
Wages wasn't nothing in those days. Not too many people had
money and those that had it were awfully close with it.

First she got an acre plowed and that became a garden.
That's an awful lot of garden, but all of us worked in it. We
didn't go to school much but we sure worked around the place.
In that garden. Then the next year she got another acre plowed
and so forth, and after that I was big enough to drive a team
around and I plowed up the rest. I can't remember just where
she got the horses. I think she must have borrowed them or

maybe rented them, because I know we didn't own them. Horses in them days was expensive. So I was behind the plow. How old was I? Oh, 1905, let me see, I'd be about 10. Yes, I was 10 years old. It must have been quite a sight to see a 10-year-old boy behind a big team of horses plowing. It wasn't good land, it was fair land, some alkali, some sand, and I plowed up the whole shooting match.

Yes, I remember now. We rented the team from the money Mother used to make working for other people. She'd get a dollar and a half a day in harvest. She would cook, sometimes for as many as 21 men during harvest.

Between her and me we proved up that homestead and everybody was saying, "Oh, they'll never make it." But Mother just kept at it, working away and getting this done one year, that done the next year. A cow, more chickens, later a team. The neighbors were real good when they saw how hard we were all working, and they come and give us a hand.

It was my mother who did it. She just said she was going to have a home for us and that's all there was to it and she went and filed on that homestead. She'd never seen it but the map showed it was on a lake and she thought that would be nice. Having a home by a lake. She said, "That's the place I want," and she got it. And then she brought out all the things we had from the place west of Calgary and she rolled up her sleeves and pitched in. She worked 18 hours a day, that woman did. And when it was all over, all those years later when she had a nice farm, if you looked at her talking with other women in town on Saturday, just as quiet and gentle and lady-like, you wouldn't have believed that she could have done it.

Beyond the Call of Duty

Marjory Bellamy

In the year 1921, I was a young nurse-in-training in my home town of Dauphin, Manitoba. One fateful morning, I was assigned to care for the post-operative patients of the day. There were several tonsilectomies slated and one listed was Joe Bellamy of the RCMP. All the while that Cst. Bellamy was recovering from his anaesthetic, he raved about the recent loss of one of the detachment's prized horses. Cst. Parsons, while on duty, was riding along the railroad tracks one night and his horse was hit by a train and killed. Cst. Bellamy's wild eulogy in tribute to this dead horse was punctuated with loud demands as to who the heck I was and what did I think about the terrible accident. There seemed to be nothing for me to do but agree with everything he said and to assure him that I was very sorry indeed about the horse. Somehow, through this stormy tirade, I became impressed with Joe Bellamy and somehow, through the fog of anaesthetic, he must have drawn a few conclusions of his own. A week after his discharge from the hospital, the constable called to ask if I would like to go to the show with him.

I saw much of Cst. Bellamy after that though his duty hours and mine, and the fact that I was still studying, didn't make our courtship easy. Then there was the time we admitted a patient with smallpox and another nurse and I volunteered to care for him in total isolation — a small house on the edge of town. I saw very little of Joe in those two months. He did what he could for us, sometimes coming to the house to bring baking from my mother. But there was no sharing of the goodies over a cup of tea. We could only chat at a distance and then, when Joe left, I would go and retrieve the parcel where he had left it by the fence.

Joe and I became engaged on October the 5th, 1922. At

that time, a constable was required to have eleven years service in the Force before he was allowed permission to marry. As Joe had joined the Royal North-West Mounted Police only in 1919, after discharge from the Canadian Army, I wondered if I would ever become a Mountie's wife! However, special consideration was sometimes given to those who showed a record of good standing and this Joe received in 1926. We were married exactly four years to the day after we had become engaged. The detachment at Hodgson, Manitoba became my home for the next three years and it was here I learned what it meant to become apart of the RCMP family.

Hodgson, then, was a small town at the end of a CNR branch line. Across our back lane, just behind the yard, was the well-known Pequis Indian Reserve. Joe had been stationed in Hodgson a year before we were married so that when I arrived as his bride, we were made welcome by the many good friends he had come to know. They had a banquet prepared for us and presented us with many lovely gifts.

One of the first things I was to learn about living with a Mounted Policeman was that, in the necessary order of things, a wife ranked somewhere below the horses. And when your policeman was away on patrol without them, the horses ranked first with you because they still had to be fed and watered, exercised and watched. It didn't take me long to become acquainted with the stable routine and, despite myself, I grew very fond of some of the horses. Two in particular became my favorites — Chubby and Old Joe. Old Joe was a wily number. He had learned to unlock the gate into our back yard. One morning, I placed a couple of hot blueberry pies on the kitchen table near the back door. While I was gone for a minute, Old Joe walked in and helped himself to a pie. I can still see him backing out of the door with a hot pie in his mouth. The pie was a loss but I use the plate to this day!

The horse would often wander away, down the railroad track eating the lovely tall grass. When the time came to bring them home, I had only to walk to the tracks and call them. They could be a quarter of a mile away but on hearing my voice, they would come sauntering back and walk, one on each side of me, nuzzling and kissing me and looking for candy.

One year, our adored Chubby came down with swamp fever. To avoid destroying him, Joe and I worked night and day boiling tubs of water to make the huge foments that we needed to save his life. We used heavy wool blankets, wringing them out by hand and putting them over the horse's hind quarters. It was exhausting work and progress was slow but we persevered and Chubby eventually recovered. Then the first day that he was ridden, we saw his hind quarters sagging and we knew that Chubby would never be a saddle horse again. As such, he was no use to the Force and orders came to sell our beautiful Chubby. He was bought by a man who hauled wood into town and had often been up in court for mistreating his horses. I couldn't watch him take Chubby away. I went into the house and had a good old "cry".

I was used to many nursing duties but nothing had prepared me for what I had to deal with the morning we were awakened at 2 a.m. by a fisherman who had come to town that day. He stood at our door with his right arm ripped wide open, slit from his wrist almost to the shoulder. He reported that he had done it by lifting a box of fish but nothing less than a broken bottle could have done such a job. We put him on the constable's bed and, finding a bottle of liquor in his pocket, gave him a good stiff drink. Joe and Jack Cameron, the constable, held coal-oil lamps in one hand and held the man on the bed with the other while, with the few surgical supplies that I kept handy, I commenced repairing that arm. I put in thirty-nine stitches all together then dressed the wound and left the man sleeping on the constable's bed. Months later, he came back to thank me. He had seen a doctor in Gimli who had checked his arm and removed the sutures. "Who fixed your arm?" he asked the fisherman. "The Mountie's wife at

Hodgson," came the reply. "Well," said the doctor, "if you ever see her again, tell her she sure did a beautiful job." That was the best thanks I ever heard.

Word soon got around the district that the Mountie's new wife was a nurse. Calls for help came at any time and from many places. My first winter there, I made a day-long trip to Birchpoint to examine a mother and baby. To get there, we travelled first by dog team — from morning until supper time — and then another thirty miles across the lake by team and open cutter. After losing our way on the trail and crossing no less than three ice fissures, we arrived at the camp safely about 10 p.m. The patients were both very ill and I knew we must get them to Winnipeg and the care of the doctors there. I prepared them as best I could for the long trip to Hodgson by heated caboose and horses. We arrived at the detachment in time for me to make us breakfast and catch the train to Winnipeg. The stretcher was placed in the baggage car and I cared for the patients as best I could from the express man's hard wooden armchair. With a big cup of coffee and a bite of toast from the crew, I finally was able to relax. I returned home by train the following morning and the mother and baby, after making a good recovery, returned home some weeks later.

Another time, a man came for me in a horse and buggy and took me sixteen miles to Fisher Branch to be with his wife who was having a difficult labour. It was a terrible trip. I was sure the buggy wouldn't last on those rough roads, the horse looked half dead and the mosquitoes were the worst I'd ever seen. There was so much mud in the farmer's yard that I had to walk across single poles to reach the house and that wasn't the worst. I entered the house to be greeted by the squeal of pigs and the cackle of chickens. The fowl were even on the kitchen table. The room where my patient lay was no better. I looked around and thought, "Dear God, what can I do here?" I could do little. The baby was stillborn and before the end of the day, I had to inform the farmer that his wife, too, was dead. I drank a cup of tea at the kitchen table among the pigs and chickens, walked back across the poles to the buggy and drove home through the swarm of mosquitoes. Months later, the man came again. He wanted to thank me and he brought me two of his chickens. I thanked him warmly but I hadn't been able to forget the sight of that house and knew I could never eat anything that had come out of it. The chickens were passed along to a neighbour.

During our years of detachment life, I had the privilege of assisting at over seventy births. Fortunately, none of the others were as unhappy as that one nightmarish experience.

Those years at Hodgson, I used to like to accompany Joe on his various duties around the country. I particularly enjoyed treaty time on the reserve. I would go along to take in the dancing and excitement during the day then hurry home at night to feed the horses as Joe had to stay on the reserve all night. Those were the days of the home brew troubles and much time was spent searching for well-concealed stills. The men liked to have me along. While they did their investigating, I could keep an eye on the woman of the house. I'll never forget one such lady. Even though it was a beautiful day and her kitchen hot from the fire in her cookstove, she was wearing several dresses and four or five aprons. When finally the men had located the still, the dear old lady just smiled and gave me a loaf of home-made bread to take away with me. Another time, we were able to locate a still simply because someone reported that a certain farmer's chickens were acting in a peculiar way. Sure enough, the men dug up a still from under the floor of the chicken house.

In 1929, we were transferred to Gypsumville to open a detachment there. We will always think of that place as "Mushroom Town". We were greeted our first day by a group of children who brought us a heaping dishpanful of fresh mushrooms. They did this almost every day and we never tired of them. In fact, we still count a good feed of mushrooms a treat.

We were only to be at Gypsumville for six months as Joe was then transferred to Ottawa to work in the Fingerprint Bureau. Those were happy months and we remember still the thrill of the Christmas party; the sleigh rides to Rockcliffe. However, Joe wasn't cut out to be a city man. He missed being out of doors and he missed the challenges of detachment life. We were moved back to "D" Division, to Emerson detachment at the border.

We were into the dirty thirties then and it wasn't uncommon to have people at the door looking for a handout. One evening while I was alone, three men came looking for a place for the night. I was a little frightened and couldn't think what to do. On impulse, I sent them over to the local magistrate. The men informed the magistrate that the Mountie's wife had said he would put them up for the night. I suppose he could have been angry but he didn't let me down. He gave them a bed for the night — in the town lock-up!

We were still using horses at Emerson. I recall once when two constables arrived on the train bringing us two new horses. I thought one of them looked familiar but the constable didn't know his name. A check of the regimental numbers proved me correct. It was Brownie who had been with us at Gypsumville.

I still enjoyed going out with the men as often as was possible. For a while we had a bad time with cigarette smugglers at the border and I pride myself in being responsible for apprehending at least three of them. I had gone out one night with Joe and Ken Coulter, the constable, while they walked the tracks — a favourite spot for smugglers to hang out. They caught one man and brought him back to sit in the car with me while they went out once more. My prisoner tried to distract me with talk but as well as being aware of the fact that he was frantically stuffing cartons under the seat, I also kept an eagle eye on the road. Suddenly, I saw three men. We had previously decided that if I saw anything suspicious, I would give a low whistle. Well! I have never been very good at whistling and now that I had to do it, it was the hardest thing in the world. I rolled down the window and gave my feeble toot. Coulter responded and was able to apprehend the three men who were, indeed, smugglers. At least, I noticed all the way to the detachment that they occasionally tossed cartons out the window. I mentioned this to Ken and Joe and before long we had to stop the car and all get out to salvage some of the evidence.

One of the most nerve-wracking episodes that I endured as a Mounted Policeman's wife, involved the harmless business of checking out the safety of the patrol car. Coulter and I had taken a woman prisoner to Winnipeg. It seemed a logical time, to him, to put the car through a necessary safety check. At the RCMP garage, I was told I could stay in the car if I wished. All went well until it came time to test the brakes. One Mountie got into the car beside me while another one stood up ahead of us in front of a big cement wall. On signal from the man up ahead, we shot forward, heading for the cement wall at a terrifying rate of speed. I was sure it would be the end of all three of us. At the last possible moment, the man we were about to run down gave us another signal and my driver slammed on the brakes. They were adequate. We stopped in time but as the years passed, I have never fogotten the terror I felt as we were hurtling toward that cement wall. I have driven cars for fifty-five years now and I can tell you, my brakes are always set up high.

In October of 1935, we received word that we were being transferred to Norway House. Luckily, the call came early in the day because we were told to have all our belongings packed and on the train that night at 11 p.m. They had to be in Winnipeg immediately in order to catch the S.S. *Keenora* which would carry our goods up the length of Lake Winnipeg to Norway House. Well, we did it. Washed the dinner dishes, brought in the washing, packed the smaller items in boxes and crated the furniture. It was all on the train that night!

Despite the rush to pack, we ended up waiting a week in Winnipeg as the water on the lake was so rough the *Keenora* couldn't get away. I made good use of the time, going from store to store ordering the supplies we would need to last our first winter in the north. I was told I would need not only food for ourselves but also enough to feed the prisoners, some of whom would be in our jail for as long as six months. I must have been a little over-exuberant in my estimates of what we would need as, months later, when the Hudson's Bay Company post ran out of flour, I was able to let them have three hundred pounds of ours!

We arrived at Norway House in late October. It had been a beautifully warm month and I thought nothing of swimming across the river for my daily exercise. Then it turned cold suddenly and within the space of one day, people had great difficulty getting through the freezing water with their canoes. Next morning, the radio operator from the fort arrived at our door with a telegram. "How did you get across the river?" I asked him. "Walked across on the ice," he said confidently. "It's quite safe." "Well," I countered, "it might be safe for you but I swam across that river day before yesterday and it will be a good long time before I walk on it!"

We walked everywhere on the ice after that. The winter trails were merely paths on the frozen rivers. We either walked or travelled by dog team and occasionally one would see a horse and sleigh from one of the missions. I'm afraid I never got used to the terrific boom that often sounded right under your feet while walking on the ice.

It was at Norway House that I got acquainted with dog teams. I learned then what wonderful animals the sleigh dogs were though I never grew to trust them enough to attempt to touch one. Still, a little sadness always crept in when one grew old or sick and had to be destroyed.

The detachment quarters at Norway House was an old log building, re-covered long since with lumber siding. The huge, heavy doors and tiny square windows had been shipped over from Scotland at the time that the house was built. The police compound included a separate office and jail. We also had a huge garden which the prisoners looked after. Tubs and tubs of vegetables were harvested off our garden each year and I was kept busy canning the produce for winter. I never knew how many hungry men would be spending the winter in our jail house!

One day, I heard the prisoners complaining about their meals. It sounded an unlikely complaint as I'd made sure they were always well fed. I investigated and found that they were hungry for bannock. I gave the men what they needed and they cooked themselves a pile of bannock, baking it in an outdoor fire that they built on the rocks. I enjoyed some for my supper that night too.

Our mail came in just whenever it managed to get there. We could count on the first plane of the winter to come before Christmas. That caused great excitement. That day, I would forget the housework and simply sit on the floor going through huge bundles of mail. And we knew then that there would be weeks to wait before the mail came again.

I went for my first plane ride at Norway House. I sat in the back of the plane amid the bags of mail and freight. There was only one seat and that was for the pilot. In contrast to flying, I used to enjoy too the trips I made with Special Constable Jim McDonald and his dog team. We would often go out onto the bay to lift the net he had set under the ice. He fished in this manner to get food for the dogs.

When the time came to leave Norway House in 1938, I stayed behind for a month as the children at the fort had been ill with typhoid. I had been helping to care for them and it didn't seem right to leave my friends while they stilled needed me.

We spent a year at "D" Division Headquarters in Winnipeg and then Joe was transferred to Kenora, Ontario.

We arrived there the day war was declared. Next day, I went with Joe and the constable out into the surrounding area locating ex-R.C.M. Policemen and asking them to rejoin the Force for the duration of the war. We found several and some of them did enlist.

Many of the policemen handled extra duties during the war. Joe's patrols now took him far away — back into the north to Fort Severn, Slave Lake and James Bay. On those long trips I would find myself alone for six weeks at a time. Our life was due for a radical change, however. In 1943, Joe was offered another job and decided to take his discharge from the Force.

Those years of service in the RCMP have left me with many memories — memories of the good times and the bad, exciting times, difficult times and times of great pleasure. It seems to me, as I look back, that there was pleasure to be found in most things. Even the dreaded "Inspection Day" brought me some of my happiest moments. I remember at Hodgson, I always looked forward to the visit of Inspector Walter Munday. The inspection routine took all afternoon but in the evening, after dinner, we would play cards — "500" or four-handed cribbage. The expressman was always invited to dinner when Insp. Munday came. The inspector and I would be partners to play against Fred and Joe. Then at Norway House, it was Insp. Belcher who came up one summer. In the evening, we decided to all go over to Playgreen Inn. The inspector, busy rowing, started to sing. My, how he could sing! He had such a beautiful voice and I can still hear him singing all the old favourites, expecially "Rose Marie".

I have been able to attend many of the RCMP Centennial events in Winnipeg and have met again some of the men who worked with us so many years ago. One man I hadn't seen for forty-three years. In particular, I enjoyed the Centennial Review but, toward the end, I felt such deep regret that Joe couldn't be there to share it with me. The Review ended and I broke down and wept.

Ma Parsons

R. D. Symons

Mrs. Parsons is about ninety if she is still alive — and I bet she is. She was young at eighty-six when I saw her last. I used to ride with her son Allen, who was older than I, and a thoroughly good cow hand. Sometimes I used to ride over to their ranch of a Sunday, and have a good feed—Allen always said his ma was a first-rate hand at pies.

I knew the family had come from the East years before, over the plains by wagon; and between yarning with Allen and asking questions of the old lady I pieced together the story, which is a remarkable epic of pioneering not so much for the adventures encountered as for the lack of them.

She was born Rowena Webb, at Horning's Mill in old Ontario, in the days when it was Upper Canada and the third concession was 'way back in the bush. She was seventeen when she married Amos Parsons who had been her father's hired man; and like most young folks of those days they planned for a farm of their own. So they went to Manitoba. "Manitoba was turrible far in them days."

Amos was from what they call pioneer stock, which means he wasn't afraid to work. If he had been he would never have been able to work for Tom Webb, let alone marry his daughter. Tom's own father had hewn out a farm from the hardwood bush. And this is almost precisely what his son-in-law did, for he chose a homestead in the wooded valley of Swan River in sight of the blue heights of the Riding Mountain; and, granted that soft white poplar and bunchy willow fall to the axe more easily than maple and ash, still it took a worker to prove-up and get title.

But I won't go into details of grubbing willow crowns and urging the ox-drawn breaker plow through the heavy sod; of the building of the log shack; of the first crop of Red Fife wheat. Nor of Rowena's long winter evenings knitting for her growing family or the equally long summer days of housekeeping, chicken rearing, and gardening. Neither shall I more than mention the many anxious nights when her man was late coming from "town", as they called the little settlement where the trading was done — nights when she sat up, keeping the kettle hot; straining her ears for the creak and whine of sleigh runners, but hearing only the hiss of the wind-driven snow as it banked against the cabin; hoping he would see the guiding rays of the lantern she had hung at the gate.

I want to tell you of Rowena's crowning triumph — The Trip, as she called it.

Well, after many years on the homestead they made good; but as the farm became well established more settlers came, and then the railroad; and presently, to use Rowena's words, "a person didn't have room to swing a cat any more."

Amos got restless first.

"They say there's first-class cattle country 'way west; good grass and lots of room." A bit too dry for wheat; but he preferred cattle anyway. And he wanted to take a look at it.

So they talked it over. Amos wanted to take a look and perhaps get work with one of the ranchers, and he figured Rowena could run the farm for a bit. Allen was thirteen now and could handle the plowing and cutting, and the littler 'uns could stook the grain and do chores. If he settled on a place she could come out later and bring the family and the stock.

Rowena, at sight of his glowing face, knew her man had already made up his mind. She belonged to a breed of wise women who know that there is a type of man who has to follow a star; and she had the loyalty as well as the love which goes with that breed. So she never for a moment even considered that there was anything else she could do but stick it out and leave him to go his way.

And so it was arranged. Amos went to Swift Current, the

jumping-off place for the cattle country of what was then Assiniboia Territory. A year later found him herding cattle on Battle Creek, just south of the rolling Cypress Hills, where Canada touches the State of Montana among broken hills and scented sage flats. To the south, sixty miles away, rose the jagged peaks of the Bear Paws; to the southwest the triple buttes of the Sweetgrass Hills; to the north the timbered coulees and level high benches of the Cypress. Towns? Havre, Montana, a wild cow town, forty-five miles to the south on Milk River. To the northeast on the Canadian Pacific's transcontinental line, Maple Creek, a booming cattle town with its neat Mounted Police barracks. Neighbours? A few ranchers — Texans, down-East Canadians, English, and Scotch; a few Mounted Policemen and some half-breed horse breakers; plenty of half-wild range cattle, mustangs, antelope, and other animals of the plains. Roads? Prairie trails — twin grooves a few feet apart, worn by freight wagons in the grassy sod, winding snake-like between the low hills and over the gentle swells.

A big land of immense blue distances and great horizons. A dry land where grass is green only briefly in May and June, scorched to tawny and yellow and pinkish-grey in fall. A land of high plateaus and clear crisp air; of balmy spring breezes and January blizzards. But, as Amos had been told, a good cattle country — the very drying of the grass on the stem being a curing process which retained in the blade all the nourishment that stock required for winter grazing.

Amos had filed on a quarter by the creek, and had a small log shack sheltered against a cut bank, a few good saddle horses, and a Cripple Creek saddle. With grazing plentiful, he had a few dollars coming in and could see his way, as he would have said, to running a "spread".

So he sent for Rowena. He didn't bother her with details and instructions as to what to sell and what to bring, or how to do it. He knew Rowena; so he simply wrote:

Dear Rowena:

I have started a ranch on Battle Crick. Sell the
Farm or tell Lawyer Robson to sell it if you can't right
away. Bring the cows and oxen and wagons and
whatever you think we need. Allen better herd the
cattle along. If you start the first grass you'll get here
before freeze-up. When you get to Maple Crick go to
Trueman's barn and he will put you on the Havre trail.
Cross through the Cypress Gap and you will come to
the Police post at Ten Mile, and the fellow there will
show you the trail to our place; it's only a few miles
further. Take care of yourself and take it easy, and tell
the kids to be good.

Hoping this finds you and the kids fine as it leaves
me, I sign myself as usual,

Your loving husband.

P. S. I should of said theys plenty of good spring water
and some reel pretty flowers here, and you will like the
place.

So Rowena sold the farm — there were plenty of buyers in
those days, what with the new railroad and all — and set about
the business of packing. This was April, and new grass meant
about the end of May — plenty of time to get ready.

First to the bank, where she was told that a branch had
been opened in Swift Current. So she had most of the money
from the sale put through to Amos's credit there, carefully
keeping enough for incidental expenses on the way. Pioneer
women are good at business, even if they seem to handle it in
a funny way sometimes — as when she parcelled up the notes
and asked the bank manager to send them by registered mail
to the branch out West. He smiled and said "Sure"; and Ma
Parsons still swears that the identical notes of "my money"
made the long trip!

Finances being shipshape, her next concern was what to take and what to leave. The big oval daguerreotypes of Pa and Ma, in their gilt frames, simply had to be taken; and great was her concern over the packing of this evidence of her good Ontario parentage. She dusted Ma's photo with great care, remembering the old lady's injunction about not packing dirty things. Then there were the big cookstove, the heater, and the most substantial pieces of furniture; the chinaware, to be packed in barrels with the spare bedding; the kitchen utensils; and the special household treasures — especially the Good Book in which were recorded her wedding day and the children's birthdays. All the miscellaneous things, cleaned and sorted and packed, soon stood ready. The cookstove, the kitchen things, and the "using" bedding would be needed to the last minute, and had to be the last things loaded; and they would continue to be used on the way.

The two wagons were got ready. Tires had to be reset by the blacksmith, the wheels had to be well greased and the woodwork repaired. Two canvas tops had to be made, of heavy rough canvas that her sewing machine could not take; so she sewed them by hand, using an old sail-maker's palm that a sea-going uncle had given her for a souvenir when she was a little girl. Funny how things always come in handy if you keep them long enough!

Came a month of methodical work — taking it easy as Amos had said — during which she was helped by thirteen-year-old Allen, who was coming into his growth; and rather hindered by the four smaller fry, two girls and two boys. A month of packing, figuring, and planning, and all was ready. The caravan — not an uncommon one in those days — left Swan River, Manitoba, on a May morning of bright sunshine that made the poplar leaves as yellow as the breasts of the meadow larks which fluttered and whistled before them.

Rowena drove the first white-canopied wagon, perched high on the spring seat and handling the heavy leather ox reins with ease — for they drive oxen like horses in Manitoba, with bridles and bits. At the rear of the wagon she had set up her cookstove, its black pipe projecting through a neatly bound opening in the canvas, her flour barrel on one side of the stove and her pork barrel on the other; and here she cooked for six, three times a day. Rowena had wanted to bring at least one brood sow, but figuring it out she realized that the beast could hardly make it on foot with the cattle, and would take up too much room crated alive; and, as she said, "I like my pigs best in the pork barrels anyways." So that settled the problems of both transportation and of meat supply on the way. Her utensils hung close to hand in friendly company, frying-pan and kettles clanking against each other with every jolt of the wheels. In this wagon, too, she kept the rolled-up bedding by day. At night it was spread on the wagon floor for her and the girls, and on the prairie grass under the wagon for the three boys.

The second wagon had the big hayrack on it, and was packed tight with furniture and hand tools. It also carried the cutting bar of the mower, the wheel part of which was slung underneath. Here was a glorious miscellany of chattels, from the protesting hens in the crate at the back to the baby's cradle wedged in the middle, its interior crammed with winter clothing. The quietest and oldest oxen were hitched to this wagon; and there being no one to drive them, they were simply fastened to the front wagon by strong halter shanks, which meant careful driving to prevent a sudden speed-up breaking the ropes.

Behind the second wagon, and drawn by the simple expedient of having its shafts lashed to the wagon axle, came the shiny family buggy. Not for anything would Rowena have parted with that buggy. It was a symbol of prosperity and horsepower, marking the transition from the homesteader's oxen to the farmer's driving horses. The one horse, a Standardbred driver, free of the shafts, carried young Allen as he brought up the rear with the driven cattle — eight or nine milch cows and a scattering of yearlings, heifers soon to be cows, and steers for the family beef.

The party travelled southwest for about two weeks, following the old Fort Ellice trail and crossing the Qu'Appelle River near Spy Hill. Then they proceeded westward parallel to the Canadian Pacific Railway, built only a few years before and still the only railroad in the whole Northwest. Sometimes they were near it, sometimes far away, according to the trail; sometimes they came close enough to one of the string of mushroom towns to camp on the outskirts and do a little small shopping or have minor repairs made to the vehicles. Some days they travelled only seven or eight miles, on others ten or fifteen; but not once did they move on a Sunday.

On the fine mornings all but the two youngest children — three-year-old Jessie and the baby, born after her father had left Manitoba — walked beside the wagons or else behind, helping Allen with the stock; sometimes running off the trail to look at a bird's nest in the grass, or pick the lovely harebells that nodded their blue heads all day. Their hard little feet, accustomed to being unshod in summer, scuffed the dust of the trail or scampered over prickly bull thistles with equal disregard. On the rainy days, or when the strong west wind whipped the grasses low and sent dust devils whirling from horizon to horizon, Rowena made them stay under cover. Rain on a bare head, she averred, never did any good and too much wind took the breath away.

And all the way across the plains this woman attended to her housework and chores in the same steady, orderly fashion that she had learnt as a girl. With one exception — wash-day was not Monday but Saturday. I have already indicated that Rowena was no "Sabbath breaker" (as she would have said), and under no circumstances would she travel on the first day of the week. But she soon found that washing hung out to dry on and about the moving wagons picked up plenty of fine black dust, and that it would be necessary to stop and camp in order to dry the weekly wash properly; so she wisely altered the old family routine and washed at Saturday night's camp, hanging the clothes on a line between the wagons. And there they stayed all day Sunday, to be gathered clean and fresh as prairie herbs early on Monday morning.

She bathed the children first and washed the clothes afterwards, reheating the water in the big pot, as the children called the rotund and heavy cauldron which had started life boiling maple sap in the far-off bush days. Sunday morning saw neat, clean children in a neat camp, gathered round their mother as she read from the Bible — stories of wanderings in strange lands, of hunger and thirst and deliverance — while the row of small garments flapped bravely on the line and the oxen lay down with contented grunts to chew their morning cud.

"It didn't hardly look right," says Rowena, "to be reading from Scripture with the kids' underwear a-flapping; but anyhow I knew them clothes hadn't been washed on a Sunda, and I weren't going to take them down on a Sunda."

After three weeks or more of travelling over the park-like prairies to the Qu'appelle, they began to leave the poplar and willow groves behind and come into more level and open plains. They missed the friendliness of the groves and they missed the hundreds of shining sloughs with their throngs of wild-fowl — green-headed mallard, graceful pintails, broad-billed shovellers, various small teal and the black-and-white scaup ducks. The grass began to get shorter and finer — real prairie wool — and they began to see birds which were strange to them — small black ones with white wing patches, which the children called at once "white-wings", not knowing that they were lark buntings.

Rowena somehow always had a bright fire in her stove and water in the barrel lashed to the wagon's creaking side. Word always seemed to go ahead that a woman and kids were on their way west, so that sometimes when Rowena asked at a homesteader's sod shack or a constructor's camp as to the best place for water or grass she found that she was already expected, and so had leave to camp by someone's well; or she might be directed to a creek or spring.

When the scanty waterside willows permitted, the smaller children were set to work gathering dry twigs and branches; but otherwise their fuel was dried dung picked up on the prairie — "cow chips" as they called them, and mighty good fuel as every old-timer knows.

In the evening the cows had to be milked and the warm milk set in pans overnight for the cream to rise. In the morning she skimmed it off and gave what was left to the calves — two of which had been dropped on the way, and were now crammed somehow into the second wagon. In addition, the morning's milk went directly to them — or at least as much as they could take. What the children and the calves could not drink had to be thrown away, as the cream would not rise during the daytime travelling. Her faithful barrel churn hung at the wagon's back, and twice a week the cream was put in it and turned to yellow butter by the ceaseless jolting and swaying of the wagon as it followed the uneven trail; so that at the evening camp it could be worked in the wooden bowl, salted, and pressed away in the big stone crocks.

As the July heat ripened the wild strawberries and saskatoons, there was many a feast of fresh fruit and cream to vary the monotony of salt pork, bread, porridge, and prunes. To smell that home-made bread and see that firm butter was almost as good as eating it; and what with a few eggs from the hens and plenty of thick cream on the breakfast oats Queen Victoria herself fared no better.

Not that things always ran smoothly. The cows drifted off one stormy night and Rowena and Allen had to thrash about in the wet till daybreak rounding them up — only to find that in their absence Jessie had walked in her sleep, upsetting the sponge for the next day's bread and putting the whole camp in an uproar. And there was the loneliness to fight, for a grown woman yearns for somebody more "talkable" that a thirteen-year-old, and a boy at that; and some of the nights were very dark, and the coyotes' howling didn't make them any better.

Some nights she would wake with a feeling that something was wrong, and reaching out her hand would touch the rough side of the wagon box and suddenly remember that she was out on the lone prairie with her small children dependent on her. But remembering Allen, almost a man, heartened her and she would sometimes call out, "Are you awake, son?" and Allen would sleepily answer that he was. "Go to sleep, Ma, everything is all right, and I'm keeping Jim covered."

Mosquitoes were a plague. On still evenings they appeared in grey clouds in the long grass around the sloughs and drove the stock almost frantic at times, as well as attacking the humans. The children's legs looked quite "measly", as they laughingly told one another. But as the drier weather and the party's arrival into the shorter grass of the cattle country thinned the humming ranks of these insects, the party got respite and were gradually able to discontinue the smudge-pot of cow chips and green grass, and the children could stop scratching their legs.

They rose early and breakfasted early. But by the time the cows were gathered and the milking done and everything packed, it was usually about eight o'clock before they were off. Oxen are no good in the heat of the day so they made noon camp about eleven o'clock, and while the oxen rested and grazed Rowena would iron or mend or sometimes take a nap, while the elder children looked for berries. At three in the afternoon they would be on the trail again till six, when it would be time to make the night camp.

So they travelled on as spring gradually turned to summer and the prairie became bright with sunflowers; and summer itself began to age, and the grasses ripened with the smell of new-mown hay; and the young gophers could be seen almost as big as their parents as they peeped and whistled from their holes.

Suns rose like molten discs from behind the horizon's rim. Day breezes freshened and swept the grass into waves and ripples, and blew the brown pipits before the wagons like autumn leaves. After a morning's run the children loved to lie back in the buggy and watch the procession of great fleecy clouds with turreted tops like castles, slowly and steadily moving overhead. Suns set slowly, gloriously, as only on the plains they can; cool nights followed burning days and sage-scented twilights.

And this woman, with her little world for which she was responsible, went on to where her man waited. Cook, house-keeper, teamster, stockman; doctor, nurse, preacher, dairy-maid — such was Ma Parsons. And she did all this in a per-fectly natural, contented, and efficient manner that left no room for stupid anxieties or useless grumbling. She knew that she could hurry along and make the trip in little more than half the time. But she also knew the cost to the cattle, the vehicles, and her own nerves (though she wouldn't have understood that word!) of hurrying and bustling and being impatient. And she reckoned to arrive with the "hull kit an' boodle" safe and sound.

So it was well into August before they got to Maple Creek, nearly 700 miles from their starting point. There Trueman took care of their animals for a day or two, while his missus took care of Rowena's youngest children so that Rowena herself could do a little shopping at Dixon's store and generally freshen up before starting on the last lap. And since one of the young policemen was making a patrol to Ten Mile, Trueman — who was well acquainted with the police through supplying fodder for their horses — asked him to let Amos Parson know that his wife and kids had arrived from Manitoba.

So it came to pass that, having been duly put on the Havre trail by their friend, they were making noon camp at Fish Creek when Amos himself rode up.

The baby was frightened of her father, but they all finally got settled down; and in the evening, talking more quietly as the children slept, Rowena may have told Amos about the nights she was a bit scared. And she was proud to show him that she had made enough butter to do them all winter in case the cows dried up with the cold weather, and knitted a full supply of winter socks and mitts and scarfs.

She did like the ranch and soon set about making the cabin more homelike. And they prospered as they deserved, in cattle and land; but better than that they had three more children, making eight in all.

Mrs. Parsons became Ma to most of the bachelors for miles around, though she was no older than most of them, and could trip it at the cowboy dances with the best — yes, and make the finest coffee afterwards while they all waited till daylight to go home.

When I last saw Ma Parsons, not so long ago, she sat in her big rocking-chair on the ranch porch, as happy and hearty and as full of fun as ever. Allen, a great hulking chap with rough red whiskers, himself the father of four or five, had stopped in as he was riding by and clanked through the kitchen and had to be spoken to by his mother who "never could abide spurs in my house".

I would hardly dare call Mrs. Parsons a heroine. She wouldn't like it. She thinks a "heroeen" is some woman who does something extraordinarily brave and marvellous.

The Enigma of Bill Miner

F. W. Lindsay

Anyone travelling from Merrit to Princeton must inevitably pass through a small settlement called Aspen Grove. This beauty spot has an added romance because not far from here lies a small ranch, once owned by a gentle, kindly man named George Edwards. Edwards was beloved by everyone. He was an expert with horses and cattle, a skilled shoe-maker who cobbled many pairs of shoes for children who would not otherwise have had any, a wonderful dancer and a virtuoso with the old time fiddle. He was a religious man who loved children and sometimes taught Sunday School. On one occasion it was said he preached an excellent sermon when the Presbyterian minister failed to arrive at the church. In short, Mr. Edwards was all that a mid-Victorian society could ask for in a citizen of British Columbia.

But Mr. Edwards, who had friends in many B.C. towns, was much more than first class citizen. He was also a first class bandit. Kentucky born and Texas raised, he served his apprenticeship in the gentle art of stage-coach robbery while still in his teens. Historians state it was he who first used the phrase, "Hands up" and that his initial stick-up netted him $75,000.

When stage coaches became obsolete, Mr. Edwards, known to the fraternity of the "road" as Bill Miner, turned his attention to trains. It is possible that his excitement-craving nature found even more thrills in holding up a train than in stopping a stage coach. Certainly it required a greal deal more advance planning and clock-work precision to stage a train hold up. The train must be secretly boarded, the engineer, fireman and perhaps the conductor or a brakeman commandeered to cut the baggage or mail car from the main section of the train at the place where waiting horses would provide a get-away; the mail clerks over-powered, the safe or strong box blown open and escape made good before other crewmen or passengers suspected anything was wrong. Both stage and train robbers required cool courage and courage was one of Bill Miner's great assets. Kindliness was another and the ability to act yet another.

Bill Miner was a badman alright, but a good badman — a gallant badman. He never intentionally caused bodily harm and his code forbade theft from an individual. His robberies were directed at large companies who he felt had gained their wealth by robbing the public. His ethics were those of a Robin Hood, his escape wizardry that of Houdini. His gentle ways and protectiveness toward women and children were recalled by Mrs. Maisie Hurley in a letter to the editor, published in the *Vancouver News Herald* in 1954. She wrote:

> I am another of Bill Miner's old pals and I back Mrs. Frampton in saying he was a fine gentleman. I knew him in Aspen Grove in 1905 as George Edwards and often rode with him. . . . I remember the time (he) made me a little skating rink by flooding a patch in Dodd's cow pasture near Ducks, B.C. and all the while lecturing me as follows: "Never be a bigot, little 'un, never interfere with a man's religion," he said. "If he prays, be thankful that he prays."
>
> Miner loved children and respected women and afterwards when I knew it was my friend they had caught at Douglas Lake for holding up the CPR at Ducks, I wept. He educated 18 children from the proceeds of his profession, never held up people, only companies. He never refused to help anyone in need.

Another story tells of his kindness to one of his neighbors in the Nicola Valley, a widow with several children. He took many presents to the children and during his time there as a rancher, the woman regularly received an envelope containing money from an anonymous friend. The money stopped coming when Bill Miner was captured.

Miner spent more than half of his life in some fifteen different penitentiaries, yet he always managed to shorten his sentence through good behavior or escape. His uncanny escapes became notorious. One was the subject of a lengthy debate in the federal parliament.

When he was nineteen years old he got three years in San Quentin for sticking up a Wells Fargo stage. This was on April 5th, 1866. The young Bill Miner, however, had such a gentle air and such a persuasive tongue that he was released by court order three months later in June of 1866. In July of that eventful year, Miner held up a stage coach in Colorado and was given five years in the pokey. He was apparently an ideal prisoner for in 1870 he was paroled with one year off his sentence for good behavior.

In 1871 Miner, who by now was becoming noted as a gentlemanly bandit, engineered the robbery of a bank in Calaveras County in the golden state of California. He was caught. An unkindly judge, one who frowned on highwaymen, sentenced Bill to ten years in jail. Again Bill wooed and won the hand of leniency, for in January of 1872 he was once more discharged from durance vile.

By this time anyone but Bill Miner, it seems, would have learned his lesson and gone into some more legalized form of banditry. Not Bill Miner. He did not hide behind legal loopholes, sharp business practices or any of the customary camouflages which make more flagrant forms of robbery acceptable. He was an honest robber who stuck to his aboveboard trade of ordering, "Hands up".

For the next job he took on a partner, joining up with a character called Billy LeRoy, an infamous Rocky Mountain stage coach robber and holdup man. Together they stuck up the Del Norte stage in May of 1872 and cleaned the strong box of $3,600. A vigilance committee cornered them in a dead-end canyon, captured Billy LeRoy and hung him. Miner miraculously escaped with the loot.

Bill should have quit when he was winning, but the art of robbery was like a drug. He hung around Del Norte, pulling a few jobs to keep his hand in and finally defied the law by pulling a second holdup of the Del Norte stage. Luck temporarily deserted him. A posse trailed him clear to Sacramento where he was captured.

This time they threw the book at him and he caught thirteen years in San Quentin. Eight years later Bill was free again, with five years off for exemplary behavior. He was quiet for most of 1880. He got out sometime in February and wasn't heard of again until 1881, when single-handed, he held up a train of the Oregon Railway and Navigation Company at a place called Corbett and took $37,000.

Again our Bill was caught and again the judge took a serious view of his activities. Twenty-five years in San Quentin prison was the sentence. Twenty-five years can make a big hole in a man's life, but Miner didn't kick about it. He became a model inmate and did the stretch in twenty years.

By now Mr. Miner at 60 was somewhat tired of the hospitality of the State of California and headed north for British Columbia, leaving his name and identity behind him. He settled in the Nicola Valley but also had a cabin down at Haney. Everybody liked the kindly rancher, George Edwards, who was able to live a completely double life, changing at will into Bill Miner, the bold train bandit.

After a few years dormancy, during which George Edwards played the star role of gentleman farmer in B.C., Bill Miner stole the show again in his role of train robber. The setting was Mission Junction, the train a crack Canadian Pacific passenger, the time a Saturday night about 9:30 p.m. on September 10th, 1904. Miner had driven a small band of horses from Aspen Grove over the Hope trail into the Fraser Valley and sold them there. He made camp on the south side of the river and after dark crossed over to the CPR main line at Silverdale, 4 1/2 miles west of Mission and pulled off the first train robbery in Canada. Miner and 2 companions handled the job with aplomb and escaped with $6,000 in Cariboo gold dust and $1,000 in currency. It was also claimed that he got an $80,000 bearer bond, which later figured in a great many rumors, but nothing was ever proved.

However, no one suspected him of having anything to do with the Mission train robbery. He breakfasted with friends the next day and nonchalantly discussed the hold-up with them.

For almost two years George Edwards lived comfortably land contentedly on his share of the take. Then in the spring of 1906 Bill Miner the bandit decided to make one last big haul and leave the stage to Edwards. He received a tip-off about a shipment of gold bars from the Nickel Plate Mine at Hedley worth $35,000 and organized a small gang which included a young unemployed Ontario school teacher named Louis Colquhoun and a poetic prospector named Shorty Dunn. Shorty was a similar type to Miner himself, except that this was Shorty's first and last adventure in train robbing. Besides the accomplice who gave the tip, there was also a horse trader, name unknown, who didn't attend to the horses properly and thus botched the escape of Miner and his companions.

That was the second and fatal error. The first mistake occurred after the 3 bandits boarded the westbound CPR mail train at Ducks, 17 miles east of Kamloops, that bright moonlit night in May 1906. Miner and Dunn climbed into the cab to cover the engineer and the fireman. Miner ordered the train stopped at the 116 mile post and there was almost an accident there. A fast-moving train cannot be brought to an immediate stop and Shorty, the novice bandit, became agitated and threatened the engineer with his gun. Fortunately the train slackened speed about then and Shorty's fears were allayed.

Miner remained in the cab with the engineer, while Shorty went back with the fireman to uncouple the mail car, being unaware (as was Miner) that there were two mail cars on that train. They cut off the first one and had the engine haul it ahead some distance to a point near where their horses were supposed to be waiting. But instead of scooping up $35,000 worth of bullion, they ended with a lousy hundred dollar take. When they discovered the gold shipment was in the second mail car, it was too risky to go back for it — and two of the get-away horses had broken loose, so the escaping bandits had only one horse between the three of them.

The train pulled into Kamloops only forty-five minutes late and the district was soon swarming with police. This was twice in two years the CPR had been hit and it rocked the powers that were. Repercussions were felt from Bay Street to the drawing rooms of stately homes in England. There were bitter denunciations in boardrooms and exclusive clubs. A reward of $12,000 was posted for the capture of train robber, William Miner.

Twelve thousand dollars in those days was enough for a man to retire on. Cowboys, trappers, miners, Indian trackers — practically everybody who could ride, walk, creep or crawl joined the hunt for the train robbers.

However, the bandits were actually captured by a group of Royal North-West Mounted Police who had been called in from Alberta to help in the hunt. Five of them were searching the bush country around Douglas Lake when Constable Fernie of the B.C. Provincial Police rode up and said he'd spotted three men who he thought were the ones wanted. He led the Mounties to the place where he'd seen their campfire and found the men eating lunch.

When accosted, the oldest of the three said they were prospectors and had a ranch near Quilchena. On being told that they answered the description of the train robbers, Shorty Dunn panicked. "Look out boys, it's all off!" he yelled and started running and shooting. One of the constables stopped him with a bullet in the leg.

And so the bandits were captured — and one of the most written-about and talked-about episodes in B.C.'s history opened to the public for a six-year run — The Case of Bill Miner. As one of the constables was searching Miner, a tattoo mark on the bandit's left thumb made him gape in astonishment. "Look at this!" he exclaimed. The officers then realized that they had captured much more than the Ducks bandits. This was Bill Miner, notorious American train robber with a $20,000 reward on his head.

The three men were bound and taken back to the Douglas Lake ranch on a passing stone boat. Graves, the ranch manager, insisted there must be some mistake. One of these men was George Edwards, he said, a rancher whom he knew well.

When the constables and their prisoners arrived at Quilchena and the bandits were placed under heavy guard in the schoolhouse, a near-lynching boiled up — lynching to rescue a man, not to hang him.

Residents of the area were incensed at the idea of their kindly neighbor, George Edwards, being accused of a train hold-up. The saloons were overflowing with indignant, gesturing men and finally had to be closed by order of the police to keep the peace.

The constables hustled their prisoners to the Kamloops jail, but even on the road they were accosted by two men in a buggy who claimed they were Provincial Police and demanded that the prisoners be handed over to them.

At their trial in Kamloops, in spite of the most positive identification and the fact that Miner was in possession of a CPR revolver, the jury disagreed and they were held over for another trial.

At a second trial they were found guilty. Bill Miner and Shorty Dunn were given life sentences. Louis Colquhoun as a first offender, was let off with 25 years.

That was 1906. A year later Bill Miner was once more

outside the prison wall. His unbelievable escape brought extras rolling off presses all over the continent. No radio bulletin or TeeVee news flash could compare with the electrifying cries of the newsboys calling, "Extry-extry! Read about Bill Miner's Escape."

It was a thrilling piece of news for the average citizen, to whom Bill Miner had become a favorite daredevil. His dual personality of gentleness and audacity was the ideal mixture for kindling affectionate admiration. His escape represented a wish-fulfillment in thousands of hearts beating out a routine existence.

But to the warden and deputy warden, guards, inspectors of penitentiaries, the Hon. Minister of Justice and many others, even including the Prime Minister, Sir Wilfred Laurier, the escape and subsequent investigations and insinuations caused endless embarrassment over a period of several years.

Miner escaped in broad daylight with 2 guards watching over 29 prisoners at work in the brick yards, while a third guard stood watch in a 150 foot high look-out tower. It was said that Miner crawled under a fence through a hole dug by a confederate, dashed across a wide field and scaled a second fence by means of a ladder, conveniently lying nearby. Another story says he slipped through the gate on which the lock had been broken. Three other men escaped with him, but their names have faded into history. Even at the time they were hardly noticed. It was Miner whom folks cared about.

Quite a few minutes elapsed before the men were missed. More time was lost while the remaining prisoners were returned to their cells for security. When the alarm finally sounded and a search began, Miner had a good head start. Dozens of rumors were followed through but not one proved to be a useful clue.

However, several days after the escape, a hospitable rancher on Nicomen Island reported having fed a man answering to Miner's description, who was suffering from foot trouble. He ate an enormous meal, stowing away a whole loaf of bread, several servings of meat and preserves and innumerable cups of coffee — and then vanished.

The warden at Okalla was ill when Miner escaped, but Bourke, his deputy, sent a telegram to the Inspectors of Penitentiaries at Ottawa, informing them that four prisoners had escaped. The following day he sent another telegram stating that Bill Miner was one of the escapees and requesting permission to post a reward.

Several days went by with no answer to his wires. Finally, when Inspector Dawson started an investigation, he is said to have given Bourke a dressing down for directing the wire to him personally instead of to "The Inspectors", claiming that since he was away when it arrived, much valuable time was lost before it received attention. Warden Bourke said he had indeed addressed it correctly to "The Inspectors" and produced a copy of the wire from the Telegraph office to prove his point. Who then had changed the address?

There appeared to be no satisfactory answer to this or many other peculiar incidents surrounding Miner's escape. Rumors were sizzling that the $80,000 bearer bond, said to have been part of Miner's haul from the first train robbery, had played an important part in Miner's escape. It was claimed that Miner had been permitted certain visitors contrary to prison regulations, that these privileges were connived at by the prison inspector and that one of these visits was from the chief detective of the CPR who called regarding the stolen bond.

This story was officially contradicted more than a year later when Mr. J. D. Taylor, MP from New Westminster, read an item in the House of Commons at Ottawa on March 2nd, 1909, during one of several hot debates on the Miner escape. Said Mr. Taylor:

> I propose to read an extract from the *Vancouver Province*, a most influential and independent newspaper published at Vancouver, a paper I may say

of the highest respectability and responsibility and which I am sure would not publish a paragraph of this kind except on the most unquestioned authority. I read from the *Vancouver Daily Province* of the 12th of February this statement. . . .

"An official who is in a position to speak authoritatively on the subject of Bill Miner's escape from the penitentiary at New Westminster this morning made the following statement for publication:

'At the time of the investigation into the escape made by Inspector Dawson, I could have told him, had I been called upon to testify, that Bill Miner did not escape from prison by crawling under the fence through the hole through which it was alleged he went. No man ever crawled through that hole for two good reasons. The first was that the hole was not large enough; the second because the hole was made only for the purpose of covering the letting out of Mr. Miner. The story of the loss of $50,000 worth of bonds or money by the Canadian Pacific Railway or anyone else in the robbery and that it had been cached by Miner was an invention in the interests of the robber himself. No one ever lost that sum; no bonds were ever stolen. Miner's friends on the outside called on him and conducted fake negotiations for his so-called escape and the securing of the cached money. Certain persons made it possible for Miner to escape, apparently on the understanding that he would divide up on the booty. These facts can easily be proved if the government makes an investigation.

Much political fodder was made of all this and other information which came to light in the months following Miner's escape on August 8th, 1907. It appeared that Miner had developed eczema which spread into his hair and beard, thus preventing the poor man from shaving or having his hair cut for several months. When he escaped, he didn't look like a convict at all. And it wasn't until four or five days had gone by that authorities remembered to correct his discrepancy in the published description of Miner. Of course if Miner stopped rubbing dirt into the scratches on his face and scalp, the eczema would disappear and all would be well.

A question was raised in parliament as to who had given permisson for Miner to let his hair and moustache grow. Another question, according to the Hansard report of March 2nd, 1909, was brought up by Mr. R. L. Borden, Leader of the Opposition, who asked:

> What is the meaning of the extraordinary apologetic attitude assumed in this House by the Minister of Justice towards this man Bourke? . . . He (Bourke) has been charging that officials for whom the Minister of Justice is responsible in this House have connived in that escape.

Deputy Warden Bourke had been "allowed to resign" after Miner's escape and received his full superannuation allowance. It was suggested in the House that he knew enough to make things politically uncomfortable for certain persons in the Department of Justice. An impartial inquiry into the whole affair was demanded by Mr. Martin Burrell, MP for Yale-Cariboo, who said:

> The capture of this convict was a credit to the police system of the country and his sentence strengthened the confidence of the public in the administration of justice in Canada and now that he has escaped . . . and in view of the unrest in the public mind about the circumstances of the escape of this notorious criminal, is it not time that we should have an impartial inquiry, not an inquiry at the hands of Inspector Dawson who

is hopelessly mixed up in it, but a thorough inquiry conducted by some impartial tribunal.

And the Prime Minister, Sir Wilfred Laurier, speaking in the House, declared:

> The question which interests the country . . . is whether there has been any connivance on the part of anybody in the escape of Miner. No more dangerous criminal, I think, was ever in the clutches of Canadian justice. It was a fact for which we took some credit that when one of these American desperados came to Canada, thinking to play with impunity in this country the pranks he had been playing on the other side of the line, he was arrested, tried and convicted. It was a shock when we heard, and we heard it with a good deal of shame also, that he had subsequently been allowed to escape the penitentiary.

In defence of his position, the honorable Minister of Justice, Mr. Aylesworth, replied:

> "No person in this country can regret the fact of his escape more than I do. . . . What is to be done about it? What can be done? Every exertion that I was able to think of was made at the time to capture the man. Only the other day one of the four men who escaped with him was recaptured and is now in custody. At any moment, any day, Miner may be recaptured.

But Miner was never recaptured — at least not by Canadian authorities. And no investigation was undertaken, nor was any attempt made to inquire whether any bonds were in fact stolen at the time of the train robbery and if so, what had become of them. No blame was fixed on anyone for Miner's escape, no punishment meted out and no reward offered for his re-capture.

While members of parliament sparred with one another

over the circumstances of Miner's escape, Bill Miner himself was far from the scenes of any of his former tilts with the law. It is said that old soldiers never die. It seems that old bandits never quit. There was a lull of four years with no news of the escaped train robber. Bill Miner fans no doubt believed they had thrilled to the last headline and witnessed the final scene of daring robbery and desperate escape by their favorite player.

Not a bit of it. In February 1911 a news story of the first train robbery in the state came from far away Georgia — like an echo of an earlier performance, and, echo-like, following in swift succession, the well-known pattern of conviction and escape. It was the old stager — the man with the tattooed thumb — Bill Miner.

In November 1911 he was recaptured. Facing a life sentence at 65, the old bandit asked permission to return to Okalla at New Westminister to serve out his time. "I never was so well treated there," he told the judge, adding "and I've been in a lot of prisons."

Had his request been granted, he would have been too late to greet one of his former Ducks accomplices. On September 23, 1911, Louis Colquhoun, the handsome young school teacher, son of a respected Ontario family, turned his face to the prison wall and died of advanced T.B. — with only 5 years of his 25 year sentence served. Thus of the 3 convicted bandits, Colquhoun, the youngest, was the only one to serve a life sentence.

The third man, little Shorty Dunn, the nervous novice, was paroled in 1918 and moved to Ootsa Lake in central British Columbia where he lived as William Grell, a respected and well liked citizen, until his death by drowning in 1927.

Bill Miner's plea to be returned to New Westminister was not granted — so he filed his shackles in the Georgia state convict farm and set out on his own. There we must leave him, for like the modern novel, this true life story leaves the ending to the reader's choice.

Some rumors floated up from Georgia that Miner had died in the prison hospital. But others, equally possible, told of his rendezvous with some old time colleagues who were headed for South America via Mexico and that Miner starred in several dramatic escapades in those countries before going to his reward.

As a Miner fan from early childhood, this writer chooses the latter ending.

Acknowledgements

The editor wishes to thank the authors and publishers for permission to include the following in this anthology:

Gordon Burles for "Bill Peyto Alone".

Calgary Power Ltd. for the following radio spots by Jacques Hamilton from "Our Alberta Heritage": "Canada's 'Indian' Senator", "Grant McConachie", "Punch Dickins", "George 'Kootenai' Brown", "C. W. Gordon (Ralph Connor)", "The Greatest Rider in the World", "The $100,000 Dream", and for "Frank Mewburn, Surgeon".

Canadian Council of Teachers of English for "Volunteer" by Debby Caplan from *Pandora's Box: A Collection of Poems by Canadian Students* (1973).

The Canadian Publishers, McClelland and Stewart Limited for "Grandfather" by George Bowering from *Touch: Selected Poems 1960-1970*. For "Bishop Bompas" by Ed Tait from *Famous Canadian Stories*.

The Centennial Book Committee for "Beyond the Call of Duty" by Marjory Bellamy from *Red Serge Wives*.

John W. Chalmers for "Tekahionwake" from *The Alberta Historical Review*, 1974.

Clarke, Irwin & Company Limited for "Emily Murphy" by Byrne Hope Sanders from *Famous Women*.

Doubleday Canada Limited for "Not a Penny in the World" by Barry Broadfoot from *The Pioneer Years: 1895-1914: Memories of Settlers Who Opened the West*, (1976).

Fitzhenry & Whiteside Ltd for "Son of a Great Nation" by Carlotta Hacker from *Crowfoot*. For "Bobby Clarke" by Fred McFadden.

Ruth Gorman for "Jimmy Simpson of Num-Ti-Jah" from *Golden West Magazine* (1968).

Helen FitzPatrick for "The Swimming Smiths".

Gage Publishing Limited for "Ranch Wife" by James M. Moir from *Family Chronicle*.

Hancock House Publishers Ltd. for "Words to a Grandchild" by Chief Dan George from *My Heart Soars*.

House of Anansi Press Limited for "the witch" by Terrence Heath from *The Truth and Other Stories*.

Hurtig Publishers for "Death of a Son" by Hugh Dempsey from *Crowfoot: Chief of the Blackfeet*. For "Goofy McMasters" by Tony Cashman from *The Best Edmonton Stories*.

Longman Canada Limited for "Ma Parsons" by R. D. Symons from *Many Trails*.

Macmillan Company of Canada Ltd. for "Jerry Potts" by Andrew Suknaski from *Wood Mountain Poems*.

Mrs. Margaret McCourt for "A War Chief Dies" by Edward A. McCourt from *Buckskin Brigadier: The Story of the Alberta Field Force*.

McGraw-Hill Ryerson Limited for "Bull Head: The Fearsome Sarcee", "Red Crow: Mekaisto of the Bloods" and for "Tom Three Persons: Cowboy Champion of 1912" by J. W. Grant MacEwan from *Portraits from the Plains* (1971). For "The Men That Don't Fit In" by Robert W. Service from *Later Collected Verse*. For "Brother Jim" by Robert W. Service from *The Collected Poems of Robert Service*.

Methuen Publications for "Dan George: A Noble Man" by Terry Angus and Shirley White from *Canadians All: Portraits of Our People* (1976).

Nancy Greene Limited for "The Gold Medal" by Nancy Greene with Jack Batten from *Nancy Greene*.

Ellen Neal for "The Cactus Bloom" from *Spirit of Canada*.

Reader's Digest Magazines Limited for "Emergency Operation!" by John Braddock (1977). For "Suzuki: The Prime-Time Scientist" by David Spurgeon (1978).

Saskatchewan History and Folklore Society for "Payepot: The Sioux-Cree Chief" by Abel Watetch from *Payepot and His People*.

Van Nostrand Reinhold Ltd. for "John Ware: A Living Legend" by Andy Russell and Ted Grant, from *Men of the Saddle: Working Cowboys of Canada* (1978).

Inge Vermeulen for "Alex Janvier".

Johanna Wenzel for "Walking Buffalo, A Man for Our Time" from *Heritage Magazine*, July/August 1977.

Western Producer Prairie Books for "Alberta Pearl" by Cliff Faulknor from *Turn Him Loose! Herman Linder, Canada's Mr. Rodeo*. For "Caroline 'Mother' Fulham: The Lady Kept Pigs" and for "Nellie McClung: Loved and Remembered" by J. W. Grant MacEwan from . . . *and mighty women too, Stories of Notable Western Canadian Women.*

While every effort has been made to trace the owners of copyrighted material and to make due acknowledgment we regret having been unsuccessful with the following selections:

"Twelve Foot Davis"
"Miss Tannahill" by Joan Hanson
"The Enigma of Bill Miner" by F. W. Lindsay
"Vancouver Speed Boy" by Helen Palk
"To A Woman" by Alexander M. Stephen
"The Face of a Thief " by Phil Thompson